T0323033

Symbolic Management

Symbolic Management

Governance, Strategy,
and Institutions

JAMES WESTPHAL AND SUN HYUN PARK

OXFORD
UNIVERSITY PRESS

OXFORD

UNIVERSITY PRESS

Great Clarendon Street, Oxford, OX2 6DP,
United Kingdom

Oxford University Press is a department of the University of Oxford.
It furthers the University's objective of excellence in research, scholarship,
and education by publishing worldwide. Oxford is a registered trade mark of
Oxford University Press in the UK and in certain other countries

First Edition published in 2020

Impression: 1

Published in the United States of America by Oxford University Press
198 Madison Avenue, New York, NY 10016, United States of America

British Library Cataloguing in Publication Data
Data available

Library of Congress Control Number: 2019957863

ISBN 978-0-19-879205-5

DOI: 10.1093/oso/9780198792055.001.0001

Printed and bound in Great Britain by
Clays Ltd, Elcograf S.p.A.

Preface

Much has been learned about corporate governance over the past thirty years. While there have been several, excellent reviews of empirical research on governance, we lack a comprehensive theoretical framework or perspective that can encompass the seemingly diverse ideas and findings of the larger governance literature. There is a particular need for theoretical synthesis of the behavioral literature. While economic perspectives on governance are largely integrated by agency theory, behavioral theory and research have remained fragmented, limiting the broader impact of our findings. As of yet, no theory has been advanced that can encompass and explain the various cognitive, political, structural, and cultural processes that have been identified in the behavioral literature. Our primary intent with this book is to develop the symbolic management perspective into just such a comprehensive and integrated theory of corporate governance. Although it could not and *should* not have the parsimony of economic perspectives such as agency theory, symbolic management is a linchpin mechanism that offers a kind of theoretical *multum in parvo*, without sacrificing the richness of the behavioral literature. Moreover, symbolic management not only offers a viable alternative to agency theory, but it subsumes and subverts economics by reconceiving agency theory as a historically contingent, institutional logic. Rather than absolute truth, agency theory is revealed as an impermanent set of cultural assumptions that motivated symbolic management activity for a period of time, and were reciprocally influenced *by* symbolic management processes.

Aside from integrating the corporate governance literature, this book is also intended to broaden the ambit of symbolic management and institutional theory. The construct of symbolic decoupling has been unduly constrained in organizational theory, limited in its application to explaining formal policies and structures at the organization level. Our theory reconceives decoupling more broadly as a separation between outward appearances and actual processes that may occur at virtually any level of analysis, from the social psychology of individual managers, to the strategic decision making of top management teams and boards, to relations between firm leaders, lower-level managers, and external stakeholders, to the operation of the governance system as a whole. Although this book integrates over twenty-five years of research on behavioral governance, it also includes new, previously unreported findings, some of which go beyond the traditional governance domain, including research on the symbolic management of strategic decision making, information technology, and diversity. Indeed, much as symbolic management promises to integrate the corporate governance literature, it also promises to integrate management and organization theory at large. Symbolic decoupling is a linchpin construct in the broader literature, because identifying and explaining the difference between what organizational characteristics appear to do, or are intended to do, and what they actually do, is (or should be) a primary objective of scholarly research on organizations.

The intended readership of this book is broad, including not only corporate governance scholars, organizational scholars, strategic management scholars, and researchers from the social science disciplines and relevant professional schools, but practitioners and policy makers as well. In fact, the theory and research described in this book can be traced in part to the first author's experience in management consulting. In spending hour after tedious hour reading proxy statements and annual reports of Fortune 500 companies, he started asking questions that his colleagues couldn't answer: Why did firms prolong the tedium of proxy analysis by providing even more information about executive compensation than was legally required? Why did they sometimes adopt executive incentive plans without actually using them (i.e., without making grants under the plan)? And why did clients frequently pay at the seventy-fifth percentile of "the market" for top executives, but at the fiftieth percentile for some lower-level positions? The second author's interest in symbolic management was motivated by his observations of companies in emerging economy: In response to new government regulations after the financial crisis of 1997 in Korea, which required at least 50 per cent of board members to be independent, firms simply reduced their board size rather than appointing more independent directors. Chinese companies listed on U.S. stock exchanges differed dramatically in their response to the request of NYSE/NASDAQ to appoint independent directors: Some companies simply rejected the idea, declaring that they follow the Chinese local jurisdictions in practice, while others embraced the idea of independent directors, at least on surface, as prescribed by the agency theorists. Our attempts to explain these phenomena, along with a great deal of help, support, and luck, ultimately led to the program of research described in this book.

While the findings of this research address the consequences of specific policies and practices, ranging from executive incentive plans, to particular board "reforms," to security analyst reports, the larger symbolic management perspective should be helpful to practitioners in understanding and anticipating the consequences of other policies and practices as well. Symbolic management theory reminds us to beware of what Merton called the "unanticipated consequences of purposive social action" (1936: 894). Seemingly innovative incentive plans may engender positive reactions from investors, even if they're not implemented, and even if individual analysts and investors have their doubts about the benefits of the plans. And even if the plans are implemented, they may lead to excessive risk aversion by top executives. A new board reform that increases the board's independence from management or constrains managerial discretion may induce political behavior by top executives that lowers the quality of board decision making. Appointing a woman or a racial minority to a high-profile leadership position such as chief executive officer or board chair may reduce the tendency for white male executives to provide advice, mentoring, and other forms of help to their female and racial minority colleagues. An understanding of the symbolic management perspective can help corporate leaders and policy makers anticipate all of these unfortunate consequences, and many more that have yet to be shown in empirical research, but which can be predicted with our theory.

We would like to acknowledge the many collaborators and colleagues who have made this book possible. The collaborators whose work is described or reflected in the book include: Michael Bednar, Steven Boivie, Mason Carpenter, Daniel Chng, Michael Clement, David Deephouse, James Fredrickson, Melissa Graebner, Ranjay Gulati, Mathew Hayward, Gareth Keeves, Poonam Khanna, Raji Kunapuli, Donald Lange, Michael McDonald, Laurie Milton, Marc-David Seidel, Guy Shani, Stephen Shortell, Ithai Stern, Katherine Stewart, Edward Zajac, Yanlong Zhang, and David Zhu.

Colleagues who have provided input to the material in this book include: Ruth Aguilera, Gautam Ahuja, Philip Anderson, Sue Ashford, Rick Bagozzi, Christine Beckman, Warren Boeker, Daniel Brass, Bert Cannella, Seth Carnahan, John Chen, Jerry Davis, Alison Davis-Blake, Jane Dutton, Sendil Ethiraj, Sydney Finkelstein, Martin Gargiulo, Scott Graffin, Adam Grant, Henrich Greve, Benjamin Hallen, Donald Hambrick, Pamela Haunschild, Andrew Henderson, Amy Hillman, Paul Hirsch, Michael Jensen, John Joseph, Matthew Kraatz, Dovev Lavie, Jeffrey Loewenstein, Michael Lounsbury, Geoffrey Love, Mark Mizruchi, William Ocasio, Donald Palmer, Timothy Pollock, Nandini Rajagopalan, Kelly Patterson, Huggy Rao, Violina Rindova, Mark Shanley, Ned Smith, Maxim Sytch, Vivek Tandon, Brian Uzzi, John Wagner, Klaus Weber, Karen Westphal, Minyuan Zhao, and Maggie Zhou.

We would also like to thank our editors, David Musson and Jenny King. David had the patience of a saint, and never lost hope that the manuscript would be completed (or was too polite to say so). We also appreciate the financial support of several institutions, including the Guanghua School of Management Peking University, Kellogg School of Management, the McCombs School of Business, the Ross School of Business, Seoul National University, and the Marshall School of Business.

This book is dedicated to our spouses, Karen Westphal and Jinyoung Yang, who sacrificed more than anyone to make this book a reality, and to our parents, Barbara Westphal, James Westphal, Sr., Youngsuk Jung, and Moonheun Park.

Contents

1

Introduction to the Symbolic Management Perspective

In this book we develop symbolic management into a comprehensive and integrative behavioral theory of firm governance. While economic perspectives on governance have long been integrated by agency theory, behavioral perspectives on governance have remained fractured. Behavioral research has addressed how political, socio-cognitive, and sociological factors influence corporate governance policy and its consequences (see Finkelstein et al., 2009; Westphal and Zajac, 2013 for reviews), but these factors have not been integrated into a single theoretical framework. Symbolic management lies at the intersection of these seemingly disparate behavioral processes. It is an agentic, political process by which organizational actors leverage norms, values, beliefs, and assumptions in the broader culture to exert influence over the perceptions and behavior of organizational stakeholders. The potential for symbolic management to integrate behavioral perspectives on firm governance has not been fully leveraged in prior theory and research. Extant perspectives suggest that firm leaders adopt governance policies and structures that symbolize conformity to prevailing cultural values, while decoupling them from actual practices in ways that serve their political interests (Westphal and Zajac, 1998; Fiss and Zajac, 2004; Westphal and Graebner, 2010). The focus of this research is on the symbolic management of firm-level policies and structures, consistent with a traditional, neo-institutional perspective on organizations (Meyer and Rowan, 1977; Scott and Davis, 2007). While this research has made important strides in developing a socio-political perspective on governance, it greatly underestimates the scope of symbolic management and its consequences, and it is largely divorced from a considerable body of theory and research on the social psychological processes of firm leadership and governance.

We present symbolic management as a broad, multi-level theory that has far-reaching implications for strategic management and organizational behavior. The mechanisms of symbolic management comprise verbal and non-verbal communications, as well as organizational processes, policies, and structures. They may derive influence from leveraging culturally specific values and beliefs, such as

Symbolic Management: Governance, Strategy, and Institutions. James Westphal and Sun Hyun Park,
Oxford University Press (2020). © James Westphal and Sun Hyun Park.
DOI: 10.1093/oso/9780198792055.001.0001

democratic or meritocratic values, and/or by leveraging more generalized cultural norms, such as the norm of reciprocity. The agents of symbolic management may include lower-level managers and third parties such as consultants, in addition to corporate leaders. And the audience or "target" of symbolic management may include board members or lower-level employees, in addition to external stakeholders.

A key tenet of our theory is that there is a pervasive separation between appearances and reality, or between symbol and substance, at each level of the governance system. In effect, symbolic management theory broadens the traditional, neo-institutional concept of decoupling beyond organizational structure and policy. While scholars have recently extended the construct of decoupling beyond failures of implementation (e.g., Bromley and Powell, 2012), the literature is still focused on decoupling at the organization level. We suggest that symbolic decoupling is a pervasive feature of organizational life which occurs at every level of analysis, from dyadic relations within organizations (e.g., relations between chief executive officers (CEOs) and directors, and between top managers and lower-level employees), to relations between firm leaders and external constituents, to relations between groups of leaders and groups of constituents. There is even a separation between appearances and reality at the level of the overall governance system. Symbolic management comprises the agentic processes by which decoupling is maintained at different levels of the system, including internal and external communications by firm leaders that conform to prevailing cultural values. Moreover, while extant perspectives focus on the firm-level consequences of symbolic conformity, our theory suggests how symbolic management can also have important consequences beyond the firm, such as bolstering the reputation of corporate leadership as a whole, and contributing to processes of institutional change. Our theory further suggests how social psychological processes at the individual, dyad, group, and community levels facilitate and perpetuate symbolic decoupling.

Symbolic management theory not only provides an integrative, behavioral alternative to economic theories of governance such as agency theory, but it also subsumes economic theory. Agency theory is reconceived as a historically contingent, institutional logic (Friedland and Alford, 1991; Thornton et al., 2012), or a set of cultural values, assumptions, and prescriptions that became institutionalized or taken for granted in the financial community for a period of time. Our research reveals a gradual shift in institutional logics of governance over time, away from the traditional agency logic, and toward an alternative "neo-corporate" logic of governance that reinterprets agency prescriptions and jettisons fundamental assumptions of agency theory. Moreover, our theory specifically indicates how the symbolic management activities of firm leaders have contributed to this historical shift in prevailing logics of governance.

The Major Forms of Symbolic Management

The Symbolic Management of Organizational Policies and Structures

The first part of our theoretical framework describes major forms of symbolic management that operate at different levels of analysis, and the second part describes social and psychological processes that determine and support symbolic management at each level of the governance system. We begin by reviewing the symbolic management of firm-level policies and structures, which have been the focus of prior theory and empirical research. Taken together, this body of research shows that as the agency logic of governance became institutionalized in the financial community over time, a series of formal policies and structures emerged as potent forms of symbolic action. Each of these policies and structures, which included executive incentive plans, financial policies, and board reforms, appeared to conform to normative assumptions of the agency logic, but were often decoupled from actual practices in ways that preserved the discretion of firm leaders. Moreover, each of these symbolic actions significantly enhanced the market value of adopting firms, despite insulating firm leaders from substantial governance reforms, thus reducing the allocative efficiency of financial markets. Symbolic management theory suggests that a fundamental irony of agency theory, and of normative, economic theories of organization more generally, is that their application tends to induce and enable social behavior that undermines the central normative prescriptions of the theories. We further contend that while the institutional status of agency theory is transient, it contributed to a lasting increase in the amount and variety of symbolic management activity by firm leaders.

The Symbolic Management of Social and Organizational Processes

We next examine the symbolic management of social and organizational processes in firm leadership and governance. We contend that the focus of neo-institutional theory on organizational structure and policy as the locus of symbolic action (Meyer and Rowan, 1977; DiMaggio and Powell, 1983) has unduly constrained theory and research on symbolic processes in organizations. Symbolic management often concerns the social and organizational processes by which policies and structures are determined and implemented, rather than the policies and structures themselves. We describe how firm leaders engage in verbal impression management about their strategic advice seeking in communicating with the board, and how the content of such rhetoric is often decoupled from leaders' actual advice-seeking behavior. We also review research suggesting how firm leaders gain reputational benefits by adopting participative strategic decision-making programs that appear to use information technology (e.g., crowdsourcing) to solicit input from lower-level managers and staff, despite decoupling these programs from the actual strategic decision-making process. In particular, top executives often solicit strategic input under these programs *after* they have effectively decided on a strategy. While decoupling is often conceived as formal adoption without implementation, symbolic action can also involve "[re]-ordering reality," including the sequence of events in decision-making processes (Feldman and March, 1981; March and Olsen, 1984; Friedland and Alford, 1991: 243). In the case of participative strategic decision-making programs, the apparent sequence of events, which involves seeking input and then considering that input in rendering a decision, may be decoupled from the actual sequence of actions (making the decision and then seeking input about it). We further explain how and why firm leaders augment the symbolic benefits of participative decision making by high-lighting the use of information technology as a means of soliciting input when they communicate with information intermediaries.

Our theory suggests that symbolic management about participative strategic decision making is a particularly efficient and effective way to enhance the reputation of firm leadership, strategy, and governance. The logic of appropriate-ness is especially likely to govern perceptions of organizational processes (March and Olsen, 1984), and participative approaches to decision making conform to implicit models of leader effectiveness in Western culture (House et al., 2004, 2013), in part because they align with the institutional logic of democratic process (DiMaggio, 1997; Friedland and Alford, 1991). We also suggest that communica-tion about the strategic decision-making process conveys a sense of transparency by giving constituents a glimpse into the "back regions" of strategic management (Goffman, 1959; MacCannell, 1973: 590–1). Moreover, we draw from contem-porary theoretical perspectives in the cultural anthropology of technology (Pfaffenberger, 1988, 1992; Hornborg, 2014) to explain why references to the use of crowdsourcing technology in executive communication about strategic decision making reinforce the symbolic value of participative processes and cause stakeholders to ignore or overlook the potential for decoupling and increase their support of firm leadership and strategy. Executive communication about participative decision making is not only a particularly effective form of symbolic management, but it is also a highly efficient one, since communication that reassures constituents about the quality of decision-making processes tends to increase their confidence in the various strategic decisions subsequently announced by firm leaders (i.e., reducing the need to manage impressions about each individual decision).

The symbolic management of decision-making processes is more complex than the symbolic management of policies or structures such as incentive plans or stock repurchases. We describe how complex forms of symbolic action such as participative strategic decision-making programs are often supported by management consultants and the colleagues of top managers at other firms who have prior experience with similar programs. Symbolic management has typically been conceived as a firm-level or dyadic phenomenon, with a particular focus on symbolic communications and other actions by organizational spokespersons toward particular internal or external audiences. This emphasis in the literature can be traced to Goffman (1959: 144–5), who defined acts of impression management as including "those who perform; those performed to; and outsiders who neither perform in the show nor observe the performance." However, this conception ignores other parties involved in symbolic action. We extend Goffman's dramaturgical metaphor in suggesting that, in complex organizations, symbolic management is often a larger production that is itself managed or directed, often with the assistance of third parties. In the case of symbolic organizational processes such as participative strategic decision-making programs, while executives are the "face" of the programs, consultants essentially direct the performance behind the curtain. We describe the specific roles that consultants play in managing these kinds of programs, and we explain how friendship ties to executives at other firms who have prior experience with such programs often play a key role in brokering the consulting engagements.

Beyond symbolic management about strategic decision making, we examine symbolic management about the diversity and inclusiveness of firm leadership. An increasingly common response by firm leaders to disappointing performance outcomes or negative appraisals by information intermediaries is to increase the demographic diversity of firm leadership, while engaging in verbal impression management about diversity in communications with external stakeholders. We describe some of the many ways that apparent increases in diversity mask the marginalization or exclusion of demographic minorities from decision-making processes and other forms of social interaction. While this form of decoupling is less categorical than adopting but not implementing policies or programs, it is also more multi-faceted.

Symbolic Management beyond the Firm Level

We next examine cooperative and collective forms of symbolic management that cross organizational boundaries. These include acts of symbolic management "support," in which leaders make positive remarks about the leadership, governance, or strategy of particular firms in communicating with information intermediaries, as well as more coordinated forms of symbolic management that occur in groups of female and racial minority leaders. We argue that these cooperative forms of symbolic management can have more influence on stakeholder assessments than firm-level impression management by CEOs about their own firm's leadership, governance, and strategy. The effectiveness of cooperative symbolic management owes in large part to its inconspicuous nature. Positive remarks by firm leaders about the leadership, governance, or strategy of other firms come across as less self-interested, more sincere, and thus more credible than conventional forms of impression management.

Our theory suggests how cooperative forms of symbolic management have not only influenced stakeholder beliefs about particular firms and their leaders, but over time they have exerted a deeper influence on stakeholders' normative assumptions about governance, or the criteria by which they evaluate the quality of governance practices. We contend that symbolic management support has contributed to a fundamental shift in the prevailing institutional logic of governance, away from the "pure" agency logic that had prevailed since the 1980s, toward a "neo-corporate" logic that subtly reasserts the autonomy and discretion of managers. The micro-mechanism underlying this change is rhetorical cooptation. In particular, the rhetoric of symbolic management support reinterpreted central prescriptions of agency theory in ways that reasserted the final decision-making authority of top management. For example, board involvement in strategic decision making was redefined as "participative decision making" and "democratic governance," and board independence from management was reinterpreted as a means of providing objective input and advice to management, rather than as a means of exerting control over management to reduce the "agency problem" created by self-interested managers. The rhetoric of symbolic management support has drawn normative legitimacy from the social logic of democratic process, rather than from the economic logic of independent control.

The second-order effect of symbolic management on institutional change is an unintentional kind of agency that represents a novel and rather insidious form of cultural entrepreneurship (Lounsbury and Glynn, 2019). Rather than an overtly political approach in which change agents highlight and perhaps overstate the contrast between existing social prescriptions and the new practices they hope to enact (Rao et al., 2003), firm leaders have instigated institutional change in governance without overtly contesting the prevailing model. Institutionalized prescriptions served as a trojan horse for changing implicit assumptions about firm governance. As testimony to the subtlety and potency of this institutional change mechanism, we provide evidence from large sample surveys that not only have normative beliefs about corporate governance significantly changed in recent years among journalists and security analysts, but also that these stakeholders are largely unaware of the change. We conclude that information intermediaries were unknowing carriers of a new institutional logic of governance that helped shift control over organizational decision making from firm stakeholders toward managers.

We also reveal an emerging form of collective symbolic management in which firm leaders highlight the sparsity of board interlock ties between firms in the same industry as evidence of competition, especially in communicating with journalists at general media outlets. Such rhetoric is particularly common in the context of merger announcements or other disclosures that could arouse anti-trust concerns, and appears to have reinforced the prevailing impression among many journalists that firm leaders have become increasingly independent of each other.

Yet, while board interlock ties between competitors are rare, our data indicate that top executives of competing firms are frequently connected by two-step social network ties, which we call "board-friendship ties," in which the personal friends of a firm's CEO serve on the board of a competitor firm. We contend that board-friendship ties dampen competition and increase firm profitability at the expense of consumers. Firm leaders are connected by other kinds of direct and indirect social ties between firm leaders as well, including shared ties to headhunters and other consultants. This analysis ultimately reveals a multi-faceted decoupling between appearances and reality with respect to the social structure of firm leadership. Although the scarcity of formal ties would appear to indicate independence between leaders that should promote competition, this apparent social structure belies a persistently high level of relational and structural embeddedness that can promote collusive behavior. Moreover, the symbolic decoupling of social structure has become more pronounced over time. While board interlock ties have become increasingly sparse, less visible, informal ties between leaders such as board-friendship ties have become more prevalent. And symbolic management by firm leaders has exacerbated the separation between external perceptions and the reality inside corporate leadership.

While social networks have been conceived as pipes and prisms, meaning channels of communication and signals of quality (Podolny, 2001), the social network ties of firm leaders have symbolic value that is largely independent of their signaling value. They are properly conceived as social constructions that are partially decoupled from organizational behavior, due in part to the symbolic management of firm leaders.

At the highest level, symbolic decoupling persists in the larger governance system. Corporate governance appears to be an interlocking system of vertical and horizontal checks and balances. Higher levels appear to exert independent control over lower levels: top managers over lower-level managers, boards over top managers, and institutional investors over boards and top managers. External control is facilitated by information intermediaries, who provide independent evaluations of the quality of firm governance. There is also redundancy in the system, to reduce dependence on any one component. If boards fail to exert independent control, it would attract a takeover threat; if security analysts fail to provide independent evaluations, it would be exposed by journalists. However, a system of checks and balances is rendered ineffective if the independence of each component is compromised. Further, the capacity for reform is compromised if each component of the system *appears* more independent than it actually is. Our theory suggests how symbolic management promotes the appearance of independence and objectivity at different levels, while compromising the actual independence of each social role in the system.

The Social and Psychological Processes of Symbolic Management

The Multi-Stage Social Influence Process in CEO–Board Relationships

The second part of our theoretical framework addresses the social and psychological determinants and supporting processes of symbolic management. We begin by explaining why the CEO's social influence over the board of directors and the social network ties of firm leaders constitute primary determinants of symbolic management. Given its boundary-spanning position, the board occupies a central position in the corporate governance system, and consequently the success of symbolic management hinges on the CEO's ability to exert social influence over the board. Empirical research has demonstrated a robust relationship between CEO influence over the board and the symbolic decoupling of governance policies and structures, including executive incentive plans, stock repurchase plans, and board reforms. We describe CEO influence as a multi-stage process that begins with director selection, is strengthened by the socialization of new directors and the ongoing interpersonal influence behavior of CEOs, and further reinforced by the social control of directors who violate social norms. Moreover, there is a distinct separation of appearances and reality at each stage of the influence process, and this decoupling can be attributed in part to the rhetoric of firm leaders.

CEO influence begins with director selection, as CEOs tend to favor board candidates who are demographically similar or personal friends, and who are especially likely to support their strategic priorities and personal preferences. They also tend to favor their friends for important committee assignments such as the board-nominating committee, which perpetuates their influence over the selection process. Yet despite evidence that average levels of demographic similarity between CEOs and new directors remain high, and that CEOs often have personal ties to multiple members of the board-nominating committee, our surveys indicate that information intermediaries and institutional fund managers tend to assume that independence from management has become a more important criterion in director selection. As a result, external pressure to reform the director selection process has abated substantially since the early 2000s.

The next stage of the influence process is socialization. Incumbent board members often mentor first-time directors about how to participate in the decision-making process in ways that reinforce the CEO's control over firm strategy and policy. Our research also indicates a separation between rhetoric and reality with respect to director mentoring. While top managers and directors increasingly describe the mentoring of new directors as a "best practice" that promotes board effectiveness, our empirical analyses indicate that directors who received participation process mentoring are much less likely to engage in deci-sion-control behaviors, and they are no more likely to provide strategic advice and input to executives.

The third stage of the influence process involves ongoing interpersonal influ-ence behavior by CEOs, including ingratiation and persuasion toward demo-graphically dissimilar directors, or directors with whom they lack friendship ties. While the rhetoric of top executives and directors emphasizes the need for CEOs to "explain" their proposals to the board, implying that CEO persuasion reflects board influence over strategy, in reality persuasion attempts provide cover for ingratiatory behavior such as flattery and opinion conformity. Our analyses indicate that CEO persuasion interacts with ingratiation toward directors to advance the CEO's agenda on a variety of issues, ranging from compensation policy to diversification strategy.

The fourth stage of CEO influence involves social control of directors who violate norms of director conduct. For example, directors who raise a concern about the CEO's strategy in board meetings without clearing the issue with the CEO beforehand are at risk of "social distancing" from other directors, a subtle form of social ostracism. While corporate directors tend to characterize social distancing as reducing "disruption" in the strategic decision-making process, thus promoting board effectiveness, in reality it deters directors from disagreeing with the CEO and ultimately reduces their influence over policy decisions. Finally, CEO influence is further bolstered by recommendations for board appointments. Although the rhetoric of corporate leaders tends to echo Fama's (1980) economic theory of director labor markets, in which the "best" directors are recommended for further appointments, the empirical evidence suggests that individuals are most likely to garner recommendations by ingratiating the CEO and their peers, while avoiding involvement in board decision control.

Moreover, the board's ability to exercise influence over strategy in particular has been further compromised by a general decline in the average strategic experience of outside directors at large and mid-sized United States (U.S.) com-panies. We report that despite evidence that prior management and board experi-ence at companies with similar corporate strategies to the focal firm is an important determinant of outside directors' ability to make valuable contributions to strategic decision making, the portion of directors who possess such experience has declined significantly since the early 2000s. This trend stands in stark contrast to the popular belief among many firm stakeholders that outside directors have become *more* qualified for board service in recent years. It is also reinforced by the rhetoric of firm leaders, which emphasizes the formal independence of directors as the single most important qualification for board service, implicitly downplaying the importance of prior strategic experience.

Social Network Ties and Symbolic Management

Social network ties between firm leaders are a second key determinant of symbolic management activity. Prior research on social networks in firm leadership and governance has focused mainly on board interlock ties between firms. The focus on board interlocks in empirical research reflects traditional, sociological perspectives on the corporate elite, which have long viewed the board interlock network as a primary indicator and determinant of social embeddedness. This literature has devoted little attention to informal social connections between leaders of different firms, whether direct friendship ties, or indirect ties through third-party service providers such as consultants, lobbyists or attorneys, or common stakeholders. Similarly, while few studies have examined the influence of social network ties on symbolic management, the limited work in this area has focused almost exclusively on board interlocks. As a result, scholars have greatly underestimated the relational and structural embeddedness of firm leadership, and by extension they have underestimated the influence of social network ties on firm leadership, including symbolic management. We further suggest that the underestimation of social embeddedness and its effects on firm leadership have become more pronounced over time as the board interlock network has become relatively sparse, while some kinds of informal ties between firm leaders have become more prevalent.

We explain how various forms of symbolic management have diffused through different kinds of social network ties between firm leaders, including (1) director ties to informal groups of firm leaders, (2) social exchange ties between leaders, (3) direct and indirect personal friendship ties between leaders, and (4) mutual ties to management consultants. These ties tend to be stronger and more personal than board interlock ties. As a result, the mechanisms by which symbolic management has spread through these informal ties are different from the mechanisms that are assumed to underlie the diffusion of practices through board interlock ties. While extant theory suggests how board interlocks facilitate diffusion by promoting awareness and social learning, we describe how informal ties have helped spread symbolic management through social identification, interpersonal trust, and social exchange between leaders. Since the mechanisms that underlie board interlock ties tend to be relatively weak and impersonal, such ties have a stronger influence on the diffusion of relatively generic forms of symbolic management that are straightforward to implement, such as decoupled stock repurchase plans. The stronger, more personal connections that we describe play a larger role in the diffusion of relatively complex forms of symbolic management such as decoupled participative decision-making programs or coordinated symbolic management. We suggest that these complex forms of symbolic management are more likely to provide a sustainable competitive advantage than the generic forms of decoupling examined in prior research, increasing the strategic value of informal ties between leaders relative to formal ties such as board interlocks.

Social Influence Processes in Leader–Stakeholder Relations

We extend our theoretical framework beyond the core determinants of symbolic management to address social and psychological processes that support and perpetuate symbolic action. We begin by describing micro-level social influence processes in relations between firm leaders and external stakeholders, focusing especially on ingratiation, favor rendering, and negative reciprocity, which our research indicates are particularly common and impactful social processes in leader–constituent relations. We explain why ingratiation is a relatively efficient, effective, and robust social influence tactic. It is efficient because it requires few social or material resources to deploy. It is effective because it exerts influence through multiple social and psychological mechanisms, including reciprocal attraction and similarity-attraction bias. And it is robust, in multiple respects: It can help secure a wide variety of outcomes, it works "in" a wide variety of organizational, social, and cultural contexts, and it works "on" a wide variety of different kinds of people. Moreover, firm leaders often engage in subtle and sophisticated forms of ingratiation that are relatively unlikely to be recognized or interpreted by the influence "target" as attempts to curry favor. We describe these sophisticated tactics, and review evidence that CEOs who deploy them exert significant interpersonal influence over information intermediaries and institutional fund managers. We also address the determinants of sophisticated ingratiation, including the vocational and socio-economic backgrounds of corporate leaders that predict their use in communications with external stakeholders.

In addition to ingratiation, reciprocity and retaliation are important social influence processes in leader–constituent relations. Reciprocity from rendering personal and professional favors is a relatively strong social influence tactic, though also a resource-intensive one. We review evidence that CEOs can exert significant influence over the evaluations of security analysts by rendering personal and professional favors, though they normally limit their use of such tactics to relatively threatening circumstances, such as the disclosure of significant performance declines or relatively controversial corporate strategies. We also explain how and why CEOs sometimes engage in negative reciprocity or retaliation against information intermediaries who render negative evaluations (e.g., by limiting or cutting off personal communication with them). While negative reciprocity is used much less often than ingratiation, and it has less influence on individual behavior than favor rendering, it nonetheless has a larger "total" effect on analyst behavior by deterring negative assessments by other analysts. Moreover, its effects appear to be very "durable" or long lasting.

Thus, micro-level social influence processes have powerful and robust effects on relations between firm leaders and external stakeholders. Moreover, they amplify the effectiveness of firm-level symbolic management by reducing the inclination of information intermediaries and powerful investors to validate policy implementation, or to verify the rhetoric of impression management. Sophisticated ingratiation in particular creates a kind of decoupling between appearances and reality in dyadic social interaction, as it disguises the intent to curry favor behind a façade of normatively acceptable communication, such that decoupling at the dyad level effectively contributes to the success of symbolic management at the firm level. Moreover, the covert nature of these social influence processes complements the more public forms of symbolic action described above. By pacifying information intermediaries and investors who are in a position to exert external control over firm governance, and doing so covertly, these micro-level processes maintain the appearance of objective and independent evaluation and control by external stakeholders, while perpetuating managerial autonomy and discretion. In effect, they reinforce the tendency toward ceremonial inspection, and the "logic of confidence and good faith" among organizational stakeholders that makes symbolic decoupling possible (Meyer and Rowan, 1977: 357), and which helps to preserve the dominance of corporate elites.

Group-Level Social and Psychological Processes that Support Symbolic Management

While behavioral governance researchers have focused on dyadic processes in CEO–board relationships and leader–constituent relations, and devoted some attention to socio-cultural processes at the organization and field levels (Thornton and Ocasio, 1999; Finkelstein et al., 2009), they have largely ignored group-level social and psychological processes. Such processes are a missing link in theory and research on governance and strategy. Our theory explains how two group-level processes—social distancing and pluralistic ignorance—contribute to a wide range of suboptimal firm strategies, policies, and practices, including the different forms of symbolic decoupling described in Part I. Both processes play key roles in supporting symbolic management because they operate at multiple levels of the governance system, from small groups within the firm (e.g., top management teams and boards) to professional communities outside the firm (e.g., communities of journalists and security analysts).

As noted above, social distancing on boards is a subtle and informal kind of ostracism in which directors who deviate from group norms are socially and psychologically isolated from affairs of the board: Their input is solicited less often and their comments are ignored during formal meetings, and they are not invited to informal meetings, subgroup activities such as preparation for analyst conference calls, and social activities such as golf outings. Social distancing not only deters directors from expressing concern about the strategic decisions of top executives in board meetings, but it also deters them from "breaking ranks" and communicating with journalists, analysts, or powerful investors in ways that might threaten managerial control (e.g., expressing support for governance reforms that would increase executive accountability to shareholders). Thus, social distancing on boards supports the persistence of symbolic decoupling, including the decoupling of policies, structures, and processes that perpetuate managerial discretion and autonomy. Moreover, social distancing is an especially powerful and efficient, yet inconspicuous form of social control. To the layperson, social influence connotes active behavior: One "exerts" or "exercises" social influence over another person. But social distancing involves the silent *withdrawal* of interaction, which makes it both insidious and efficient as a mechanism for enforcing illegitimate social norms.

We also explain how social distancing occurs in relations between firm leaders and information intermediaries. Unlike other forms of social influence in leader–constituent relations, which are dyadic in nature, social distancing is a group-to-group form of influence. It involves collective behavior toward an individual constituent that affects the behavior of that individual *and other constituents* toward leaders *as a group*. In relations between CEOs and journalists, for example, social distancing often involves a lack of response from multiple CEOs to a journalist's requests for an interview or meeting (e.g., not returning the journalist's phone calls). In relations with security analysts, it can involve a reduced willingness of executives from multiple different firms to speak privately with an analyst after public conference calls, communications that are highly valued by analysts (Brown et al., 2015).

We contend that journalists who engage in negative coverage of the leadership and strategy at a particular firm tend to experience social distancing from multiple CEOs, due to the multiple potential bases of social identification among firm leaders, including demographic similarity, social identification with the corporate elite, and personal friendship ties. Social distancing in turn has a strong influence on the valence of journalists' subsequent reporting about firm leaders as a group. Moreover, it not only influences the coverage of journalists who directly experience distancing, but it also influences the coverage of journalists who become *aware* of the distancing experienced by *another* journalist. We further explain how social distancing "cascades" across communities, such that social distancing of a journalist by CEOs is related to subsequent distancing of the journalist by their colleagues. The combined effects of these different forms of distancing on subsequent journalist behavior are very strong in magnitude.

Social distancing on boards and between CEOs and information intermediaries supports symbolic management by deterring directors, journalists, and analysts from investigating and objectively evaluating and reporting on the implementation of firm policies, structures, and decision-making processes. In effect, social distancing contributes to symbolic decoupling by motivating ceremonial forms of monitoring and evaluation at multiple levels of the governance system.

A second group-level dynamic that supports symbolic management is pluralistic ignorance, a social psychological bias in which most group members have private concerns about the group's norms, policies, or practices, but underestimate the extent to which their concerns are shared. Pluralistic ignorance creates an "attitude-behavior disjunction," in which groups persist with policies or practices that most members have reservations about (Miller et al., 2000: 103). We describe the subtle social and psychological dynamics that create pluralistic ignorance on corporate boards, including the perceived risk of expressing a minority point of view, and social influence tactics in which executives tend to exaggerate the level of support for current policies and practices. Pluralistic ignorance among outside directors is associated with the persistence of multiple forms of symbolic decoupling, including the decoupling of stock repurchase plans and board independence from management.

Pluralistic ignorance also occurs among external stakeholders, including information intermediaries. We explain how pluralistic ignorance among security analysts has contributed to the persistence of positive reactions to symbolic policy adoptions such as stock repurchase plans. Analysts systematically underestimated the extent to which fellow analysts shared their reservations about the value of stock repurchase plans, and this bias in social perceptions led them to react more positively to newly adopted plans, despite accumulated evidence of decoupling. We also describe how social network ties moderate pluralistic ignorance among outside directors and information intermediaries. Directors and analysts exhibit less pluralistic ignorance to the extent that they have a dense ego network of strong social ties to their colleagues.

We extend our discussion of group-level dynamics to reveal a common social psychological profile for the leadership of relatively low-performing organizations, characterized by pluralistic ignorance among outside directors and top managers below the officer level, and symptoms of groupthink among the inside directors and other corporate officers. Whereas pluralistic ignorance is a failure to recognize shared concerns about a policy or practice, groupthink involves collective over-confidence in the policy. In effect, there is often a core-periphery structure to the social psychological profile of leadership in low-performing firms, in which the inner core of corporate leaders exhibit symptoms of groupthink, while lower-level managers and outside directors who play a more peripheral role in decision making exhibit pluralistic ignorance.

We further suggest that there is a parallel core-periphery structure to beliefs about some corporate governance policies among information intermediaries. Security analysts who communicate with top executives most frequently (e.g., in private conversations outside conference calls (Brown et al., 2015)) express significantly more confidence in the governance practices of firms that they cover, relative to the majority of analysts who rely mainly on conference calls and other public sources for information. The minority of high-status analysts who have privileged access to top executives exhibit bias about certain governance policies *and* bias about the beliefs of other analysts. Whereas most analysts tend to underestimate the extent to which their reservations about decoupled policies such as stock repurchase plans are shared, this minority of privileged analysts exhibited a reverse kind of ignorance: They *over*estimated the degree to which their *confidence* in the value of the policies was shared by other analysts.

Thus, while group-level social and psychological processes have received relatively little attention from corporate governance scholars, they play a key role in the persistence and success of symbolic action. Given the central importance of these dynamics to firm governance and strategic management, we consider the prospects of ameliorating group-level biases and negative social influence processes. We suggest that while social distancing and groupthink are inherently difficult to reduce or avoid, pluralistic ignorance may be easier to correct. We ultimately recommend increasing awareness of pluralistic ignorance and exposing shared concerns about decoupled policies and practices, and leveraging this awareness to combat the more insidious biases and behaviors that we have described.

The Social Psychological Dynamics of Symbolic Management

We also examine how the individual-level, cognitive tendencies of firm leaders support symbolic management processes. In particular, we consider how different forms of self-regulated cognition by executives and directors enhance the effectiveness of social influence processes in symbolic management. We describe a form of self-regulated cognition in which executives and directors reflect on personal and social characteristics that they have in common with a colleague, while avoiding thoughts about characteristics not shared, shortly before interacting with the colleague. We explain how such cognitions increase the efficacy of ingratiation toward high-status, demographically dissimilar colleagues, whether directors, analysts, or representatives of institutional investors, by self-inducing more genuine feelings of liking and respect for the influence "target." Self-regulated cognition helps resolve the "ingratiator's dilemma" that the most attractive targets of social influence tend to be particularly vigilant for insincere flattery (Jones and Pittman, 1982; Leary,

1995; Schlenker, 2003). Aside from increasing interpersonal influence, self-regulated cognition has other important psychological and social benefits for firm leaders, including reduced symptoms of burnout and lower interpersonal conflict in diverse executive teams.

In addition to self-regulated cognition about high-status colleagues prior to social interaction, firm leaders also sometimes engage in self-regulated cognition about organizational characteristics, including firm strategy and governance, prior to opportunities for impression management. In particular, top executives and directors sometimes engage in a sequential process of reflection prior to meetings with security analysts and institutional investors that involves first considering possible weaknesses and vulnerabilities of the current strategy and governance, then reflecting on advantages and strengths, and finally affirming to themselves and each other that the strengths outweigh the weaknesses. We explain how self-regulated cognition of this kind can enhance the efficacy of impression management by preparing top executives to express genuine confidence in the firm's strategy, governance, and performance prospects. Such cognitions help resolve the broader dilemma facing firm leaders that the most attractive targets of social influence tend to be particularly vigilant for exaggerated claims about the leader's strategy, especially under conditions of low firm performance when impression management is most needed. As Suchman (1995: 577) noted, "managers rarely convince others to believe much that the managers do not believe themselves." We report evidence that self-regulated cognition about strategy and governance has spread and evolved to become a more group-oriented activity over time.

These various forms of self-regulated cognition not only enhance the effectiveness of social influence processes in symbolic management, but they also create predictable patterns of oscillation in the social and strategic perceptions of firm leaders. Executives and directors report significantly higher levels of liking and respect for their colleagues shortly before and after interacting with them, and they report significantly more positive attitudes about firm strategy and governance shortly before and after meeting with powerful stakeholders. In effect, self-regulated cognition creates a subtle kind of decoupling between leaders' perceptions about their colleagues at times of social interaction, or their perceptions about strategy and governance at times of impression management, and their perceptions at other points in time. We suggest that such decoupling reduces the tendency for symbolic management to bias strategic decision making, and otherwise helps top executives to compartmentalize symbolic management from their internal leadership roles.

Thus, our theory suggests that symbolic management is the common denominator of organizational governance. It can be found at every level of the governance system, and it explains the reciprocal influence of micro-level, social psychological processes and macro-level, sociological factors. It also links the psychology and behavior of small groups within the firm, such as top management teams and boards, with professional communities in the external environment, such as journalists and security analysts. Moreover, by integrating institutional and social psychological theories of governance, symbolic management fulfills the promise of both perspectives. Although institutional theory is typically characterized as a cognitive perspective on organizations, it has always lacked specificity about the cognitive processes that underlie institutional maintenance and change (DiMaggio, 1997). Conversely, with few exceptions social psychological perspectives on governance have devoted much more attention to psychological processes than to social influences, especially beyond dyadic relations. Few studies have considered how social structural and cultural factors determine or moderate the cognitions of organizational leaders. In specifying the cognitive processes that underlie institutionalization and institutional change, as well as the social and cultural influences on managerial cognition, symbolic management theory offers a truly socio-cognitive perspective on organizational governance.

PART I

THE MAJOR FORMS OF SYMBOLIC MANAGEMENT

In this part we describe major forms of symbolic management that occur at multiple levels of the corporate governance system. In Chapter 2 we review theory and research on the symbolic management of firm-level policies and structures, including executive incentive plans, financial policies, and board reforms. This literature shows that as the agency logic of governance became institutionalized in the financial community over time, firm leaders adopted a series of formal policies and structures that appeared to conform to normative assumptions of the agency logic, while often decoupling them from actual practices in ways that preserved their discretion and autonomy. The cumulative effect of these symbolic actions was to substantially increase the market value of adopting firms, while compromising the allocative efficiency of financial markets, and stemming the diffusion of corporate governance reforms. While the institutional status of normative agency theory has waned, its impact on organizational behavior has persisted, though not in the way its propagators anticipated. In particular, it has contributed to a lasting increase in the level and variety of verbal impression management and symbolic decoupling by corporate leaders. Our research reveals a fundamental irony in the research and practice of corporate governance: The successful propagation and institutionalization of normative agency theory motivated and enabled the very symbolic management activity that undermined core prescriptions of the theory, including incentive alignment policies and board reforms that increase board independence from management.

The next two chapters develop symbolic management theory into a multi-level perspective on corporate governance, leadership, and strategy. While neo-institutional theory has focused the attention of organizational scholars on firm-level structure and policy as the locus of symbolic action, symbolic management often addresses the internal processes by which structures and policies are developed and implemented. Moreover, extant theory and research has largely ignored cooperative forms of symbolic action in which leaders from different firms engage in joint impression-management activities with the intent of influencing the reputation of individual leaders and firms, or the reputation of corporate leadership and governance at large. In Chapter 3 we describe the symbolic management of strategic decision-making processes, including verbal impression management by firm leaders about their strategic advice seeking, and the adoption of participative strategic decision-making programs that appear to use crowdsourcing technology to solicit input from lower-level managers and staff on strategic options. We explain how the symbolic rhetoric about these processes is often decoupled from actual strategic decision making, which tends to be substantially less participative than advertised, and yet it is both effective and efficient in influencing constituent assessments of firm leadership and strategy. We contend that rhetoric about participative forms of strategic decision making bolsters the reputation of firm leadership by conforming to implicit models of leader effectiveness in Western culture, which are rooted in the institutional logic of democratic process. Such rhetoric enhances the legitimacy of firm leadership by conveying the impression of transparency. We also draw from theoretical perspectives in the cultural anthropology of technology to explain why rhetoric about participative decision making is especially effective to the extent that leaders highlight the use of crowdsourcing technology to solicit strategic input. Finally, we consider how and when firms manage impressions about the diversity and inclusiveness of firm leadership, in particular, increases in racial and gender diversity of top management and boards, and how such rhetoric may also be decoupled from actual decision-making processes.

In Chapter 4 we describe different forms of symbolic management beyond the firm level that cross organizational boundaries, including symbolic management "support" in which individual leaders issue positive comments about the leadership, governance, or strategy of particular other firms in communicating with information intermediaries. We also describe a coordinated form of symbolic management in which groups of female and racial-minority CEOs help manage the reputations of individual leaders. We explain why these cooperative forms of symbolic management are often more potent than the firm-level forms of impression management examined in prior research. Our theory and findings suggest that symbolic management support not only exerts a strong influence on constituents' beliefs about particular firms and their leaders, but over time exerts a deeper influence on normative assumptions about governance, including the implicit criteria by which information intermediaries evaluate the quality of firm leadership. We contend that symbolic management support has contributed to institutional change in corporate governance through a process of rhetorical cooptation, in which firm leaders subtly reinterpret agency prescriptions that had become taken for granted among firm constituents in ways that reassert their autonomy and discretion.

In addition, we reveal how firm leaders have increasingly engaged in symbolic management that addresses characteristics of the larger governance system, including the social structure of corporate leadership. We suggest that such symbolic management may have contributed to a kind of decoupling between the apparent social structure of corporate leadership, as indicated by the increasingly sparse network of interlocking directorates, and the *actual* social structure, which is characterized by persistently high levels of social embeddedness among firm leaders.

2

Symbolic Management of Policy and Structure

In this chapter we examine the symbolic management of formal policies and structures in corporate governance. Formal policies and structures acquire symbolic value when they appear to conform to prevailing institutional logics of governance, or taken-for-granted assumptions about normatively appropriate forms of organization. We review theory and research suggesting that over a period of several decades, a series of policies and structures emerged as potent forms of symbolic management as the agency logic of governance became institutionalized in the financial community. We ultimately argue that the institutionalization of the agency logic not only contributed to the reinterpretation of particular governance policies and structures, but increased the symbolic importance of corporate governance at large. The agency logic reduces and simplifies complex organizations down to particular governance characteristics, such as incentive policies that align executive and shareholder interests, and board structures that increase the board's independence from management. We also contend that the institutionalization of the agency logic contributed to a lasting increase in symbolic management activity by firm leaders, both in terms of the frequency of symbolic management and the variety of its forms. The agency logic places a premium on external, financial control over organizations and managerial accountability, which spurred an increase in symbolic management by firm leaders in order to preserve their power and discretion. While the theory and research presented in future chapters ultimately suggests how prevailing institutional logics of organization have evolved from the pure agency model, the increased symbolic importance of corporate governance and the increased intensity and variety of symbolic management activity are major legacies of the agency logic of governance that first emerged in the late 1970s and early 1980s.

We begin by reviewing the shift in institutional logics of organization from the so-called corporate logic, which prevailed in the 1960s and early 1970s, to the agency logic that became institutionalized thereafter. We then describe how the agency logic contributed to the reinterpretation of specific corporate governance policies and structures, and how this increased the need and opportunity for symbolic management by firm leaders.

Symbolic Management: Governance, Strategy, and Institutions. James Westphal and Sun Hyun Park,
Oxford University Press (2020). © James Westphal and Sun Hyun Park.
DOI: 10.1093/oso/9780198792055.001.0001

Shift from the Corporate Logic to the Agency
Logic of Organization

The shift that occurred in the late 1970s and early 1980s from the corporate logic to the agency logic of organization entailed a paradigmatic change in prevailing assumptions about the nature of the firm and the role of managers in organizations (see Table 2.1). The corporate logic was founded on the assumptions of managerialist theory: It conceived the firm as an institution with distinct core competencies, and managers as trained professionals who possess critical knowledge for the efficient allocation of resources (Chandler, 1962). Top managers in particular were viewed as stewards of the firm who play a critical role in value

Table 2.1. Agency logic versus corporate logic of organization

	Agency logic	Corporate logic
Assumptions about...		
Top managers	Relatively fungible agents of shareholders; pursue strategies that advance personal interests at expense of shareholders	Professionals with unique strategic knowledge that is required for efficient allocation of corporate resources; stewards of their organizations
The firm	A nexus of contracts; legal fiction	An institution with unique core competencies
Concept of resource allocation	Investor capitalism: Shareholders can diversify better and more easily than firms	Managerial capitalism: Top managers have primary responsibility for allocating resources to different businesses in the corporation
Links to high-order cultural frames	Logic of capitalist markets	Norms of professional autonomy
Links to theories of organization	Agency theory (Jensen and Meckling, 1976)	Managerialist theory (Chandler, 1962)
Implications for governance policies:		
Compensation	Use incentives to align management and shareholder interests	Use salary and other rewards to attract and retain scarce management talent
Allocation of cash flow Boards of directors	Redistribute to shareholders Adopt structures that enable independent control over management.	Retain and reinvest Recruit directors who can secure critical resources and provide valuable input and advice to management.

Source: Adapted from Zajac and Westphal (2004: 436)

creation by developing business and corporate strategies that leverage and develop the firm's core competencies. The agency logic proceeds from fundamentally different assumptions about the firm and the role of managers that are rooted in economic theories of organization (Alchian and Demsetz, 1972; Jensen and Meckling, 1976; Fama and Jensen, 1983). The firm is conceived as a nexus of contracts; it is a "legal fiction" that does not exist apart from contractual relations between owners, individual employees, and other suppliers and customers (Jensen and Meckling, 1976: 310). The agency logic questions managerial motives, and implicitly discounts managerial capabilities. Rather than trained professionals with uniquely valuable knowledge and experience, managers are conceived as relatively fungible "drones" or agents of shareholders (Useem, 1993: 21). And rather than responsible, well-intentioned stewards that seek to leverage distinctive capabilities in ways that differentiate the firm and create value, managers are thought to pursue self-interested strategies such as unrelated diversification and self-interested behavior such as perquisite consumption that generate agency costs and reduce shareholder value. Moreover, according to the agency logic, the purpose of organizational structures and policies is not to execute managers' strategies, but to control managers and mitigate the agency costs that otherwise result from their self-interested activities. In addition, agency assumptions supported a new model of economic resource allocation, sometimes described as "investor capitalism," as distinct from managerial capitalism (Davis, 2005; Davis and Thompson, 1994; Useem, 1996: 1; Westphal and Zajac, 1998). If managers are simply fungible agents, and if firms are legal fictions without unique core competencies, then economic resources can be allocated by institutional fund managers and individual investors in capital markets, rather than by managers in corporations.

The agency logic is a highly parsimonious and radically individualistic perspective on organizations. The main function of organizations is the governance of contracts, and the main mechanisms of governance are financial incentives and the board of directors. Managers and other agents are viewed as individual actors; there is little concern with management groups or teams. The board is similarly conceived as a unitary actor; the agency logic discounts the importance of group or subgroup dynamics on boards or board committees.

There is considerable evidence to suggest a shift in the prevailing institutional logic of organization from the corporate logic to the agency logic among members of the financial community in the late 1970s and into the 1980s. Useem's (1993) qualitative research on institutional investors, our archival research on communication in proxy statements (Westphal and Zajac, 1998; Zajac and Westphal, 1994, 1995), and Davis and colleagues' analyses of various Securities and Exchange Commission documents, court decisions, and publications of various investor groups (Davis and Thompson, 1994; Davis, 2005) all provided evidence for a dramatic shift in prevailing assumptions about top executives and resource allocation over this time period. More recent research has also documented the influence of agency theory in the curricula of U.S. business schools during the late 1970s, and its subsequent influence on corporate strategy as former students ascended to leadership positions (Jung and Shin, 2018). Studies have also provided evidence that this shift toward an agency logic occurred not only in the U.S. but in other countries where managerialism had predominated (Fiss and Zajac, 2004; Meyer and Höllerer, 2010).

In the following sections we discuss how this radical shift in assumptions about the firm, managers, and resource allocation led to different interpretations of corporate governance policies and structures, and provided both the need and opportunity for specific forms of symbolic management.

Executive Compensation Policy and Symbolic Management

The agency logic places particular importance on managerial incentives as a determinant of firm performance. From the agency perspective, incentive compensation is the primary means of aligning the preferences of managers with the interests of owners, in order to mitigate the agency costs that otherwise result from managers' self-interested decision making. The agency logic focuses especially on the incentive compensation of CEOs as a solution to firm-level agency costs, reflecting the extreme methodological individualism of organizational economics, on which the agency logic is founded. From the preceding corporate logic of organization, compensation policy is one element of strategic human resource management, which has the fundamental, broader objective of attracting and retaining managerial talent (Milkovich and Newman, 1984; Pfeffer, 1994). Whereas the agency logic implicitly treats managers as fungible agents, the corporate logic presumes that managerial talent is scarce, such that the purpose of compensation policy and other human resource policies is to compete with other companies for talented managers. Executive incentive plans, including short-term incentive plans (or "bonus" plans), and long-term incentive plans (or "LTIPs"), are viewed as means of attracting and retaining a team of top managers who have the native talent and acquired experience to develop strategies that effectively leverage and build the firm's distinctive capabilities. Whereas the agency logic interprets incentive plans such as LTIPs primarily as a means of reducing agency costs by controlling individual executives (especially the CEO), the strategic human resource perspective contained in the corporate logic views these plans as a means of rewarding and retaining executives who create value for the organization's stakeholders.

The assumption that managers are the source of agency costs, together with the focus on CEO incentives as a primary solution to the agency problem, created the impetus for symbolic management of CEO compensation. Our research has showed that as the agency logic became predominant in the financial community, there was a significant increase in the frequency and intensity of verbal explanations for CEO incentive plans, and a shift in the content of these explanations (Zajac and Westphal, 1995; Westphal and Zajac, 1998; see also Wade et al., 1997). Firms provided explanations for CEO LTIPs such as stock option plans and restricted stock plans in proxy statements on a more frequent basis after 1980, and the average length of these explanations more than doubled from 1976 to 1990. Moreover, the content of LTIP explanations changed in accordance with the shift in institutional logics. Prior to 1980, firms tended to justify LTIPs in terms of the corporate logic. AT&T, for example, explained its plan as follows: "The Board believes that adoption of the Plan will enhance the Company's ability to attract and retain individuals of exceptional managerial talent upon whom, in large measure, the sustained progress, growth and profitability of the Company depends" (Zajac and Westphal, 1995: 285). By the mid-1980s, most firms were using an agency-based justification, as in the following example from Alcoa's 1988 proxy statement:

Alcoa's Board of Directors has decided to place an increasing share of management's overall compensation at risk rather than in fixed salaries. The new approach to compensation was recommended by the Board's compensation committee, which is composed solely of outside directors. The board believes that granting stock options, performance shares and [bonuses] will create a more appropriate relationship between compensation and the financial performance of the company in order to increase key employees' personal financial identification with interests of the Company's stockholders.

(Zajac and Westphal, 1995: 285)

Moreover, the data indicated a transition period during the early 1980s in which many firms used a hybrid explanation that combined elements of both logics.

At the same time, while firms were providing more frequent, lengthy, and agency-based explanations for LTIPs, they were also increasingly decoupling these plans from actual compensation packages. In particular, firms were increasingly adopting LTIPs that appear to make CEOs pay more contingent on shareholder performance, but without actually making grants under the plans, or making very small grants that represent a trivial portion of the CEOs' total compensation. Moreover, firms were especially likely to provide agency-based explanations for LTIPs while decoupling the plans when the potential for shareholder concern about agency costs was relatively high. In particular, firms were especially like to engage in these forms of symbolic management when recent stock returns and firm profitability had been relatively low.

Our analyses showed that the symbolic management of LTIP compensation was generally effective in influencing shareholder opinion. Event study analysis indicated that the adoption of LTIPs elicited a positive stock market reaction across a variety of time intervals, regardless of whether the plans were implemented (i.e., regardless of whether grants were made under the plans). Moreover, the market reactions were significantly stronger when firms provided an agency-based explanation for the LTIP in proxy statements, again irrespective of whether the plans were implemented.

There was also evidence that symbolic management of LTIP compensation can alleviate shareholder pressures to enact other corporate governance reforms. In particular, LTIP adoption interacted with the level of ownership by institutional investors to reduce the likelihood of two specific changes in board structure that were assumed to increase board control over management: separation of the CEO and board chair positions, and increases in the ratio of outside to inside directors (Westphal and Zajac, 1998). Agency theorists, policy makers, and members of the financial community have generally agreed or assumed that allocating the CEO and board chair positions to separate individuals will enhance the board's ability to exercise independent control over firm strategy and policy (Beatty and Zajac, 1994). It is assumed that CEOs who also hold the board chair position can more easily control the agenda of board meetings and suppress open challenges to their decision making (though the actual effects of board leadership structure are contingent on the performance context, among other factors (see Krause and Semadeni, 2013; Krause, 2017)). Finance scholars, regulators, and financial market actors have also generally assumed that outside directors are better able than inside directors to independently evaluate and control management decision making, such that increases in the ratio of outside to inside directors are thought to increase board control and reduce agency costs (Fama and Jensen, 1983). Agency theory posits a partial substitution effect between incentive alignment and behavioral control mechanisms: compensation that aligns the interests of agents and principals (e.g., CEOs and investors) and reduces the need for independent control of agent behavior (Jensen and Meckling, 1976; Eisenhardt, 1989; Beatty and Zajac, 1994; Rediker and Seth, 1995). Our analyses suggested a *symbolic* substitution effect between incentive alignment and behavioral control mechanisms. The adoption of LTIPs reduced the likelihood of subsequently separating the CEO and board chair positions or increasing the ratio of outside to inside directors, regardless of whether the LTIPs were implemented. This substitution effect was especially pronounced when firms provided an agency-based explanation for LTIP adoption, and when the level of ownership by institutional investors was relatively high. As the agency logic became institutionalized in the financial community, powerful institutional investors increasingly exerted pressure on firm leaders to enact governance changes to ensure that managerial interests do not dominate shareholder interests. Symbolic increases in incentive alignment, in the form of decoupled LTIPs with an agency-based explanation, alleviated pressure from powerful institutional investors to enact board reforms that were thought to increase board independence and reduce managerial discretion.

An ironic feature of agency theory, and of normative, economic theories of organization more generally, is that when accepted by organizational stakeholders, it facilitates symbolic management activity that helps to falsify the theory. The agency logic reduces the complexity of organizations down to only a few characteristics, especially incentive alignment and structural independence. It assumes that these formal characteristics determine the extent of agency costs in the organization, which in turn largely determines organizational efficiency and economic returns to shareholders. By extension, the agency logic implicitly ignores the potential for political behavior or social influence activity to offset the effects of formal contracts (incentive alignment) and formal structure (independence) on performance. Thus, as the agency logic became institutionalized in the financial community, symbolic management became more efficient *and* effective. Rather than managing impressions about a broad range of organizational characteristics, firm leaders could go a long way toward reassuring investors about the quality of firm governance and the prospects for strong economic returns by adopting a single policy. Moreover, investors would likely be satisfied by formal adoption alone, so that firms could elicit positive, and often very strong market reactions, without even implementing the plans. As a result, the rate of decoupling increased over time as the agency logic became institutionalized in the financial community: As the agency logic became increasingly accepted, and even taken for granted among financial market actors, the adoption of incentive plans increasingly had no discernible impact on agency costs or organizational efficiency. While academic theory often lags practice, in this case it actually led market behavior, though not in a positive way. Scholars in financial economics had assumed that LTIPs would reduce agency costs and improve organizational efficiency, and empirical studies on CEO compensation continued to equate LTIPs with lower agency costs until the mid-1990s (Kumar and Sopariwala, 1992; Brozovsky and Sopariwala, 1995).

Stock Repurchase Plans and Symbolic Management

The historic shift in prevailing logics of organization from a corporate logic to an agency logic also led to the reinterpretation of financial policies such as stock repurchase plans. From the corporate logic, as discussed above, top executives are trained and experienced professionals who have acquired unique strategic knowledge that enables them to allocate firm resources efficiently. As a result, they will tend to allocate free cash flow only to profitable corporate projects. If profitable projects are unavailable, the free cash would be returned to shareholders to be invested in other companies. Accordingly, based on the corporate logic, a stock repurchase plan can be viewed as a negative indicator that a firm lacks promising investment opportunities, thus eliciting a negative reaction from investors. The agency logic is predicated on the assumption that managers tend to favor projects that serve their own personal interests at the expense of shareholders, such that repurchase plans were viewed positively as a means of preventing managers from incurring agency costs. As articulated by Jensen (1989: 64), agency theory suggests that when executives have free cash flow to spend, they are "tempted to waste it on empire-building projects or other perks that benefit themselves at the expense of shareholders." As a result, shareholders and other stakeholders are thought to benefit from policies that return free cash flow to investors, who can be expected to allocate the financial resources more efficiently. According to the agency logic, therefore, the adoption of repurchase plans indicates strong corporate governance, which can elicit a more positive market reaction.

In fact, our analyses revealed a significant shift in stock market reactions to repurchase plan adoptions during the 1980s. Whereas market reactions were negative on average from 1980 to 1982, they shifted from negative to positive over the period 1983 to 1985. At the same time, our research and other studies revealed that firms may formally announce a repurchase plan, but without subsequently repurchasing any stock, or they may buy back only a small portion of the shares targeted for repurchase in the plan (Stephens and Weisbach, 1998; Westphal and Zajac, 2001). We suggested that non-implementation of repurchase plans can be a form of institutional decoupling, in which executives symbolically conform to the agency logic of governance by formally adopting a repurchase plan, and then neglect to distribute free cash to shareholders in order to preserve their discretionary control over the allocation of corporate resources. Moreover, our analyses indicated that firms were more likely to adopt and decouple repurchase plans when the potential for shareholder concern about agency costs was relatively high. In particular, firms were especially likely to engage in symbolic adoption of repurchase plans when firm performance had been poor, and when visible indicators of board independence from management were lacking (e.g., when the CEO also occupied the board chair position, and the level of director stock ownership was low).

Our data also indicated both a sharp increase in repurchase plan adoptions during the mid-1980s and an increase in the rate of decoupling, during a period in which the agency logic of governance prevailed. In effect, repurchase plans became more symbolic and less substantive over time. This provides another example of how the growing acceptance of agency theory in the financial community ironically facilitated symbolic management activity that served to falsify normative prescriptions of the theory. At the same time, the decoupling of repurchase plans in order to preserve managerial discretion is consistent with the premise of agency theory that managers cannot be trusted to pursue shareholder interests on their own volition, but are prone to engaging in self-interested behavior that reduces organizational efficiency and violates shareholder preferences. Thus, the growing acceptance of agency theory and rising shareholder concern about agency costs has also ironically contributed to untrustworthy management behavior (i.e., the failure to implement repurchase plans) that is consistent with the *descriptive* assumptions of the theory. In effect, the behavioral assumptions of agency theory became a self-fulfilling prophecy through its promulgation in the financial community. Regrettably, agency theory was self-confirming where we would like it to be disconfirmed, and self-disconfirming where we would like it to be confirmed.

In a possible conflating of hopes and expectations, financial economists responded to these findings by suggesting that positive market reactions to decoupled repurchase plans were a short-term outcome, and that market reactions would correct themselves in the medium or long run as evidence of non-implementation accumulated. They proposed that, from a market-learning perspective, as more firms neglected to implement their repurchase plans over time, the expected efficiency benefits of adoption should diminish, and the stock market's reaction to the adoption of new plans should diminish in tandem. Instead, our analyses showed an *increase* in stock market reactions to repurchase plan adoptions over time, despite accumulating evidence of decoupling. After controlling for corporate governance characteristics, year and industry effects, firm performance, and other firm-level financial characteristics, the number of prior implemented *and non-implemented* repurchase plans were significantly and positively associated with excess stock returns from adopting a repurchase plan over the period 1980 to 1994.

These results were consistent with an institutional perspective on stock market reactions, wherein repurchase plans acquired symbolic value over time, despite an increase in decoupling, through a process of institutionalization. Policies are more likely to become institutionalized if they resonate with a higher-order belief system that provides a favorable interpretation of the policy (Scott, 2001; Thornton et al., 2012), and the emergence of the agency logic provided a more favorable interpretation of repurchase plans. From the cognitive perspective on institutions, policies can acquire symbolic value through a process of "reciprocated interpretations," wherein the policy is presented to organizational constituents as consistent with their values, and this interpretation is validated by the constituents (Scott, 1987: 496; 2001). As this process is repeated over time, the policy becomes more closely integrated with the belief system, and may ultimately become taken for granted as a symbol of the higher-order logic. Large-sample, empirical evidence for this institutionalization process remains rare; few studies have been able to fully control for efficiency or other performance benefits from adoption. By showing increasingly positive constituent reactions to a decoupled policy, our findings provided rare, large-sample evidence for the institutionalization of symbolic value.

Financial economists typically assume that stock market reactions reflect semi-strong market efficiency, wherein all publicly available information about a policy at the time of its adoption is reflected in the market's reaction (Brealy and Myers, 1991; Fama, 1970). From this perspective, the stock market would seem to be an unlikely context in which to observe the institutionalization of symbolic value. In actuality, however, the dynamics of stock market reactions are well suited to institutionalization. Because market reactions to the announcement of policy adoptions occur quickly, and are predicated on imperfect communication, they are governed by a socio-historical estimation process in which investors estimate the response of other investors by referring to prior market reactions to similar events. As more firms adopt a policy that receives a positive reaction from the market, each investor's uncertainty about the market's response to the current event is diminished, which tends to induce a more positive response. In this way, the market value of the policy can increase over time, despite evidence of decoupling. Thus, the social referencing process that guides investor reactions to material events can perpetuate and amplify market reactions to policy adoptions, contributing to the institutionalization of corporate policies that do not necessarily increase organizational efficiency.

We also examined whether stock market reactions to repurchase plan adoptions might be influenced by prior adoptions of LTIPs. The event study literature has tended to treat different policies and strategies as independent events. Individual studies focus on market reactions to particular events, without considering how investors might be influenced by prior responses to related events. The larger literature on firm–stakeholder relations has also tended to focus on constituent reactions to particular policy and strategy initiatives, without examining how these reactions might be conditioned by constituents' prior experience with related policies and strategies. However, investors' reaction to a specific policy is likely to be influenced by their recent experience with other policies that had similar rationales. In this case, market reactions to repurchase plans could be influenced by investors' prior experience with other policies that were ostensibly adopted to mitigate agency costs. Prior to widespread decoupling of repurchase plans beginning in the mid-1980s, in the early 1980s many firms had adopted LTIPs without implementing the plans. Many firms explicitly invoked an agency logic in presenting LTIPs to shareholders, as discussed above. Thus, from a market-learning perspective, as more firms adopt LTIPs and then neglect to implement the plans, investors should not only discount the expected value of LTIPs, but they may also lower their estimates for other policies that are alleged to control agency costs, such as stock repurchase plans. Instead, our analyses showed that, after controlling for a range of factors, including corporate governance characteristics, year and industry effects, firm performance and other firm-level financial characteristics, and previously decoupled repurchase plans, the number of firms that had previously adopted LTIPs with an agency explanation but not implemented the plans was *positively* and significantly associated with the market's reaction to repurchase plan adoption at a focal firm.

An institutional perspective on constituent reactions would suggest that as more firms adopted LTIPs with an agency explanation, the agency logic itself acquired normative legitimacy as a socially acceptable rationale for corporate policy initiatives. Thus, as LTIPs diffused widely in the mid-1980s, firms could increasingly realize legitimacy benefits from adopting related policies that appeared to mitigate agency costs. In effect, repurchase plans borrowed symbolic value from agency explanations for LTIPs. This can occur despite an increase in decoupling of LTIPs due to the socio-historical estimation process that drives investor reactions.

Board Independence and Symbolic Management

The third pillar of efficient corporate governance according to the agency logic is independent monitoring and control of management by the board of directors. From the agency perspective, independent directors are optimally positioned to exercise control because they have access to reliable and timely information about management decision making, but are not dependent on top managers for their compensation or employment (Fama and Jensen, 1983).[1] The proposition that greater board independence from management improves firm governance by increasing the board's ability to control management was "conventional wisdom" in the financial community from the 1990s through the 2000s (Langevoort, 2006: 1553), such that board independence was *equated* with board control (e.g., Corporate Board, 2006). A large-sample survey of analysts and investors showed that "a well-governed company was defined by investors as a company with a majority of outside directors on its board" (Investor Relations Business, 2000: 1; Coombes and Watson, 2000; Ocasio and Joseph, 2005; Joseph et al., 2014).

Increasing board independence should enhance the legitimacy of firm leadership and governance along each of the three dimensions of legitimacy described by Suchman (1995). It enhances pragmatic legitimacy, which relates to the self-interest of constituents, as independence is assumed to indicate board control on behalf of shareholder interests. It enhances normative legitimacy, since increasing board independence is a central injunctive norm of the agency logic. And, as the agency logic became institutionalized in the financial community, greater board independence conferred cognitive legitimacy by reducing the complexity of organizational governance to one simple metric. Thus, by increasing board independence, firm leaders enhance the legitimacy of firm governance with analysts

---

[1] Although the definition of an independent director has varied somewhat in the agency literature, in recent years the most common definition among scholars, regulators, and practitioners is a director "whose only business relationship with the firm is their board members" (Anderson and Reeb, 2004: 324; Langevoort, 2006).

and investors, which should prompt more positive analyst appraisals of strategic decisions and reduce the likelihood that institutional investors intervene in strategic decision making, mandate reductions in executive play, or force changes in leadership in response to weak firm performance.

As with CEO incentives and stock repurchase plans, however, the agency logic ironically provides both the need and opportunity for executives to engage in symbolic management. While the agency logic focuses on the board's formal or contractual independence from management, a large body of behavioral research has now shown that the board's *social* independence from the CEO is a much stronger predictor of policies and strategies that promote shareholder interests (Joseph et al., 2014; for reviews, see Finkelstein et al., 2009; Lynall et al., 2003). This literature suggests that directors who have friendship ties to the CEO are likely to feel conflicted about blocking the CEO's preferences, and they are likely to be biased toward the CEO in evaluating his/her decision making and in making attributions about firm performance (Finkelstein et al., 2009; Westphal, 1998; Zhu and Westphal, 2014). Powerful leaders therefore have an opportunity to separate substance from symbolism in the domain of board control by favoring the appointment of directors who lack contractual ties to the firm but who have friendship ties to top executives, increasing the board's formal independence without increasing (or even decreasing) its social independence. Symbolic decoupling is facilitated not only by the focus of agency theory on formal contracts versus social relations, but also by information asymmetry in relations between firm leaders and external stakeholders. Social ties between executives and directors and behavioral dynamics in management–board relationships are difficult for firm stakeholders to ascertain.

Top executives can also enhance the cognitive and normative legitimacy of their firm's governance by proclaiming that their boards monitor and control management decision making on behalf of shareholders. By framing board conduct in the language of agency theory, firm leaders create the perception of "procedural conformity," defined as conformity to "institutionally defined means-end chains an organization is [expected] to follow to realize desired objectives" (Meyer and Rowan, 1977; Scott, 2002: 196).

Verbal impression management (IM) is known to be especially persuasive when it contains simple and succinct accounts of organizational activity (Elsbach, 1994; Ashforth and Humphrey, 1997; Elsbach and Elofson, 2000; Bansal and Kistruck, 2006). Schlenker and Weigold's (1992: 144) classic research on verbal IM shows that "People think 'truth' comes in tidy packages." The agency logic allows simple and succinct accounts of firm governance because it reduces the complexity of firm leadership and governance to a few prescriptions—incentive alignment and independent board control. It also conceives these mechanisms as partial substitutes, as noted above, such that the presence of one reduces the need for the other (Jensen and Meckling, 1976; Eisenhardt, 1989; Beatty and Zajac,

1994). Accordingly, the agency logic facilitates verbal IM that is both efficient and persuasive. Moreover, in enhancing the legitimacy of firm governance, executives also ensure more favorable impressions of subsequent policy and strategy initiatives. Thus, top executives can go a long way toward persuading constituents about the quality of firm governance, policy and strategy by referring to independent board control over management.

Two-stage regression analyses showed that while increases in the proportion of board members who are formally independent of management were positively associated with security analysts' earnings forecasts and stock recommendations, a validated measure of board control derived from survey responses of CEOs and outside directors was not significantly related to these outcomes (Westphal and Graebner, 2010). Moreover, a validated measure of CEO verbal IM about board control in communications with individual analysts, which is derived from survey responses of CEOs and analysts (e.g., "In talking with [this person] about your board over the past year, to what extent has your objective been to give [him/her] the impression that the board engages in independent control over management?"), was also positively associated with earnings forecasts and stock recommendations of those same analysts, again independently of our survey measure of actual board control. In addition, there was a positive and significant interaction between increases in board independence and verbal IM by the CEO in predicting these outcomes, consistent with evidence from the social psychological literature that verbal IM can amplify the effects of socially legitimate attributes on an actor's image by making those characteristics more salient to a relevant audience (Cialdini and Goldstein, 2004; Siegel and Brockner, 2005). The magnitude of these effects was also quite strong. For example, if the level of verbal IM toward an analyst is relatively high (one standard deviation above the mean), adding two formally independent directors increases the likelihood of an upgrade by the analyst by 36 per cent on average, and reduces the chances of a downgrade by 45 per cent on average.

Our analyses also provided uniquely strong evidence that increases in the ratio of outside to inside directors and CEO communication with analysts about board control often represent deliberate acts of symbolic management. Our analyses showed that relatively low consensus earnings forecasts and relatively negative stock recommendations by analysts interacted with a validated survey measure of CEO influence over the board nominating committee to predict (1) the addition of formally independent directors, and (2) reductions in the number of non-independent directors. Low earnings forecasts and negative stock recommendations by individual analysts also significantly predicted the level of subsequent verbal IM about board control directed at the same analysts by the CEO.

We also validated our interpretation of the results using multi-item survey scales that measure the criteria used by board-nominating committees to evaluate director candidates. One scale gauged the weight given to board candidates' appearance of independence (e.g., one question asked the extent to which the committee looked for a board candidate who will appear to external constituents to be independent of management). Additional multi-item survey scales gauged the weight given to whether a candidate (1) had a social tie to the CEO and (2) appeared likely to support the CEO's leadership rather than control management. Each measure had strong inter-item and inter-rater reliability. Supplemental analyses provided strong evidence that the weight given to board candidates' appearance of independence mediated the interactive effect of CEO influence and low earnings forecasts on subsequent increases in the board's formal independence from management (this mediated relationship also held for negative stock recommendations). Further, these effects were also significantly and positively mediated by the weight given by the nominating committee to whether board candidates had a social tie to the CEO and appeared likely to support the CEO's leadership rather than control management. Moreover, the survey of verbal communication about board control directly measures the CEO's intent to manage impressions. Overall, therefore, the results provided perhaps the most direct evidence to date for agentic, symbolic management activity by firm leaders.

We were also able to corroborate evidence for the effectiveness of symbolic management using survey responses from security analysts. Our analyst surveys included a multi-item measure of perceived board control (e.g., "To what extent do you believe that the board of [company name] exercises independent control over management?"). Analyses indicated that this measure significantly mediated the effects of formal board independence and verbal IM by CEOs on analysts' subsequent earnings forecasts and stock recommendations (Westphal and Graebner, 2010).

Verbal IM about board control is directed disproportionately at analysts who have a relatively high status in their profession. For example, the frequency of verbal IM about board control directed at analysts who have been selected as members of the "All-America Research Team" by *Institutional Investor* magazine is almost double the frequency of IM directed at other analysts. Such IM exerts indirect influence over other analysts, since high-status analysts serve as opinion leaders whose forecasts and recommendations are followed more closely by their colleagues (Stickel, 1995; Hayward and Boeker, 1998). In effect, status differentiation in the professional community of analysts increases the efficiency of IM. An ironic implication of this social influence process is that analysts who have the highest status are most likely to be "taken in" by symbolic management. That is, they are more likely to believe in decoupled governance policies such as increases in formal board independence that do not actually increase board control, or to express high levels of confidence in such policies, because they are a primary target of verbal IM by top management. Others are more likely to follow the lead of the high-status analysts, regardless of any personal skepticism they may have about the policy.

Accordingly, our theory and findings suggest a new interpretation of studies in financial economics and the related strategy literature on boards of directors and corporate governance. A fairly large body of research in these literatures appears to provide evidence for agency theory or related financial economic perspectives on governance by showing that (1) changes in board composition elicit a positive stock market reaction, which is interpreted as suggesting that greater board independence increases organizational efficiency and performance; (2) low firm performance and/or the level of ownership by institutional investors is associated with subsequent increases in board independence, which is interpreted as suggesting that firms increase board independence to improve organizational efficiency and performance, and that powerful owners require firms to make these reforms; (3) board independence is negatively associated with executive incentives that are thought to align executive interests with the interests of shareholders, which is interpreted as showing a substitution relationship between independent board control and financial incentive alignment (e.g., firms have less need for incentive alignment when boards are formally independent); and (4) board independence is correlated with higher bond ratings, which is also interpreted as evidence that independent directors improve organizational efficiency (for reviews, see Anderson et al., 2004; Bhojraj and Sengupta, 2003; Hillman and Dalziel, 2003). Given the symbolic separation of formal board independence from actual board control over management, however, positive stock market returns and higher bond ratings in response to board independence are best interpreted as reflecting financial market actors' *impression* or perception that firms have improved corporate governance and increased efficiency by controlling agency costs. Relatively low firm performance and/or high institutional ownership spurs such symbolic decoupling. And, as discussed previously, the negative association between board independence and incentive alignment indicates a *symbolic* substitution between independent board control and incentive alignment, rather than an actual substitution between alternative control mechanisms.

Evidence that formal board independence is associated with higher firm profitability is mixed at best, with a number of studies finding weak or null results (Dalton et al., 1998; Bhagat and Black, 2001). Thus, financial economic theory appears to be more helpful in explaining how financial market actors assess boards of directors than in explaining how boards actually work. Overall, our findings have revealed a consistent pattern of symbolic policy adoptions and verbal IM across the primary domains of corporate governance policy emphasized by agency theory and financial economics. Symbolic management with respect to executive incentive alignment, financial resource allocation, and board control over management has been generally successful in enhancing the legitimacy of firm governance and strategy in the financial community and helping to preserve managerial power and discretion, but without substantially improving organizational efficiency.

The Social Psychology of Stock Market
Reactions to Symbolic Action

A longstanding criticism of neo-institutional theory is that it proceeds from a fairly simplistic and naïve perspective on social cognition (DiMaggio, 1997). Policies and structures are thought to become institutionalized when they are assumed or taken for granted among organizational constituents as normatively appropriate elements of organization. While social actors are generally portrayed as either "cultural dopes" (Garfinkel, 1967: 68–75) or heroic "change agents" (Strang and Sine, 2002: 503–7) by institutional theorists (Powell and Colyvas, 2008: 277), recent work has begun to develop a more nuanced perspective on the cognition of social actors in institutionalized environments. As Powell and Colyvas (2008) have pointed out, however, this literature has generally been focused on the micro-foundations of institutional change (also Thornton et al., 2012). We lack a nuanced, cross-level perspective on social cognition in explanations of institutional maintenance.

Neo-institutional perspectives assume that financial market actors are rather unreflective about the value of established policies and structures. It seems unlikely that most security analysts and large investors would assume that governance policies are always implemented, or that most would remain blithely ignorant of accumulated evidence for decoupling. In fact, Zhu and Westphal (2011) showed that most security analysts in a large representative sample had reservations about the value of stock repurchase plans during a period in which adoptions were consistently eliciting very positive stock market reactions. For example, the average response to the questions, "How confident are you that stock repurchase plans will be implemented?" and "How confident are you that stock repurchase plans reflect well on a firm's corporate governance?" was less than 3 on a five-point Likert-type scale. Yet our analyses showed that repurchase plan adoptions had a positive and statistically significant effect on security analysts' earnings forecasts and stock recommendations (i.e., upgrades) during the survey period.

Why would most analysts react positively to repurchase plan adoptions, despite having significant reservations about the economic value of the plans? We theorized that positive reactions to repurchase plans have persisted in part to a social psychological bias known as pluralistic ignorance. Pluralistic ignorance is a systematic tendency for individuals in a group or community to underestimate the extent to which other group members share their concerns or reservations about group practices, policies, or events (Allport, 1924; Merton, 1957; Miller and Nelson, 2002). It leads to a "disjunction" between attitudes and behavior, wherein groups or communities continue to implement or endorse practices that most individuals have reservations about (Miller et al., 2000: 103). We describe the social psychology of pluralistic ignorance in more detail in Chapter 8. A key precondition of pluralistic ignorance is some level of perceived risk in expressing a minority position. In the presence of such risks, individuals look to the behavior of other group members for some indication that their opinion is shared before taking a public position. In the context of security analysts' reactions to repurchase plans, analysts will consider the recent reactions of other analysts to similar plans in discerning whether their reservations are shared, and they will find that other analysts generally reacted favorably to these plans. Social attribution bias then causes most analysts to overattribute the positive reactions of other analysts to confidence in the economic value of the plans, resulting in pluralistic ignorance (see Chapter 8).

In fact, our survey data indicated that while most analysts expressed private reservations about the value of repurchase plans, most also believed that other analysts lacked such reservations. For example, the modal response to the question, "How confident do you believe *other* analysts are that stock repurchase plans reflect well on a firm's corporate governance?" (italics added) was 4 on a five-point Likert-type scale. Moreover, our analyses showed that pluralistic ignorance contributed to analysts' positive reactions to repurchase plans. The effect of an analyst's private reservations about repurchase plans on the likelihood of issuing more positive earnings forecasts and upgrading a firm's stock following repurchase plan adoption was significantly reduced to the extent that the analyst perceived that other analysts did not hold such reservations. In most cases, therefore, analysts did not respond positively to repurchase plans because they took the value of these plans for granted, but because they assumed other analysts saw value in the plans. By extension, the institutionalization of market value was not driven primarily by cognitive bias about the policy, in which the value of the plans became increasingly taken for granted by individual analysts. It was driven instead by increasingly biased *social* perceptions, i.e., perceptions *about the beliefs of other analysts*: Analysts increasingly underestimated the extent to which their concerns about repurchase plans were shared as positive market reactions to adoption persisted despite accumulating evidence of decoupling. In Chapter 8 we explain how pluralistic ignorance has contributed to the persistence of symbolic value in other domains of governance policy, including board independence from management.

Thus, pluralistic ignorance provides a cross-level, social psychological explanation for the maintenance of institutional value, as it explains how individual-level biases in social cognition contribute to institutionalization at the market level. In Chapter 8 we further explain how pluralistic ignorance occurs at multiple levels in the governance system: in small groups within the firm, such as boards and top management teams, and in large groups and communities outside the firm, such as the community of security analysts. We suggest that pluralistic ignorance even occurs at the level of the governance system, as actors in particular roles underestimate the extent to which actors in different roles share concerns about particular policies and structures. We also explain how social networks moderate pluralistic ignorance. Whereas conventional, cognitive perspectives presume that network ties amplify institutionalization (Scott, 2001), we suggest how network ties among actors who occupy evaluative roles in the governance system have the potential to stem institutionalization by reducing pluralistic ignorance. However, while the leaders of large firms are connected by a variety of informal network ties that have facilitated the spread of different forms of symbolic management, as discussed in Chapter 6, the professional community of security analysts is marked by much lower levels of social cohesion, allowing pluralistic ignorance to persist.

Conclusion

We have described how a shift in prevailing, institutional logics of organization contributed to the symbolic management of formal policies and structures over the last several decades. As the agency logic of governance became institutionalized in the financial community, a series of policies and structures emerged as potent forms of symbolic decoupling: the adoption of CEO incentive plans, stock repurchase plans, and increases in board independence from management. Each of these policies and structures acquired symbolic value by leveraging a central, normative prescription of the agency logic.

A fundamental irony of agency theory, and of normative, economic theories of organization in general, is that they tend to motivate and enable social behavior that undermines normative prescriptions of the theories. The emphasis on top executives as a source of agency costs motivated formal policy adoptions, accompanied by verbal IM, which gave the appearance of accountability and commitment to shareholder value, while the focus on formal contracts enabled different forms of decoupling that undermined any efficiency benefits of the policies. Moreover, the simplicity and parsimony of agency theory increased the efficiency of symbolic management: The determinants of economic value creation were reduced largely to incentive alignment (especially for CEOs), minimizing free cash flow and increasing board independence, which provided focal points for symbolic management and increased the expected returns from each symbolic policy adoption. Deepening the irony, we explained how the symbolic value of decoupled policies increased over time through an institutionalization process in which many market participants harbored private reservations about the value of the policies, but increasingly underestimated the extent to which their reservations were shared by other actors.

Symbolic decoupling can be ephemeral in some contexts, and may even trigger events that lead to coupling or substantive implementation over the long term (Tilcsik, 2010; Bromley and Powell, 2012). However, this does not appear to be the case for policies and structures that affect powerful firm leaders. CEO incentive alignment is no higher now than in the 1970s and 1980s, as executives and compensation experts continue to devise new means of decoupling incentive plans, some of which have been discovered (e.g., stock option backdating and repricing (Pollock et al., 2002; Bizjak et al., 2009; Heron and Lie, 2009; Greve et al., 2010)), and others that remain little known (Aguinis et al., 2018). Our surveys also indicate that average levels of independent board control over management remain low and essentially unchanged since the 1990s (Westphal and Park, 2012). While the agency logic has recently been eclipsed by other logics of organization, as discussed in subsequent chapters, its legacies include an increased focus on firm governance as a core driver of economic value, and a lasting increase in the amount and variety of symbolic management activity by firm leaders.

3

Symbolic Management of Process

In this chapter we examine the symbolic management of social processes in firm leadership and governance. While extent theory and research has focused largely on symbolic management of particular organizational policies and structures, we suggest that the symbolic management of organizational processes may be an especially potent means of influencing constituent opinion. Such symbolic management takes a variety of different forms, and derives legitimacy from multiple institutional logics that go beyond the agency logic of governance described in Chapter 2. We explain how firm leaders engage in verbal IM about their strategic advice network, and how such communication is decoupled from their actual advice-seeking behavior. We also reveal that the potency of such IM has increased over time. We go on to describe how firms gain legitimacy by adopting participative strategic decision-making (PSDM) programs that conform to the institutional logic of democratic process, despite decoupling the programs from actual strategic decision making. In communicating about these programs, firm leaders sometimes highlight the use of information technology to solicit input about strategy. We explain why such IM is less likely to elicit skeptical reactions from constituents. We then consider how and when firms manage impressions about the diversity and inclusiveness of firm leadership, and how such rhetoric may also be decoupled from actual decision-making processes. We ultimately conclude that the symbolic management of social and organizational processes in firm leadership is among the most efficient and effective means of increasing the legitimacy of firm governance and strategy.

Symbolic Management of CEO Advice Seeking

We begin by examining the symbolic management of strategic decision-making processes. The symbolic management of decision-making processes, and the symbolic management of organizational processes more generally, has received surprisingly little systematic research attention. Yet, the symbolic value of engaging in normatively legitimate decision-making processes may be greater than the symbolic value of adopting normative policies and structures. March and Olsen (1984) suggested that the logic of appropriateness is especially likely to govern perceptions of organizational processes. One possible reason for this lack of research attention is that the symbolic management of decision making is typically more subtle than the symbolic decoupling of the formal structures and

Symbolic Management: Governance, Strategy, and Institutions. James Westphal and Sun Hyun Park,
Oxford University Press (2020). © James Westphal and Sun Hyun Park.
DOI: 10.1093/oso/9780198792055.001.0001

policies considered thus far. While the symbolic management of governance policies such as LTIPs and repurchase plans often involved formally adopting the policies without actually implementing them, the symbolic management of decision making often involves the implementation of procedures or routines that violate the spirit or stated objectives of the strategic decision-making process.

A longstanding and fairly pervasive form of symbolic management involves verbal communication about strategic advice seeking by the CEO in response to low firm performance. McDonald and Westphal (2003) found that CEOs of large public companies often responded to relatively low performance by changing the composition of their advice network. In particular, they sought more strategic advice from executives at other firms who were personal friends, or who had similar professional backgrounds (e.g., similar functional backgrounds or employment in the same industry), while seeking less advice from executives outside their friendship circle or who had substantially different backgrounds. Thus, rather than seeking advice from executives who might be expected to provide a fresh perspective or an objective point of view on the strategic challenges facing their firms, most CEOs responded to significant performance declines by engaging in a kind of confirmation-seeking behavior: They sought strategic advice from personal friends and similar others who were especially likely to share their biases and to affirm the value of their strategies. Further analyses showed that advice seeking from executives at other firms who were personal friends, or who had similar functional or industry backgrounds, was negatively related to changes in corporate strategy (e.g., changes in product market or geographic diversification) following declines in firm performance, while advice seeking from non-friends and dissimilar others was positively related to strategic change. Thus, low firm performance often prompted CEOs to constrict their advice-seeking network in ways that contributed to strategic inertia. This pattern of findings has been replicated for more recent samples, and for samples of smaller public companies.

At the same time, our analyses indicate that CEOs often respond to unexpectedly low or declining performance by highlighting their advice-seeking behavior in communicating with board members. For example, following negative earnings surprises, CEOs are 92 per cent more likely on average to mention their strategic advice seeking from top executives at other firms. Responses to open-ended and Likert-type survey questions indicated that CEOs often characterize the purpose of their advice seeking as soliciting an "independent" or "objective" perspective on the strategic issues facing their firms. When asked how he characterizes the objective of his advice-seeking interactions from fellow executives in communicating with outside directors, one CEO whom we interviewed gave the following, representative account:

> I convey to [the directors] that I'm ... seeking input, objective input, on the
> challenges and opportunities in front of us. Executives who have faced similar

challenges at other firms, or who are dealing with them now, are important sources of input. This is especially important [to convey] if results have been disappointing. I let [the directors] know that I'm looking more broadly for objective input... that the process is more open than before... that I want my assumptions to be challenged.

Our analyses showed that CEOs who described their strategic advice seeking from top executives at other firms in communicating with outside directors shortly before or after negative earnings surprises subsequently received fewer questions, comments, or directives from independent board members on strategic issues. In effect, CEOs' verbal IM about their advice seeking was negatively related to indicators of board control following an unexpected decline in firm performance, and positively related to indicators of board support for the CEO's leadership. Moreover, these relationships were robust to controlling for the frequency of CEO advice seeking and the composition of the CEO's strategic advice network (e.g., the proportion of advice sought from (1) friends versus acquaintances and (2) executives with similar functional and industry backgrounds). In fact, the composition of the CEO's advice network was unrelated to indicators of board control over strategy or board support of the CEO's leadership.

When this research is considered together with research on verbal impressions about board control in communications with information intermediaries (see Chapters 2 and 7), it becomes apparent that CEOs often engage in symbolic management successfully at multiple levels of the governance system. In the same way that CEO verbal IM about board control in communications with security analysts tends to induce more positive analyst appraisals independently of actual monitoring and control behavior by directors, CEO IM about advice seeking in the decision-making process tends to reduce board control and increase board support of the CEO's leadership independently of the CEO's actual advice-seeking behavior. While the agency logic of governance suggests that boards of directors are central control mechanisms in the corporate governance system, our theory and research suggests that boards are central to symbolic management activity. They are the subject of external IM, and the target of internal IM. Moreover, the result of these communications is symbolic decoupling, or a separation of appearances and reality, at multiple levels of the governance system. There is a separation of appearances at the institutional level of organization from actual relations at the managerial level, and there is also a separation between appearances in the external, institutional environment, and actual relations inside the organization.

Our analyses also indicate that the effects of verbal IM about CEO advice seeking on board support of the CEO's leadership have become stronger over time. The positive relationship between such IM and board support was 31 per cent stronger in 2006 than in 1999, and 68 per cent stronger in 2011 than in 1999 (the 2006 and 2011 samples were similar in size to the original sample and both were representative of the larger sample frame of large U.S. industrial and service firms).

Although further research on this phenomenon is clearly needed, several factors may explain the increased potency of IM about CEO advice seeking. First, as discussed further in Chapter 6, our interviews and surveys suggest that social networks have become a more prominent component of prevailing implicit models of leader effectiveness among corporate directors. In our 2011 survey of directors at large and mid-sized public companies, 78 per cent of respondents rated social network ties as one of the five most important drivers of leader effectiveness. In the 2001 survey, only about 40 per cent of respondents rated social networks as one of the most important determinants of leader success. We also asked directors, "To what extent would you have more confidence in the leadership of a CEO who regularly solicits strategic advice from top executives at other firms?" In 2001, the modal response was a "4" on the five-point scale, with a majority also agreeing that "it would depend on other factors to some extent." In response to an open-ended question about factors that determine the value of strategic advice seeking, directors often mentioned characteristics of the advisees, such as the extent or diversity of their prior experience, and their access to novel information. In 2011, the modal response to this question was a "5" (i.e., the highest level on the survey scale), with only a minority agreeing that it would depend on other factors. In effect, the value to firm leaders of having a large and diverse social network that includes strong ties to knowledgeable colleagues and powerful stakeholders appears to have become taken for granted among most corporate directors in recent years. By extension, the symbolic value of highlighting strategic advice-seeking behavior in communications with the board has increased markedly over this period. In our interviews conducted in the mid-1990s, executives and directors sometimes remarked that strategic advice seeking from other managers or directors could be viewed as an indication of weakness, or that the CEO lacks confidence in their strategy. In our more recent interviews, executives and directors are much more likely to characterize advice seeking as an indication of confidence and strength.

Second, and related to the perceived importance of social network ties to firm leadership, the normative legitimacy of engaging in relatively open and inclusive strategic decision-making processes has also increased since the 1990s (Chesbrough and Appleyard, 2007; Gast and Zanini, 2012; Hautz et al., 2017; Whittington et al., 2011). Due in part to advances in information technology, as discussed further below, many corporate directors and powerful stakeholders no longer perceive a tension between efficiency and broad participation in strategic decision making.

A third consideration is that, while outside directors of large companies tend to be more independent of management in 2011 than in 2001, they also tend to have less first-hand experience with strategic decision-making processes at large companies, and they tend to be less cognizant of the potential for symbolic management by CEOs. The proportion of outside directors comprised of top managers from other large and mid-sized companies was much smaller in 2011 than in 2001 (Mizruchi, 2013; Chu and Davis, 2016). As a result, outside directors are much less likely to consider the potential for CEOs to use advice seeking as a means of confirming their strategies, and they are less likely to consider the composition of the CEO's advice network as a contingency factor in assessing the value of advice seeking on strategic issues. For example, when asked whether CEOs obtain an independent perspective on firm strategy by seeking strategic advice from executives at other firms, an outside director with a background in law responded, "you bet, that's a good way to avoid biased advice from the 'yes men and women' on your team." When asked if the advice is necessarily independent, he added, "why not, it's outside the firm, right?" When asked the same question, a former CEO who also served as outside director at other firms responded, "maybe it's independent, maybe not." When asked what it depends on, he replied, "how close are they? Friends aren't independent. How close are the advisers to each other? Ideally you want independence and diversity in advisers." Thus, outside directors as a group increasingly value broad-based input seeking in the decision-making process, but they are increasingly unsophisticated about the nuances of advice seeking in the context of strategic leadership, raising the potential for CEOs to separate substance and symbolism in their advice-seeking behavior.

Participative Strategic Decision Making as Symbolic Management

In recent years a new form of symbolic management has emerged that extends the IM of strategic advice seeking discussed above. Since 2009 a segment of U.S. companies has adopted PSDM programs that purportedly use crowdsourcing technology to solicit input from managers below the executive suite on strategic options open to the firm (Westphal and Zhu, 2019a). The philosophy of these programs is founded on the participative approach to strategic decision making first described by strategy researchers such as Mintzberg (1983) and Bartlett and Ghoshal (1994), and more recently by management consultants (Gast and Zanini, 2012). The ostensible purpose of these programs is to improve the quality of decision making by "inject[ing] more diversity into [the] strategy process...get [ting] leaders closer to the operational implications of their decisions, [and] avoid [ing] the experience-based biases and orthodoxies that inevitably creep into small groups at the top" (Hamel, 2007; Gast and Zanini, 2012: 3). The programs are also described as making strategy setting more "transparent" to lower-level employees (Segev et al., 2014; Stieger et al., 2012; Hautz et al., 2017: 1).

Consultants describe PSDM programs as "social strategy setting" (Gast and Zanini, 2012: 2), in which crowdsourcing technology lies "at the heart of the process" (Segev et al., 2014: 47). Lower-level managers and staff are invited to participate in an asynchronous, "digital dialogue" in which they provide input on one or more strategic options using a digital-networking platform (Gast and Zanini, 2012: 10). At one firm, for example, the strategic options included increased marketing to a particular customer segment (urban millennials), expansion into a new geographic market, and increased spending on research and development in a particular product market. Participants could comment on these options, and comment on each other's input. Our interviews and surveys indicated that management consultants play a central role in designing and implementing these programs. They work with top managers to solicit participation on the digital-networking platform, aggregate and summarize the input, and advise top managers on how to communicate about the program to internal and external stakeholders (Bonabeau, 2009; Stieger et al., 2012). These programs have been touted by management consultants, information technology experts, and strategy gurus as a highly effective approach to strategic decision making.

Yet, our preliminary interviews and surveys suggested that these programs can be decoupled from actual strategic decision making (Westphal and Zhu, 2019a). In particular, top management may decide on a strategic option *before* soliciting input about it from lower-level managers and staff. We measured decoupling of PSDM programs by conducting longitudinal surveys of top executives that include questions about the timing of strategic decisions. We considered a program to be decoupled if top executives reported having decided on a strategic option at one point in time and then in a subsequent survey reported that they had solicited input from lower-level managers and staff under a PSDM program on whether to adopt that option or an alternative. Moreover, our interviews and surveys indicated that consultants played a significant role in the spread of decoupled PSDM programs. In particular, our preliminary interviews revealed that a large management consulting firm (firm A) pioneered the use of crowdsourcing technology in PSDM in 2009, and our later interviews and surveys indicated that three other consulting firms developed a very similar approach over the subsequent two years (all three of these firms employed consultants who had previously worked at firm A). These four consulting firms proceeded to spread PSDM programs among a segment of large and mid-sized U.S. companies over the subsequent six years. Our longitudinal surveys of top executives conducted since 2009 indicated that 92 per cent of PSDM programs implemented with the assistance of one of these consulting firms were decoupled: Top executives sought input on strategic options that had already been decided.

The decoupling of these programs is somewhat different from the decoupling of governance structures and policies described in Chapter 2. Whereas the decoupling of executive incentive plans or repurchase plans typically involves formal adoption of the plans without implementation, the PSDM programs that we examined were implemented, in the sense that input on strategic options was solicited from lower-level employees. Nevertheless, our surveys of different parties, including lower-level managers, outside directors, and security analysts, confirmed a distinction between the ostensible purpose of PSDM programs as presented to lower-level employees and external stakeholders, and the actual purpose of the programs as described by consultants and top executives in communication with each other. Whereas the ostensible purpose of the programs as described to employees and external stakeholders was to solicit input in the process of *making* strategic decisions, the actual purpose as described among top managers and consultants was to increase confidence in firm leadership and support for strategic decisions among key firm stakeholders. Our surveys consistently indicated that lower-level managers, outside directors, and external stakeholders such as security analysts understood the purpose of these programs as soliciting input to strategic decision making, and not as informing the implementation of decisions that had already been made. In this sense, the PSDM programs developed by these consulting firms were fully decoupled from actual strategic decision making, as the input rarely had any impact on strategic decision making by top executives.

Friedland and Alford (1991: 243) suggested that symbolic action can involve "[re]-ordering reality," including the sequence of actions in the decision-making process (also Feldman and March, 1981; March and Olsen, 1984). In the case of PSDM programs, it involves a symbolic separation between the apparent sequence of actions, which involves seeking input and then rendering the decision, and the actual sequence of events, in which top executives make the decision and then solicit input about it (Westphal and Zhu, 2019a).

Moreover, our interviews revealed that the design and implementation of PSDM programs can facilitate decoupling in several ways. First, as a number of top managers whom we interviewed acknowledged, consultants who originally developed PSDM programs emphasized the importance of encouraging "trusted" managers to "set the example" by providing input early in the participation process. These trusted managers were more likely to share the strategic perspective of top executives, and thus were especially likely to endorse the strategic option already decided by the CEO. Second, top managers also acknowledged that consultants sometimes anonymously comment themselves on input provided by lower-level managers, especially early in the process, with the ostensible purpose of reinforcing participation and increasing the engagement of managers and staff with the program. Such comments may also be sympathetic to top management's strategy, and may reinterpret critical comments about top management's strategy as concerns about implementation, rather than concerns about the strategy itself. Third, consultants are typically responsible for "aggregating" or summarizing the input, which furnishes another opportunity to (re)interpret critical comments as concerns about how to properly implement a strategic option, as opposed to a criticism of the strategic option itself.

There is also a subtle kind of decoupling between rhetoric about the use of technology in PSDM programs and the actual operation of the programs. While top managers and consultants often highlight the use of crowdsourcing technology in these programs in communicating with outside directors, security analysts, and other external stakeholders, frequently referring to the programs as "crowdsourcing enabled," the actual solicitation of strategic input generally does not make full use of the available technology. As one top manager who previously worked at a firm that implemented a PSDM program told us, "They called it 'crowdsourcing enabled,' but it wasn't really an 'idea market' or anything fancy like that. It was basically a glorified discussion board. But whenever [top managers] talked about crowdsourcing technology to people outside, they got excited."

Legitimacy Benefits of Verbal Impression Management about PSDM Programs

Westphal and Zhu (2019a) draw from implicit leadership theory in suggesting that verbal IM about PSDM programs has the potential to enhance the legitimacy of firm leadership and strategy with the board and external firm stakeholders, where legitimacy is defined as "a generalized perception or assumption that the actions of an entity are desirable, proper, or appropriate within some socially constructed system of norms, values, beliefs, and definitions" (Suchman, 1995: 574; MacLean and Benham, 2010; Suddaby et al., 2017). Implicit leadership theory suggests that in assessing leadership, people apply an implicit model or preconscious schema of leader effectiveness. This implicit model is manifested in a prevailing prototype of the "good" or effective leader (Lord and Maher, 2002; Dorfman et al., 2004; House et al., 2004). Implicit leadership theory scholars have further suggested that implicit models of leadership are rooted in certain core, taken-for-granted assumptions about effective leaders, which in turn are influenced by norms and values in the wider culture (Dorfman et al., 2004; House et al., 2004, 2014). In Anglo-Saxon cultures, a core, taken-for-granted assumption about effective leadership is that it entails a participative approach to decision making (House et al., 2004; 2013). A participative decision-making style, defined as the "use of decision procedures that allow [employees] some level of influence over the leader's decisions" (Yukl, 2006: 82), is central to the Western prototype of an effective leader. Participative leaders are presumed to make better decisions, and to implement them more successfully. Moreover, participative decision making is viewed as normatively legitimate in part because it resonates with democratic values (House et al., 2004, 2013). Westphal and Zhu (2019a) suggest that participative decision making is an important component of the culturally endorsed, implicit model of effective leadership, and will tend to be accepted by organizational constituents on a preconscious level as normatively appropriate, because it resonates with the institutional logic of democratic process (DiMaggio, 1997: 277; Friedland and Alford, 1991). To the extent that constituents accept the decision-making process as normatively appropriate, moreover, they are more likely to have confidence in the subsequent strategic decisions of firm leaders. When leaders conform to one important element of the culturally endorsed prototype of an effective leader, moreover, observers tend to automatically assign "default values" of other prototypical leader characteristics to the individual, such as decisiveness and integrity (Lord et al., 1982; House et al., 2013).

Verbal IM about PSDM programs can therefore provide an effective and efficient way for top executives to enhance their broader reputation as effective leaders, and to bolster the confidence of external constituents in firm strategies. Because participative decision-making processes tend to be accepted on a preconscious level as normatively acceptable, constituents are unlikely to raise questions about PSDM programs. Meyer and Rowan (1977: 349) observed that "the incorporation of institutionalized elements provides an account (Scott and Lyman 1968) of its activities that protects the organization from having its conduct questioned. The organization becomes, in a word, legitimate." Verbal IM about PSDM programs provides one such legitimating account, reducing questions from external constituents about executive decision making.

PSDM programs also create the impression of transparency in firm leadership. Verbal IM about participative decision making offers constituents a glimpse into the "back region" of strategic management (Goffman, 1959; MacCannell, 1973: 590–1), giving the appearance of transparency. Transparency increases trust in firm leaders and appears to validate the participative process, since transparency and democratic processes are commonly assumed to coincide, though in actuality one need not imply the other (Hollyer et al., 2011). Consequently, such IM is less likely to elicit skepticism, even though the appearance of transparency is illusory to the degree that PSDM programs are decoupled from actual strategic decision making. The potential for this approach to IM to create the perception of transparency was suggested by our interviews with directors and security analysts. For example, one analyst whom we interviewed told us, "[The CEO] talked about their process of involving [lower-level] managers to inform the strategy. I was impressed by that—not just because it's a good process ... a thorough process, but I liked the transparency of it. A CEO who tells me what goes into the strategy is someone I can trust." In addition, constituents may be especially unlikely to raise questions about the implementation of PSDM programs to the extent that firm leaders highlight the use of crowdsourcing technology in the solicitation of strategic input. Crowdsourcing technology is commonly described as a means of "democratization," and sometimes even *defined* in those terms (Hamel, 2007; Stieger et al., 2012: 44; Brabham, 2012: 406). It is also widely viewed as an efficient means of seeking broad-based input and leveraging diversity (Hamel, 2007; Rosen, 2011; Stieger et al., 2012: 46). Thus, crowdsourcing technology concretizes the institutional logic of democratic process, and the corollary that broad and diverse participation increases decision-making quality. As a result, firm leaders bolster the cultural legitimacy of PSDM programs by highlighting the use of crowdsourcing technology (Westphal and Zhu, 2019a).

Moreover, theoretical perspectives on technology in cultural anthropology of technology offer further insight into why highlighting the use of crowdsourcing technology may reduce skepticism about the rhetoric of participative decision making. Pfaffenberger (1988, 1992) invokes the Marxian notion of fetishism in contending that technologies in Western society are implicitly assumed to be "autonomous" or disembedded from social relations, which he describes as a sort of cultural "dualism" (also Hornborg, 2001). Whereas the sociology of technology describes modern technology as socially constructed and mediated, the anthropology of technology goes further in addressing prevailing cultural assumptions about technology. In particular, it identifies a systematic tendency for observers in Western culture to discount or ignore the role of social relations in mediating and moderating the outcomes of modern technology. Winner pointed out that "[modern] technology seems to operate beyond human control and appears to embody the result of an automatic, inevitable process" (1977, 1986; Pfaffenberger, 1988: 238; Latour, 1993). Winner (1986: 98) used the term "mythinformation" to describe the growing tendency for powerful actors to successfully exploit information technology to create the appearance of democratization while obscuring and preserving power differences (also Morozov, 2012). Thus, invoking modern technology in descriptions of organizational processes obscures the potential for decoupling by powerful actors that preserves their discretion over policy and strategy. In the present context, when executives frame participative decision making in terms of crowdsourcing technology, it lowers the likelihood that constituents consider how powerful social actors (e.g., top executives) and their agents (e.g., consultants) may mediate the solicitation of input. As a result, such framing leaves constituents especially unlikely to consider the potential for decoupling PSDM programs.

The potential for references to crowdsourcing technology to pre-empt questions about the implementation of PSDM programs was evident from our interviews with directors and security analysts. For example, when we defined decoupling and asked whether a particular firm's PSDM program could be decoupled from actual strategic decision making (without having mentioned crowdsourcing technology), one analyst responded, "In principle I guess so, but they used crowdsourcing [technology] to gather input. They automated the process, took [executives] out of it. That makes the process more trustworthy." Thus, verbal IM about PSDM programs may bolster the reputation of firm leaders and enhance constituents' confidence in firm strategy despite the potential for decoupling of PSDM programs from actual strategic decision making. Our empirical analyses of longitudinal surveys collected from top executives and outside directors over the period 2009 to 2015 provided strong support for this proposition. For example, our analyses indicated that, after controlling for a variety of executive-level and firm-level characteristics known to predict CEO dismissal (Park et al., 2011), verbal IM about PSDM programs by top executives in their communications with outside directors is negatively associated with the likelihood of CEO dismissal during periods of low firm performance. Moreover, this relationship did not depend on whether the PSDM program was decoupled from strategic decision making, i.e., it did not depend on whether executives implemented the PSDM program (i.e., solicited lower-level input on strategic options) before or after deciding on a strategic option, even though decoupling of a PSDM program is *positively associated with IM about the program*. Further analyses showed that, after controlling for IM about strategy content (cf., Westphal, 1998), IM about PSDM programs is also negatively associated with the propensity for outside directors to ask questions about firm strategy, either in formal board meetings or during informal communications with executives and staff. Again, this relationship did not depend on whether the PSDM program was decoupled.

Analyses further indicated that the negative relationships between verbal IM about PSDM programs and (1) CEO dismissal and (2) the propensity for outside directors to ask questions about firm strategy were especially strong to the extent that executives highlighted the use of crowdsourcing technology as a means of soliciting input from lower-level managers and staff. These analyses controlled for the total amount of IM (i.e., the number and duration of IM episodes). Moreover, these relationships also did not depend on whether the PSDM program was decoupled from actual strategic decision making. In addition, the effects of verbal IM about PSDM programs were long lasting and far reaching, in that they reduced the propensity for outside directors to ask questions about strategic decisions that were communicated to the board more than a year later, and which were not the subject of participation under the PSDM program. These results further suggest that IM about participative decision making is a relatively efficient and effective form of social influence, in comparison to managing impressions about particular strategy and policy issues.

The surveys included additional questions to help validate the theoretical mechanisms underlying these relationships. Toward the end of the study period directors were asked to what extent they had thought about whether the strategic input sought by top executives from lower-level managers and staff was considered in making strategic decisions. At firms where executives engaged in verbal IM about PSDM programs but did not highlight the use of crowdsourcing technology (i.e., mentioning such technology only briefly or not at all), 39 per cent of responding directors gave at least some thought to whether the strategic input sought by top executives was considered in making strategic decisions. At firms where executives engaged in verbal IM about PSDM programs but *did* highlight the use of crowdsourcing technology, only 8 per cent of responding directors gave any thought to whether the strategic input was considered in making decisions.

Verbal IM about PSDM programs was also strongly associated with survey measures of board trust in firm leadership, and this relationship was especially strong to the extent that executives highlighted the use of crowdsourcing technology as a means of soliciting input. Again, these relationships were not contingent on implementation of the PSDM program. Interestingly, our results indicated that while IM by top executives about strategy content was negatively associated with the likelihood of CEO dismissal and positively associated with measures of board trust in firm leadership, IM about PSDM programs had significantly stronger effects on both outcomes.

Survey responses to a question about the perceived integrity of firm leaders were especially revealing. While verbal IM about strategy content was not significantly related to director responses to the question "To what extent are you confident in the integrity of firm leadership?" there was a positive and statistically significant relationship between verbal IM about PSDM programs and responses to this question. An increase in verbal IM about PSDM programs of one standard deviation is associated with an average increase in the confidence of directors in the integrity of firm leadership of nearly one point on the five-point Likert-type survey scale. Responses to an open-ended question in one iteration of the surveys provided further insight into the micro-mechanisms that may underlie this relationship. After the question about integrity, directors were asked to comment on the reason for their response. There was a very strong relationship between IM about PSDM programs and references to "transparency" and "inclusion" or "inclusiveness." Moreover, IM that highlighted the use of crowdsourcing technology was also strongly associated with language related to "democratization." These relationships are particularly striking given that IM about a PSDM program is positively associated with decoupling of the program from actual decision making. Overall, our analyses of the longitudinal survey data provided substantial validation of theoretical arguments regarding the legitimacy benefits of verbal IM about participative decision making by firm leaders.

Symbolic management about participative decision-making processes is unique from other forms of symbolic management that have been documented in the organizational literature. Policies and practices are typically assumed to acquire symbolic value as they become more prevalent in a population (Strang and Soule, 1998), and this was the case for the corporate governance policies and practices discussed in Chapter 2. However, our research suggests that the symbolic management of PSDM programs has thus far been limited to a minority of large and mid-sized public companies in the U.S. Our theory would suggest that firms derive symbolic value from IM about PSDM programs by conforming to the institutional logic of democratic process, rather than by conforming to prevailing norms of strategic decision making in the population. In fact, this approach allows firms to enhance the legitimacy of strategic decision making while also *differentiating* their leadership processes from those of most other firms, both of which increase the reputation of the firm and its leaders.

Accordingly, the symbolic management of PSDM programs appears to reconcile the apparently competing strategic imperatives of differentiation and conformity (Deephouse, 1999): In Chapter 6 we explain why this form of symbolic management is still confined to a minority of public companies. Whereas other forms of symbolic management have diffused broadly through a "circuit" of weak network ties such as board interlocks (Westphal and Zajac, 2001; Bromley and Powell, 2012: 11), Westphal and Zhu (2019a) show that the symbolic PSDM programs appear to have diffused in a more limited fashion through relatively strong ties, such as personal friendship ties between CEOs. Friendship ties to CEOs who have adopted PSDM programs not only increase awareness about the programs, but they also provide referrals to the small set of consultants who have specialized knowledge and experience in the implementation of "crowdsourcing-enabled" PSDM programs. Given the small number of consulting firms involved, all of which are directly connected to the one firm that pioneered these programs, the symbolic management of PSDM programs is relatively homogeneous across firms. This may bolster the normative legitimacy of the programs, without losing the benefits of differentiation from non-adopters.

The symbolic management of PSDM programs also appears to be a relatively durable form of symbolic action, not only in the sense that its reputational benefits are long-lasting, as noted above, but also in the sense that decoupling of these programs appears to persist. There was no evidence that PSDM programs tended to become a more substantive influence on strategic decision making over time. Tilscik (2010) provided compelling evidence that decoupled policies can become more substantive over time as organizations recruit and promote employees with specialized knowledge and skills pertaining to the policies. The professional ideologies of these recruits lead them to "couple" the policies more tightly to actual organizational practices as they acquire more power in the organization over time. In the context of PSDM programs, however, firm leaders hire consultants to facilitate implementation. The consultants not only lack power to couple the programs, but they are referred and hired specifically for their proven expertise in symbolic management. Thus, consultants play a critical role in instituting and maintaining this form of symbolic management. The role of consultants in other forms of symbolic management, including the symbolic management of governance policies discussed in Chapter 2, is a promising topic for future research. There is certainly anecdotal evidence that executive compensation consultants often serve the interests of powerful top executives in developing compensation plans (Crystal, 1991). It seems likely that they played a seminal role in the decoupling of executive incentive plans.

More generally, extant theory and research has conceived symbolic management as a strictly dyadic phenomenon, and has given little consideration to the possible role of third parties in facilitating or constraining social influence. Goffman defined the parameters of IM theory in suggesting:

> Given a particular performance as the point of reference, we can distinguish three crucial roles on the basis of function: those who perform; those performed to; and outsiders who neither perform in the show nor observe it... [T]he three crucial roles mentioned could be described on the basis of the regions to which the role-player has access: performers appear in the front and back regions; the audience appears only in the front region; and the outsiders are excluded from both regions.   (1959, pp. 144–5)

To extend Goffman's (1959) dramaturgical metaphor, in complex organizations, IM is often a larger production that is itself managed or directed. IM researchers have focused on the actors and audiences in symbolic management, to the exclusion of other parties involved in the production. In the case of symbolic PSDM programs, consultants essentially direct the performance. While executives are the "face" of the programs, consultants manage the production behind the curtain. They design the crowdsourcing platform, orchestrate the online dialogue on strategic options, and direct top executives on how to communicate about the program with lower-level managers, board members, and external constituents.

Another way in which the symbolic management of PSDM programs is distinct from other forms of symbolic action examined in prior research is the importance of technology to enhancing the symbolic value of the programs. There is surprisingly little theory or research on the role of technology in symbolic management. Some theory and research has addressed the reverse relationship. In particular, several studies have examined how symbolic management can facilitate the legitimation of new technologies. Benner and Ranganathan (2012) provided compelling evidence that policy announcements are used to manage negative external reactions to new technologies, and the literature on cultural entrepreneurship suggests how symbolic discourse can facilitate innovation (Lounsbury and Glynn, 2019). The symbolic management of PSDM programs suggests how ostensibly "new" technology is used to manage stakeholder reactions to strategic decisions.

On another level, while Benner and Ranganathan examined how policy announcements are used to reduce skepticism about new technologies, this research reveals how communication about technology is used to dampen reservations about a longstanding practice. In particular, while participative decision making has cultural legitimacy from its resonance with the logic of democratic process, as discussed above, it also has limitations that are fairly well known among corporate leaders and at least some external constituents. Most notably, participative decision making has traditionally been viewed as a time-consuming, labor-intensive process that may delay adaptation to environmental change (Mintzberg, 1983; House et al., 2004; Yukl, 2006). Moreover, from this traditional perspective, the broader and more inclusive the participation, the more time consuming and expensive the decision-making process is assumed to be, resulting in a trade-off between enhanced quality and employee commitment from broader participation, and the efficiency of a more centralized process. However, the use of information technology ostensibly resolves this trade-off. The digital networking platform is believed to allow asynchronous participation from virtually any location, and as discussed above, constituents tend to discount the role of consultants and other personnel in mediating the technology. As a result, the use of crowdsourcing technology makes a broad-based, participative process appear much more efficient than traditional approaches that involved some combination of interviews, focus groups, and other kinds of face-to-face discussion (Gast and Zanini, 2012; Afuah and Tucci, 2012; Stieger et al., 2012). In effect, the use of crowdsourcing technology increases the "pragmatic legitimacy" (Suchman, 1995: 577) of participative decision making by increasing the perceived efficiency of the process, as well as increasing the normative legitimacy of firm leadership and strategy by reinforcing the linkage to democratization and inclusion.

The greater speed of an online process is appealing to top executives, as well as to board members and external constituents. Even if the PSDM program is decoupled, such that input from lower-level managers and staff has no bearing on actual strategic decisions, a lengthy process of input seeking can delay implementation of top executives' strategies (though our interviews and surveys indicated that top executives sometimes begin implementing strategies even before the participative process is concluded). While the use of crowdsourcing technology clearly does accelerate the input-seeking process, the executives and consultants whom we interviewed consistently told us that it does not necessarily reduce the overall expense of a participative process, relative to the traditional approach. Whereas some of the other forms of decoupling that we described at least reduce the immediate costs of implementation (e.g., decoupled LTIPs avoid the costs of incentive grants, though they also lose any long-run benefits of incentive alignment), decoupled PSDM programs entail many if not all the financial costs of implemented programs, but without many of the benefits to strategic decision making.

Some recent research suggests that, at least in some domains, firm leaders give close consideration to the benefits *and costs* of IM. Jeong and Kim (2018) showed that efficiency concerns are an important constraint on the level of corporate giving, as one type of legitimacy management. Evidence regarding the symbolic management of PSDM programs would also suggest that firm leaders are mindful of efficiency in deciding on the form and level of symbolic management, but they appear mainly concerned with the time and effort required (especially the time and effort required of top managers). There was little evidence that choices about symbolic management activity reflected a comprehensive cost-benefit analysis. For example, while the use of crowdsourcing technology in symbolic PSDM programs ostensibly saves managerial time and effort, the consulting fees for these programs are considerably higher than those for traditional approaches. Although top managers acknowledged uncertainties and concerns about PSDM programs, some of which were assuaged by network ties to prior adopters (see Chapter 6), there was no evidence from our interviews and surveys that top managers considered the increased cost of consulting services in assessing the merits of these programs.

Our surveys indicate that in the last several years the rhetoric about strategic decision making has evolved to include references to "new" techniques and processes that supposedly complement or enhance crowdsourcing, including "machine learning." Future research should examine how references to machine learning and other technological advances in communications about strategic decision making may influence the perceptions of external constituents. Our preliminary interviews and responses to open-ended survey questions suggest that while security analysts find the idea of using machine learning in participative decision making quite appealing, many do not have a good understanding (or *any* understanding) of how machine learning would actually be used in crowdsourcing. At the same time, the consultants whom we interviewed have consistently reported that references to machine learning in participative decision making are deceiving. For example, one consultant told us:

> Yes [the term] "machine learning" is routinely thrown around now, but this is misleading in a number of respects. First, the automated text analysis is really basic. It's usually a basic sentiment analysis looking at whether the comments [e.g., on a particular strategic option] are overall positive or negative. This is an ancient, simple analysis, but when they say "machine learning," people get excited. Second, it's not really machine learning at all, because the program isn't getting smarter...it's not getting better at understanding sentiment. Third, there's a lot of human interpretation going on in parallel, or in place of text analysis.

References to machine learning disavow the substantial role of consultants and top executives in processing and aggregating strategic input from managers and staff, thus reinforcing the "dualist" perspective on technology that views crowdsourcing as autonomous and disembedded from powerful actors. More generally, by periodically highlighting the use of technological innovations in participative decision making, top executives associate their leadership and strategy with technological progress, and focus the attention of constituents away from evaluating the benefits of past decision making. As another consultant suggested,

> Today it's machine learning. Artificial intelligence is coming, blockchain, who knows what's next. Every so often you can relaunch the [decision-making process] with a new technology, keeping it fresh and innovative. Is it really new? Maybe, probably not as much as it looks. Is it really better? Maybe, probably not much. But it makes [firm leaders] look current, and it puts [constituents] in an optimistic frame of mind.

Highlighting the use of innovative information technology in strategy processes may be particularly effective in communicating with financial market actors such as security analysts and institutional investors. While these constituents are especially likely to appreciate the value of technologies that allow decision makers to collect more extensive information in an efficient manner, most lack specialized expertise in cutting-edge information technologies. As a result, executive communications that highlight the use of "new" information technologies in strategic decision making may be especially likely to elicit optimism, and especially unlikely to elicit critical questions from these constituents.

The Symbolic Management of Strategy Execution

Another form of symbolic action that complements IM about PSDM programs involves communication by top executives about the process of executing firm strategies. Our preliminary interviews and surveys indicate that in recent years a growing number of firm leaders have characterized strategy execution as a learning process in communicating with external stakeholders. For example, leaders have increasingly adopted the language of "test and learn" to describe their process of executing strategy. This approach involves a trial period in which various kinds of market feedback are collected, and the strategy is revised to varying degrees in response. At some companies the test and learn process is explicitly described as "experimentation," "validation," and even "hypothesis" testing. This approach resonates with Mintzberg's (1973, 1983) normative and descriptive accounts of strategy execution, as well as Eisenhardt and colleagues' perspective on strategic decision making in high-velocity environments (Brown and Eisenhardt, 1997). From this perspective, while strategic decisions are improved by soliciting broad-based, diverse input from individuals who have first-hand knowledge of firm capabilities, customer needs, and the capabilities of suppliers and other partners, they are also improved by gauging the responses of customers and other partners to new initiatives, and modifying strategic plans accordingly. While a PSDM program conveys an openness to input ex ante, a test and learn approach conveys an openness to feedback post hoc. Moreover, both approaches appear to enhance quality without sacrificing efficiency. While PSDM programs save time and expense through the use of crowdsourcing technology, the test and learn approach uses beta testing and market experimentation to save time and expense relative to traditional market surveys, interviews, and focus groups.

Although these two processes are complementary and together form a consistent narrative about openness to information and learning in strategic decision making, IM about each process derives symbolic value from distinct sources. Although further research is clearly needed on the effects of these forms of symbolic management, it seems that while communication about participative decision making and the use of crowdsourcing technology derives symbolic value from the institutional logic of democratic process, communication about the test and learn approach to strategy execution derives symbolic value from the institutional logic of the scientific method. Direct or indirect references to the scientific method provide an effective "mode of justification" in Western culture (Barley and Kunda, 1992; DiMaggio, 1997: 277; Boltanski and Thévenot, 2006). Moreover, tendencies toward scientism, or excessive confidence in the power of scientific knowledge and techniques in Western societies, may reduce skepticism about practices that are framed in terms of scientific discourse (Latour, 1993). Latour suggested that scientific discourse tends to obscure power relations; it creates the impression of an objective, dispassionate, fact-based process that does not play favorites. As a result, rhetorical forms that employ scientific representations have become popular instruments of power. Thus, references to scientific concepts such as "testing," "hypotheses," "experimentation," and "validation" not only increase the procedural legitimacy of strategic decision-making processes, but also obscure the roles of powerful executives in strategy execution.

There would be value in future research that examines how firms actually collect and use feedback from test and learn processes in strategy execution. Our preliminary interviews and surveys suggest that test and learn processes rarely prompt significant revisions to the strategies of powerful top executives. A combination of sample selection biases (e.g., beta testing on a relatively favorable customer subsegment) and attribution biases in the interpretation of market feedback may reduce the likelihood or extent of revisions to executives' strategies. In a sample of 362 strategic initiatives that were presented to security analysts as the first step in a test and learn implementation process, less than 5 per cent had been "changed" or "substantially modified" two years later, based on the survey responses of top executives. Thirty-two per cent were "refined," and the majority were "unchanged."

Thus, while the test and learn process builds on Mintzberg's classic model of strategy execution, it can also be seen as a perversion of that model, in several respects. Whereas Mintzberg viewed strategy execution as a process of regular improvement and change, questioning the very distinction between strategy formulation and execution, firm leaders have effectively exploited Mintzberg's model for its rhetorical and symbolic value, while continuing to follow a fairly traditional approach to strategy execution. Moreover, whereas Mintzberg developed a postmodern perspective on strategic decision making as an inherently subjective process, and was skeptical about the application of traditional, scientific methods to strategic decision making (or to strategic management research), rhetoric about the test and learn process ironically exploits scientism for its symbolic value with firm stakeholders. Finally, whereas Mintzberg viewed strategic decision making in large firms as distributed and decentralized, with firm leaders operating more as strategic architects than decision makers in the traditional sense, symbolic management about PSDM programs and the test and learn process gives the appearance of a distributed and decentralized process, when actual strategic decision making remains quite centralized in the executive suite.

Symbolic Management of Diversity and Inclusion

While symbolic management about PSDM programs derives legitimacy from the perceived value of diverse input to decision making, firms also engage in symbolic management that directly addresses diversity in firm leadership. As with the other kinds of symbolic management that we have described, this form of symbolic action entails both verbal IM and decoupling. However, decoupling in this case does not necessarily involve the (non-)implementation of a formal policy or program, but rather a symbolic separation between appearances and rhetoric on the one hand, and actual organizational processes on the other. Moreover, while the other forms of decoupling that we have described are at least partly strategic or agentic in nature, the decoupling of diversity appears to be largely driven by social psychological biases. As a result, while this form of decoupling is less categorical than symbolic LTIPs or PSDM programs, it is also more multi-faceted. In this section, we describe some of the many ways that the appearance of diversity, or apparent increases in diversity, mask the marginalization or exclusion of demographic minorities from decision-making processes and other forms of social interaction.

An increasingly common response by firm leaders to poor firm performance, or negative assessments of firm leadership, strategy, or performance prospects by security analysts, is to increase the demographic diversity of firm leadership, while engaging in IM about diversity in communications with firm stakeholders. Empirical analyses for a representative, longitudinal sample of over 500 large and mid-sized U.S. companies from 2011 to 2016 indicate that multiple measures of low firm performance are associated with statistically significant increases in (1) the representation of women and racial minorities among top executives and board members, and (2) verbal IM about the diversity of firm leadership in communicating with security analysts and journalists (Westphal, 2019), measured over the subsequent year or two years. Relatively negative appraisals of firm leadership, strategy, or performance prospects by security analysts are also significantly associated with increases in racial and gender diversity of top management and boards, as well as verbal IM about the diversity of firm leadership in communicating with information intermediaries.

In general, such verbal IM does not directly reference firm performance, or external concerns about firm leadership, strategy, or performance prospects that appear to prompt increases in diversity. Instead, such communications typically highlight the firm's commitment to diversity, and especially in communicating with analysts, the benefits of diversity to strategic decision making, firm leadership, and/or firm performance. Yet, our empirical analyses also indicate that the same independent variables that predict increases in demographic diversity and IM about diversity are associated with reduced involvement of female and racial minority managers and directors in strategic decision making, and reduced access of minorities to social and professional benefits that normally accrue to firm leaders. They are also associated with an increase in certain kinds of negative treatment of female and racial minority leaders. In effect, our findings reveal a broad pattern of social discrimination against female and racial minorities in firm leadership that is worsened under conditions of economic adversity or threats to firm reputation. In the subsections below we describe each of these forms of social discrimination. We then suggest that the divergent effects of economic and reputational adversity on demographic diversity and IM on the one hand, and minority involvement in decision making and access to social and professional benefits on the other, suggest a pervasive form of decoupling in organizations.

Demographic Minority Status and Involvement in Strategic Decision Making

Our early research on minority involvement showed that female and racial minority directors tended to exert less influence on strategic decision making than their white male colleagues, particularly when they lacked common board memberships with white male directors at other firms (Westphal and Milton, 2000). These results held after controlling for prior management and board-level experience, other determinants of power and influence such as stock ownership, and other demographic characteristics (e.g., age, functional background, and industry background). The negative effect of minority status on director influence was reduced to the extent that white male directors had prior experience in a minority role on other boards (e.g., they were the only director with a particular functional background). We theorized that prior experience in a minority role would render majority (e.g., white male) directors more empathetic toward female and racial minority directors, and thus more likely to include minorities in strategic decision making. However, the negative effect of minority status on director influence was significantly increased under conditions of poor firm performance. Moreover, female and racial minority directors needed more common board appointments with white male directors to achieve the same level of influence in strategic decision making to the extent that firm performance was relatively poor.

Low firm performance had an especially strong, negative effect on minority involvement in decision making on relatively broad, strategic issues, even though the overall level of board involvement in strategic decision making tends to be higher during periods of low performance (Lorsch and MacIver, 1989). It had a much weaker, only marginally significant effect on involvement in the minority director's main area of expertise. For example, under conditions of poor perform-ance, the CEO or other board members are just as likely on average to seek the input of a female attorney on the board about a particular legal matter, but less likely to seek the director's input on whether to diversify into a new product market. At the same time, low firm performance was *positively* associated with the participation of minority directors in external communication with certain stake-holder groups, including conference calls with security analysts. This pattern of results is consistent with the view that, under conditions of poor performance, minority directors are valued more for their potential contributions to symbolic management, and less for their substantive contributions to corporate policy and strategy. As one former director recalled, in describing the involvement of a racial minority director on a board where they had served together,

> When profits took a serious fall, they trotted him [the minority director] out, put him in front of analysts. That became his main role for a time. [When asked why:] When profits take a dive they [top management] would rather talk about diversity... having [the minority director] there obviously helps. Or they thought it did.

Demographic Minority Status and Professional Support from Colleagues

Our research has provided consistent evidence that female and racial minority top executives and directors tend to receive less professional support from their colleagues, in comparison to white males. One study revealed that female and racial minority first-time directors (i.e., directors who receive their first board appointment at a public U.S. company) receive significantly less "participation process mentoring" from experienced board members about normatively appro-priate ways to contribute to board discussions (McDonald and Westphal, 2013). For example, white male first-time directors are significantly more likely to be advised by experienced board members that they should clear any concerns that they may have about firm strategy with the CEO before raising them in board meetings (i.e., not raising a strategic issue or concern in a formal meeting without getting the CEO's "okay" informally beforehand). Participation process mentoring is positively and significantly associated with receiving additional board appointments at other public companies, and this relationship is mediated by lower levels of decision control behavior by directors in board meetings (as perceived by other directors and the CEO).

Moreover, while lower firm performance increases the likelihood of appointing a woman or racial minority to the board, as noted above, it is also associated with lower subsequent mentoring of female and racial minority first-time directors. This relationship holds for minorities who are appointed before or after the decline in performance, but is especially strong for minorities appointed after the decline (there is no significant effect of performance on mentoring of white male first-time directors). Accordingly, the effect of firm performance on mentoring of minorities may be driven by a selection effect, as well as by intergroup bias. In particular, the results are consistent with a kind of tokenism in which firms, under conditions of low performance, are more likely to appoint minority directors as a symbolic act of commitment to diversity, and less likely to appoint minorities for their potential contributions to firm strategy and policy. In addition, incumbent directors may be less likely to trust new minority directors with sensitive information, such as information about norms of director conduct that would likely be controversial if conveyed to the wrong third parties, especially during periods of poor firm performance.

We have also found evidence across multiple studies that, controlling for the strength of personal ties and other individual, dyadic, and contextual factors, white male top executives provide less task-related advice to female and racial minority colleagues and subordinates than they provide to other white males (McDonald and Westphal, 2010; McDonald et al., 2018). For example, white male CEOs provide significantly less advice on strategic issues to minority CEOs of other firms than they provide to other white male CEOs. They are also less likely to provide minority CEOs with personal referrals to third-party sources of advice and counsel, and they are less likely to provide them with names of potential candidates for executive-level positions and outside directorships. In effect, white male CEOs are less willing to give minority CEOs access to their professional network. Moreover, there is a crossover interaction between demographic differences and firm performance, such that white male CEOs are especially unlikely to provide strategic advice (or access to third-party sources of advice) to minority CEOs of poorly performing firms, while they are significantly *more* likely to provide strategic advice to other white male CEOs whose firms are performing poorly. Thus, whereas white male CEOs can obtain more help from fellow CEOs to address performance problems at their firms, female and racial minority CEOs have less access to strategic advice from fellow CEOs when they need it the most. The results suggest that helping behavior toward demographically different peers is more instrumental and contingent than helping behavior toward similar others, and consequently minority leaders' access to professional support networks is relatively precarious.

In addition, white male top managers tend to provide less mentoring to minority subordinates and less task-related help to minority peers and subordinates; they are also less likely to recommend minority peers for board seats at other firms (McDonald et al., 2018). This research further indicated that white male top managers were especially unlikely to provide various forms of work-related help to minority peers and subordinates following the appointment of a female or racial minority CEO, and during periods of low firm performance. These relationships were mediated by lower levels of organizational identification among white male top managers. That is, white male top managers reported significantly lower levels of social identification with the organization following the appointment of a female or racial minority CEO, based on validated survey measures of organizational identification (e.g., items asked managers to indicate the degree of overlap between their self-image or identity and the organization (Mael and Ashforth, 1992)). Lower levels of organizational identification, in turn, were associated with subsequent reductions in work-related help provided to peers and subordinates, especially women and racial minorities. Thus, while the appointment of a female or racial minority CEO is often viewed as a highly visible signal of organizational commitment to diversity, and is often assumed to portend better opportunities for women and racial minorities at lower levels, our results suggested that apparent commitments to diversity at the CEO level are associated with an increase in social discrimination at lower levels of the organization.

Female and racial minority CEOs also receive significantly less "impression management (IM) support" from other CEOs, where IM support includes positive comments about the CEO's leadership and strategy and external attributions for low performance at the CEO's firm (e.g., attributing low firm performance to industry and macro-economic factors beyond the CEO's control) in communicating with information intermediaries (Westphal et al., 2012). As discussed in Chapter 4, our research indicates that IM support by other CEOs in their communications with journalists can have a substantial influence on the valence of media reporting about firm leadership and strategy, especially during periods of low firm performance. We describe the provision of IM support by CEOs for fellow leaders as a social exchange network that is characterized by different forms of reciprocity, including direct reciprocity and various kinds of generalized reciprocity (e.g., "paying it forward") and social indirect reciprocity in which CEOs who provide support in one period are more likely to receive support from third parties in future periods (see Chapter 4). Female and racial minority CEOs are less likely to be included in this social exchange network, after controlling for other kinds of social ties, executive-level, and firm-level characteristics. White male CEOs are less likely to reciprocate IM support provided by a female or racial minority CEO, either directly or indirectly. In particular, they are less likely to provide IM support for a minority CEO who provided them with support previously, and they are less likely to support a minority CEO who previously supported multiple other CEOs.

Separate analyses further showed that the provision of IM support by white male CEOs for female or racial minority CEOs is less likely to be reciprocated by other white male CEOs in future periods. In effect, IM support by minorities *or for minorities* is "worth less" in social exchange. The findings are consistent with an intergroup relations perspective on social exchange in which largely preconscious out-group biases cause white male leaders to discount the value of help provided by minorities, and the deservingness of minorities as help recipients. However, the findings are also consistent with a more deliberate form of social exclusion in which white male leaders restrict access to social exchange networks in order to preserve status differences in corporate leadership. The informal exclusion of minority CEOs from IM support networks helped spur the formation of "minority support groups"—formal groups of minority CEOs in the same industry who cooperate in supporting each other's reputations as leaders (see Chapter 4; Westphal et al., 2019).

Further analysis showed that minority leaders are also less likely to receive a different kind of support by other CEOs in their relations with information intermediaries (Shani and Westphal, 2016). CEOs not only provide fellow leaders with IM support that results in more positive coverage of firm leadership, but they also engage in "social distancing" of journalists who engage in negative coverage of fellow leaders. Social distancing is the reduced willingness of social actors to communicate or otherwise interact with another actor or group (Maner et al., 2007; Williams, 2009). As discussed further in Chapter 8, our research has shown that negative statements by a journalist about the leadership or strategy of a particular firm are associated with social distancing of the journalist by other CEOs who are demographically similar to the focal firm's CEO. Social distancing of a journalist is associated with more positive subsequent coverage of firm leadership and strategy by that journalist and other journalists who become aware of the distancing. We characterize social distancing of negative journalists as a kind of "bounded solidarity" among corporate leaders, which is an important form of social capital at the community level (Portes, 1998: 8, 2010). Our analyses indicate that female and racial minority leaders are less often supported due to the social distancing behavior of other CEOs, and therefore do not have full access to this form of social capital. Again, this lower level of support is especially pro-nounced for minority CEOs of firms with the lowest levels of firm performance. Social distancing of journalists who engage in negative coverage of firms with white male CEOs is entirely unaffected by firm performance.

Overall, our research indicates that while poor firm performance is associated with elevated rhetoric about the firm's commitment to diversity, it is also associated with reductions in various forms of professional support provided to female and racial minority directors, CEOs, and other top managers, both in an absolute sense and relative to the professional support provided to white males. This pattern of results suggests a systematic separation between rhetoric and reality with respect to corporate commitment to diversity in firm leadership.

Moreover, each kind of professional support has been shown to substantially benefit firm leaders: Mentoring enhances the task performance of top managers and directors (McDonald and Westphal, 2013; McDonald et al., 2018), strategic advice and other task-related help improves the quality of strategic decision making by CEOs and top managers (McDonald and Westphal, 2010), and IM support and social distancing of journalists who engage in negative coverage of firm leadership protects the reputations of CEOs and likely other members of top management teams (Westphal et al., 2012; Shani and Westphal, 2016). Thus, the total professional costs to female and racial minority leaders from reduced access to professional support from colleagues at the same firm and other firms are very large. Our findings therefore provide an alternative explanation for the "glass cliff" phenomenon, which has mainly focused on selection factors (e.g., women are more likely to be hired into precarious positions due to a prevailing tendency to "think crisis—think female"), and which have focused on gender-specific biases (Ryan and Haslam, 2007). We suggest that the glass cliff phenomenon and its analogue for racial minority leaders is attributable in part to systematic reductions in access to professional support that are especially pronounced during periods of relatively low firm performance, when mentoring, advice, other task-related help, and reputational support are most needed.

Demographic Minority Status and Personal Support from Colleagues

In other research we found that female and racial minority CEOs receive less social support from fellow leaders. In particular, they were less likely to be invited by a fellow executive or director to join an informal support group of firm leaders or "ISG" that meets periodically with the purpose of helping each other cope with problems in their personal lives (McDonald and Westphal, 2011). Our interviews and surveys showed that these groups are intended to help leaders cope with significant personal problems such as marital difficulties, the health problems of a loved one, or a strained relationship with a child, by providing informational support (e.g., specific advice, referrals, or other information on how to address the problem), as well as moral or emotional support (e.g., expressing confidence that the problem can be resolved or mitigated). The CEOs and former CEOs of large companies whom we interviewed consistently suggested that leaders of large firms face unique challenges that place strains on their personal lives, and that fellow CEOs are uniquely able to appreciate and help each other cope with these difficulties. One CEO whom we interviewed offered the following, representative point of view:

> Why do these groups [ISGs] form? Because it's lonely at the top ... Being a CEO of a large company and serving on boards of other big companies is incredibly demanding and involves many pressures that pose challenges for our personal lives. Who understands this best? Other CEOs of large companies, many of whom have experienced the same problem. So we can help each other deal with personal problems, like marital problems and other relationship problems, in a way that no one else can.   (McDonald and Westphal, 2011)

Minority leaders had significantly less access to such support than white male CEOs. They not only had less access to social support in ISGs, but they also received less ad hoc personal support from colleagues (e.g., they were less likely to receive support from fellow directors at firms where they served on the board).

Our empirical analyses provided evidence that receiving social support of this kind significantly dampened the negative effects of a CEO's personal problems on their effectiveness as a leader. In particular, social support from members of an ISG or fellow board members reduced the negative relationship between significant problems in a CEO's personal life and their engagement in a range of interpersonal behaviors that are known to enhance leader effectiveness, including (1) the mentoring and encouragement of lower-level managers, (2) seeking input from lower-level managers in making strategic decisions, (3) seeking information from lower-level managers about their progress on implementing corporate strategies, and (4) soliciting advice and counsel from outside directors on strategic issues. Supplemental analyses of our survey data further indicated that the moderating effects of social support were mediated by reduced symptoms of depressive mood and anxiety, based on multi-item survey scales that have been validated in organizational contexts. Our survey data indicated that significant personal problems were not rare among CEOs in our sample: Over half (52 per cent) reported experiencing one or more of the personal problems described above at a moderate or higher level of severity at some point during the period of our study. Moreover, reductions in firm performance were associated with an increase in the strain caused by at least some kinds of personal problems reported by CEOs, including marital problems and the health problems of a loved one.

In combination with our studies on different forms of professional support, this research suggests that minority leaders are especially unlikely to have access to both professional and personal sources of support when they need it most. The reduced access to these different forms of support may interact in ways that create a downward spiral. Limited access to support from colleagues such as strategic advice and IM support places more of the burdens of leadership on the CEO, and makes it more difficult for the CEO to adapt successfully to environmental threats that are putting downward pressure on firm performance. Such burdens will likely exacerbate the strains of any personal problems the CEO may be experiencing, making it even more difficult for them to stay fully focused and engaged in their leadership roles. Aside from compromising their effectiveness as leaders, lower access to personal and professional support likely has serious side effects on the personal well-being of female and racial minority leaders. Limited access to social support in coping with a personal problem is not also associated with symptoms of depressive mood and anxiety, but with reduced physical health and well-being.

Demographic Minority Status and Differential Access to Benefits

There is little systematic evidence that female or racial minority leaders at large public companies receive less monetary compensation or other tangible rewards than their white male counterparts. However, our research has now provided considerable evidence that minority top managers and directors do tend to receive fewer intangible rewards and opportunities in exchange for their contributions to firm governance and strategy. For example, female and racial minority directors need to provide higher levels of strategic advice and input to the CEO to have the same chance of receiving a fellow director's recommendation for a board appointment at another firm (Westphal and Stern, 2007). The results were consistent with a form of intergroup bias known as the "ultimate attribution error," wherein observers attribute the contributions of in-group members to dispositional causes, while attributing the contributions of out-group members to external causes or temporary conditions (Hewstone, 1990; Pettigrew, 1979: 461). White male directors are more likely to attribute high levels of strategic advice provided by other white males to superior knowledge and expertise, while attributing similar behavior by a female or racial minority colleague to fortuitous circumstances or special advantage (e.g., efforts by the CEO to involve the director in strategic decision making, or an especially good fit between the director's main area of expertise and strategic challenges currently facing the firm). Due to this biased pattern of attributions, minority directors receive less credit than white male directors for any given level of contribution to strategic decision making.

In response to open-ended questions about the contributions of their colleagues on the board, white male directors are more likely to mention contributions to strategy or policy-related issues by their white male colleagues, while mentioning participation in external communications with certain stakeholder groups (e.g., conference calls with security analysts) by female and racial minority colleagues. This pattern of responses is consistent with separate evidence discussed above that minority directors are valued more for their potential contributions to symbolic management than for their substantive contributions to corporate policy and strategy.

Minority directors also benefit less from engaging in social influence behavior. Ingratiation by white male directors toward the CEO or fellow directors has a very strong, positive effect on receiving a colleague's recommendation for a board appointment. For example, an increase in ingratiation toward a fellow director that includes (1) complementing the director about his/her contributions to the board two more times during the past twelve months, (2) disagreeing with the director's point of view on a strategic issue one less time, and (3) doing one more personal favor for the director during that period increases the likelihood of receiving an appointment at another board where that director serves on the nominating committee or as CEO by 72 per cent. Moreover, the effect of ingratiation on receiving additional board appointments is much stronger on average than the effect of providing advice and information to the CEO. Yet, for female and racial minority directors, ingratiation toward the CEO or fellow directors significantly *reduces* the likelihood of receiving a colleague's recommendation for a board appointment. One manifestation of the ultimate attribution error is a tendency to attribute greater sincerity to the behavior of in-group members, while adopting a more cynical view of behavior by out-group members (Hewstone, 1990). Such attribution bias may lead white male directors to interpret flattery, agreement, and favor doing by female and racial minority colleagues as insincere attempts to curry favor, while giving other white males the benefit of the doubt in interpreting similar behavior.

Demographic Minority Status and Differential Exposure to Sanctions and Blame

While demographic minorities tend to receive fewer benefits and opportunities in exchange for their contributions, they also tend to be penalized more for engaging in counter-normative behavior and to receive more blame for negative firm outcomes. Our research has shown that outside directors who participate in changes that increase board control over management at a particular firm, such as changes in board structure that increase board independence and reduce CEO power, experience "social distancing" from directors at other companies: They are less likely to be invited to informal meetings of the board, their advice is solicited less frequently, and others are less likely to build on their comments in discussion (Westphal and Khanna, 2003). In effect, participation in board control over management violates prevailing norms of director conduct, which engenders social sanctions from members of the corporate elite. In a later study, we found that outside directors who violate prevailing norms of director conduct by engaging in independent decision control (e.g., requesting information from the CEO or another inside director for the purpose of evaluating management's performance, or criticizing a strategic proposal put forth by management) were significantly less likely to receive a colleague's recommendation for a board appointment at another public company (Westphal and Stern, 2007). This research has further shown that female and racial minority directors are significantly more likely to be penalized for counter-normative behavior. In particular, the negative effect of engaging in independent decision control on the likelihood of receiving a colleague's recommendation for a board appointment is significantly stronger for minority directors. Moreover, minority directors who participate in changes that increase board control over management at a particular firm are more likely than white male directors to experience "social distancing" from directors at other companies.

Our research has also shown that minority CEOs receive disproportionate blame for negative firm outcomes. Specifically, white male CEOs are significantly more likely to make "internal" attributions for low performance of firms with female or racial minority CEOs in communicating with journalists, whereby they attribute disappointing results to internal factors such as mistakes in strategic decision making or weak leadership rather than external factors such as adverse conditions in the industry environment (Park and Westphal, 2013). These effects are also moderated by the CEO's status in the corporate elite. Whereas white male CEOs who occupy relatively high-status positions are especially unlikely to be the target of internal attributions for low performance by other corporate leaders, female or racial minority CEOs who occupy high-status positions are *more* likely to be the subject of such derogatory attributions in communications with journalists. The results are consistent with intergroup envy in social evaluations. When people make upward social comparisons with in-group members, known as "upward assimilative comparisons," they are guided by the preconscious sentiment "that could be me," while in making upward social comparisons with out-group members, or "upward contrastive comparisons," they are guided by the sentiment "that should be me" (Cuddy et al., 2007: 632; Fiske, 2010). Such envy toward higher-status out-group members reflects intergroup bias, and may be manifested as derogatory performance attributions in communicating with third parties such as journalists.

Given evidence that negative commentary by firm leaders exerts particular influence on the valence of journalists' reports, and that such reports in turn influence the reputation of corporate leaders across a range of stakeholder groups (Chen and Meindl, 1991; Pollock and Rindova, 2003; Graffin et al., 2008), the results reveal an especially damaging form of social discrimination in corporate leadership. A fundamental principle in the status literature is the "Matthew effect," wherein high-status actors ostensibly receive more rewards than low-status actors for comparable accomplishments, and they receive fewer sanctions or penalties for substandard performance (Merton, 1968; Podolny, 1993; Rao, 1994). Our research suggests that while the Matthew effect may operate for the in-group (white males), an *inverse* Matthew effect appears to operate for women and racial minorities who occupy corporate leadership positions, at least in regards to the social evaluations of fellow leaders and media coverage of firm leadership. Since the volume of media reporting about firm leadership increases exponentially with the status of the firm's CEO, the reputational consequences of the interaction between the CEO's status in the corporate elite and the CEO's minority status are amplified further. White males not only have easier access to leadership positions than women and minorities, but IM support and more favorable media coverage makes it easier for them to build on their early successes.

Evidence that appointment of a female or racial minority CEO reduces the provision of mentoring, advice, and other kinds of professional support to female and racial minority managers below the CEO level (McDonald et al., 2018) is another way in which the Matthew effect does not apply to minority leaders. Classic research on the "generalized Matthew Effect" suggests that when an individual member of a particular social group acquires a prominent, high-status position, the benefits can "trickle down" to other members of the group who occupy lower-status positions (Cole and Cole, 1973: 201; Cole, 1979; see also Graffin et al., 2008). Our research provides evidence for a kind of *reverse* generalized Matthew effect for minorities, whereby the appointment of an individual who belongs to a minority social category to a prominent, high-status position actually disadvantages other category members (i.e., fellow racial minority and female managers) who occupy lower-status positions in the hierarchy, due to the biased cognitions and behavioral responses of white males. For example, white male top managers provided significantly less task-related help to female and racial minority colleagues, and less mentoring to minority subordinates, following the appointment of a minority CEO (McDonald et al., 2018).

Not only are minority leaders more likely to be the target of negative commentary by leaders of other firms, but there is even evidence that female and racial minority leaders are more likely to be the subject of negative commentary by top managers *at the same firm*. Our research has shown that such negative commentary can be traced to an unexpected source: ingratiation in relations between top managers and CEOs (Keeves et al., 2017; see Chapter 7). We argued that engaging in ingratiatory behavior threatens positive self-regard, because it contradicts normative ideals of authenticity, autonomy, and meritocracy, and this triggers resentment toward the target of ingratiation (e.g., the CEO). We further argued that top managers would tend to feel resentment toward the CEO for the flattery that he or she receives from other top managers, in part due to feelings of envy. Analysis of our survey data showed not only that ingratiation by the focal manager and other managers toward the CEO is associated with resentment, but that these relationships are especially strong when the CEO is a racial minority or a woman.

One manifestation of intergroup bias is a tendency for white males to perceive women and racial minorities as less qualified for leadership, including leadership of business organizations, due in part to stereotypic perceptions: "being white [and being male] is perceived to be an attribute of the business leader prototype" (Rosette et al., 2008: 758; Stoker et al., 2012). Out-group biases toward minority leaders are also fueled by the widespread, often unspoken assumption among white male managers that successful minorities have profited from preferential selection processes at various stages of their lives and careers (Kluegel and Smith, 1986; Kane and Whipkey, 2009). As a result of such biases, white male managers may tend to perceive a given level of flattery toward the CEO as relatively undeserved when the CEO is a minority, increasing resentment.

Moreover, when one interacts with out-group members who occupy higher-status positions and observes the status benefits they enjoy, one is particularly likely to feel "that should be me" (Cuddy et al., 2007: 632; Fiske, 2012; Smith, 2013). Thus, stereotypic perceptions of business leaders coupled with generic out-group bias will tend to amplify feelings of resentment toward female and racial minority CEOs. White male top managers are especially likely to feel "that should be me" when they interact with minority CEOs and witness the status benefits they enjoy, including flattery and opinion conformity that endorse the CEO's leadership capability and strategic judgment. The moderating effects of race and gender on resentment are strong in magnitude: The effect of an increase in compliments to the CEO by other top managers of one standard deviation is approximately 31–36 per cent greater if the focal manager is a white male and the CEO is a woman, and 39–44 per cent greater if the manager is a white male and the CEO is a racial minority, than if the manager and CEO are demographically similar.

Feelings of resentment from ingratiation toward a minority leader may increase the likelihood that top managers engage in negative commentary about the leader in communicating with third parties (see also Chapter 7). Discrete emotions have distinctive profiles of cognitions, associated feelings, and action tendencies (Frijda, 1986; Roseman et al., 1994). Resentment that results from the perception that another person has succeeded undeservedly can prompt ruminative thoughts about the resented person being "cut down to size," thoughts which elicit anticipatory schadenfreude (Smith and Kim, 2007). Resentment is an "insidious" emotion that causes "preconscious inclinations to do harm" to the resented person (Heider, 1958: 289; Leach et al., 2003; Smith and Kim, 2007: 56). Observing negative outcomes for a resented person activates regions of the brain associated with "valuation" and "motivation (e.g., urges to inflict harm)" (Cikara et al., 2011: 307). There is specific evidence that resentment can motivate social undermining behavior that "hinder[s] the ability of others to establish and maintain favorable reputations" (Duffy et al., 2012: 643; Smith, 2013).

Our analyses revealed that top managers' feelings of resentment toward the CEO are associated with social undermining of the CEO in communicating with journalists. For example, resentment was associated with faint praise of the CEO's leadership, statements about other persons or firm characteristics that reflect negatively on the CEO's leadership (e.g., references to greater monitoring or control of the CEO by the board, or involvement in strategic decision making of other top managers, the board chair, or other directors, implicitly due to concerns about the CEO's leadership or strategy), and relatively direct negative statements about the CEO's leadership. Moreover, the CEO's minority status significantly moderated the mediated relationship between ingratiation, resentment, and each form of social undermining. That is, ingratiation toward the CEO had an especially strong, indirect effect on social undermining of the CEO through heightened feelings of resentment when the CEO was a racial minority or a woman.

Negative commentary about firm leadership is more newsworthy than positive commentary, and negative commentary about the CEO's leadership by firm insiders is likely to appear relatively objective and credible to journalists, even though our research shows that such commentary is influenced by negative emotions. Thus, we would expect a strong effect of social undermining of the CEO by top managers on media coverage of firm leadership. In fact, separate analyses showed a very strong relationship between a focal manager's resentment and subsequent negative commentary about the CEO's leadership that was attributed to a firm insider in articles by journalists with whom the focal manager had communicated (in virtually all such cases attributions were made without revealing the insider's name). Moreover, the adverse reputational effects of social undermining are especially severe under conditions of low firm performance, because media coverage of firm leadership and strategy is more intense following the disclosure of low corporate earnings (Westphal and Deephouse, 2011). Accordingly, social undermining of minority CEOs by top managers in their communications with journalists is a particularly insidious and damaging form of social discrimination.

Overall, our research has provided evidence that female and racial minority CEOs, other top managers, and directors are subjected to a wide range of different forms of social discrimination, including reduced access to various forms of professional and personal support, less benefits from their contributions to governance and strategy, greater exposure to sanctions and blame for counternormative behavior, and a greater risk of being the target of social undermining behavior. Each of the many forms of social discrimination that we have discussed has non-trivial, adverse consequences for the careers of female and racial minority leaders. Most forms of discrimination are amplified under conditions of poor firm performance and/or negative assessments of firm leadership, strategy, or performance prospects by security analysts, when firm leaders are most in need of assistance and most vulnerable to adverse career outcomes. While it is difficult to aggregate these discrete forms of discrimination into a "total" effect of minority status, the overall disadvantage faced by women and racial minorities in leadership positions is clearly immense. This helps explain higher "churn" rates for female and racial minority leaders (McDonald and Westphal, 2013; Tinsley et al., 2017). Minority leaders have higher average turnover rates, not only at the firm level, but also at the level of the corporate elite. Our data indicate that from 2008 to 2015, female and racial minority corporate officers and outside directors disappeared from the sample frame of large and mid-sized public U.S. companies at over twice the rate of white males.

While female and racial minority leaders are especially disadvantaged under conditions of low firm performance and negative analyst appraisals of firm leadership, strategy, or performance prospects, such adverse conditions are also especially likely to prompt managerial and board appointments that increase demographic diversity. In effect, economic and reputational adversity prompts the appointment of minority top managers and directors who tend to receive relatively little professional and personal support, though they are placed at greater risk of reputational harm. Moreover, firm leaders are especially likely to highlight the firm's commitment to diversity in their external communications with analysts and other information intermediaries under such conditions. These communications tend to make broad claims about the benefits of diversity to the quality of strategic decision making, firm leadership, and/or firm performance outcomes. As one top manager told us,

> [The CEO] would periodically testify to [the firm's] commitment to increasing diversity in leadership, particularly in the wake of an earnings miss. He would point to specific hires and appointments—executive appointments, director [appointments], committee chairs. And talk about the benefits to our strategic thinking. Did it re-direct the conversation? Sometimes. Did it help avoid difficult questions about strategy? I would say it did.

Thus, the very same conditions that tend to prompt increases in social discrimination against women and racial minority managers and directors also prompt firm leaders to engage in IM about their commitment to diversity. Our longitudinal surveys of corporate officers and security analysts confirmed that CEOs are significantly more likely to reference their firm's "commitment to diversity" following negative earnings surprises. Our most recent surveys also show an increase in references to "inclusion" and "inclusiveness" in regards to diversity and decision making under such circumstances. In 2015 a top manager suggested, "Diversity and inclusion is the new buzzphrase. [When asked when and with whom leaders use this language]: Increasingly with everyone: analysts, employees, media. As to when, it's when they would rather not talk about [recent] performance." Moreover, our analyses have provided some evidence that IM of this kind reduces external criticism of firm leadership and strategy. In particular, when

CEOs mention the firm's commitment to diversity and reference recent appointments that increase demographic diversity of the top management team or the board of directors in communications with a security analyst, the analyst is less likely to ask questions about firm strategy or performance in subsequent conferences calls. CEOs are especially likely to provide specific information about strategic decision-making processes and appointments that increase diversity in private communication with security analysts. Recent research has shown that private communication with management has a significant influence on analysts' earnings forecasts and stock recommendations; in fact, information provided in these communications may have a stronger influence on analysts' appraisals than their own primary research (Brown et al., 2015). While executives cannot provide individual analysts with "nonpublic material information," such as information about strategies and performance (Brown et al., 2015), many appear to act on the assumption that information about strategy processes is merely "contextual," and thus non-material. The provision of such information through private communications may not only influence an analyst's confidence in firm leadership and strategy, but it may also enable firm leaders to develop stronger professional relationships with analysts that influence the valence of their future appraisals. As one former CEO told us,

> Private conversations with analysts have two types of benefits. You can provide specific information that results in more accurate reports, more favorable and optimistic reports in the near term. And maybe more important, you're developing a relationship with the analyst that helps over the long term. Analysts naturally feel privileged to get information through a private channel rather than through a public channel like a conference call—they feel like they're getting special access. That's a powerful way to build a relationship.

Thus, IM about strategy process provides an opportunity for firm leaders to build social capital with information intermediaries in ways that IM about strategy and performance does not. Our empirical analyses have not fully captured these long-term benefits, suggesting a promising direction for future research.

Conclusion

The symbolic management of social and organizational processes in firm leadership and governance is a relatively efficient and effective means of gaining the support of organizational constituents. The various forms of symbolic management that we have described, including IM about executive advice seeking, participative decision making, and diversity, can influence how constituents react to a variety of subsequent strategic decisions and environmental changes by enhancing confidence and trust in firm leadership. These second-order benefits substantially increase the efficiency of symbolic management activity. Moreover, some of these forms of symbolic management have the potential to influence a broad array of firm stakeholders. Whereas the agency logic appeals primarily to analysts and investors, the logic of democratic process appeals more broadly to external stakeholders beyond financial market actors, and to internal stakeholders below the board level. Thus, symbolic management about participative decision making, diversity, and inclusion has broader reach than the symbolic management about particular policies and strategies examined in most prior research. In addition, our theory has suggested that some forms of symbolic management about process, such as communication about PSDM programs, convey a sense of transparency and enhance trust in leadership, despite the potential for decoupling, which further bolsters their effectiveness. Although these forms of symbolic management are less clear cut than the decoupled policies and structures examined in prior research, making them more challenging to identify empirically, their subtlety renders them especially potent in influencing stakeholder opinion.

4

Symbolic Management beyond the Firm Level

Thus far we have examined different forms of symbolic management at the firm level, symbolic management about corporate policies, structures, or decision-making processes. In this chapter we describe forms of symbolic management that cross organizational boundaries, including symbolic management by firm leaders about the leadership, strategy, and governance of particular other firms, and symbolic management by and for larger groups of leaders and their firms. While these cooperative and collective forms of symbolic management have received relatively little scholarly attention, they have significant consequences for the reputation and legitimacy of firm leadership and governance, sometimes greater than the consequences of firm-level symbolic management. Moreover, they turn out to be an integral component of the larger corporate governance system.

We begin by describing a form of symbolic management "support" in which leaders make positive remarks about the leadership, governance, and/or strategy of particular other firms in communicating with journalists and security analysts. We explain why this form of symbolic management can have a stronger influence on evaluations of firm leadership than more conventional IM by CEOs about their own firm's leadership and strategy. We then describe a distinct form of symbolic management support provided by groups of female and racial minority leaders, referred to as minority support groups or "MSGs." Whereas firm leaders normally do not coordinate with each other in providing symbolic management support, the support provided in MSGs is carefully coordinated among group members. We explain why this coordinated form of support may have an especially strong influence on constituent opinion. We then go on to suggest how symbolic management support not only has a significant impact on constituents' beliefs about particular firms and their leaders, but over an extended period of time it has also had a deeper influence on the normative assumptions of journalists and analysts about governance, or the implicit and explicit criteria by which they evaluate the quality of governance. In particular, we explain how symbolic management support has contributed to a shift in the prevailing institutional logic of governance, away from the traditional agency logic described in Chapter 2, toward a "neo-corporate" logic that subtly reasserts the autonomy and discretion of firm leaders. Finally, we reveal how firm leaders have increasingly engaged in symbolic management about the social structure of corporate leadership in

Symbolic Management: Governance, Strategy, and Institutions. James Westphal and Sun Hyun Park,
Oxford University Press (2020). © James Westphal and Sun Hyun Park.
DOI: 10.1093/oso/9780198792055.001.0001

their communications with information intermediaries. We suggest that such communications may have contributed to a growing separation or decoupling between the social structure of corporate leadership as it appears to external constituents, and the *actual* social structure, which is characterized by high levels of relational and structural embeddedness.

Symbolic Management Support

As organizational scholars have long acknowledged, there is a major limitation to many of the conventional forms of IM that have been examined in the empirical literature. Specifically, the communication "target" or audience may perceive IM tactics as self-serving, which can limit their credibility and persuasiveness (Jones and Pittman, 1982; Schlenker and Weigold, 1992; Lam et al., 2007). This limitation is likely to be especially serious for reactive forms of verbal IM in which the self-interest of the communicator is relatively obvious, such as external attributions for low performance by firm leaders in their letters to shareholders or conference calls with security analysts (i.e., attributing low performance to adverse conditions in the industry or macro-economic environment over which firm leaders have little control) (Staw et al., 1983; Salancik and Meindl, 1984). Our research suggests that limitations to conventional forms of verbal IM have given rise to symbolic management support, whereby corporate leaders make positive statements about the leadership, governance, and/or strategy of other firms, or make favorable attributions about the performance of those firms that reflect well on their leaders (Westphal et al., 2012), in communicating with journalists and security analysts. Symbolic management support is typically provided for leaders of other firms in the same industry, broadly defined to include leaders of current or potential buyers and suppliers, as well as competitors.

Symbolic management support is not a rare event at large and medium-sized U.S. companies. On average, CEOs in our samples have been the beneficiaries of symbolic management support such as positive statements about their firm's leadership, governance, or strategy, or external attributions for low performance of their firm, over three times per year. Our empirical analyses suggest that symbolic management of this kind in communications with journalists has significantly more impact on the tenor of media coverage of firm leadership and strategy than IM by CEOs and other top managers about their *own* leadership and strategy. For example, among firms that announced a negative earnings surprise, an increase in symbolic management support from the mean level that included two more positive statements about a focal firm's leadership and two more external attributions for the firm's low performance by other firms' CEOs in communicating with a journalist reduced the number of negative statements by the journalist about the firm's leadership by approximately 74 per cent; an equivalent increase in IM by the focal firm's CEO only reduced negative statements by the journalist about the firm's leadership by approximately 23 per cent.

The relative efficacy of symbolic management support is consistent with theory and research on persuasion in cognitive psychology, which suggests that the perceived self-interest of the source is an important heuristic cue in assessing the veridicality of a persuasive communication (Petty and Cacioppo, 2012). There is even evidence from this literature that people tend to overweight self-interest as a criterion of message veridicality. When the source is not obviously motivated by self-interest, or when an ulterior motive is not salient, audiences are less likely to reflect on counterarguments or solicit different points of view. CEOs have a less obvious self-interest in persuading journalists and analysts about the quality of other CEOs' leadership, governance, and strategy than in making similar claims about their own firms. Moreover, the psychological literature on persuasion suggests that audiences are especially prone to rely on perceived self-interest as a heuristic cue when they face knowledge and information asymmetries about the subject of communication (Petty and Cacioppo, 2012). Journalists and analysts face significant knowledge and information asymmetries relative to firm leaders in making attributions about firm performance (Tuchman, 1972; Brown et al., 2015). Thus, symbolic management support by firm leaders is especially persuasive to these information intermediaries. In Chapter 6 we explain how symbolic management support has diffused through mechanisms of generalized social exchange among firm leaders to become common in the external communications of CEOs at large and medium-sized U.S. companies.

The symbolic management support described so far is uncoordinated: Individual CEOs provide support for individual CEOs at other firms. Our research has also examined a coordinated form of symbolic management support that occurs in MSGs, which are informal groups of three to eight racial minority or female CEOs from the same industry, broadly defined. Leaders in these groups work together to develop a persuasive message about the quality of leadership and strategy at an individual member's firm, and then contact influential journalists to convey the message (Westphal et al., 2019). Group members rotate in giving and receiving support, often quarterly. In constructing the message, leaders exchange information about industry conditions and the strategic positions of competitors. As a result, they can develop a narrative that is not only well supported, but coherent and consistent in its reasoning and evidence. As one MSG member told us, "We get our stories straight. If [the journalist] hears the same arguments from each of us separately, not just general assertions that the CEO and strategy are good, but for the same reasons, it's a lot more convincing... it's also easier for [the journalist] to write it up" (Westphal et al., 2019: 11). The literature on persuasion in cognitive psychology suggests that people rely on a consensus heuristic in assessing persuasion attempts (Wood, 2000; Tormala et al., 2009). They tend to devote less critical scrutiny to claims they have heard before from other sources, and they tend to interpret ambiguous data in ways that validate the apparent consensus. Conversely, repeated exposure to narratives that vary in their reasoning or evidence tends to spur critical scrutiny or cognitive elaboration that reduces attitude change (Weisbuch et al., 2003). Moreover, the process of constructing a persuasive argument as a group, or "collective rationale construction," bolsters individuals' confidence in the veridicality of the argument (Heath and Gonzalez, 1995: 307; Patalano and LeClair, 2011), and conveying a sense of certainty about a position is known to increase persuasion (Reinhard, 2002; Leippe et al., 2009). In addition, while most forms of symbolic management are reactive, occurring in response to performance problems, scandals, or other crises that threaten organizational legitimacy or firm reputation (Elsbach, 1994; David et al., 2007; Desai, 2011; McDonnell and King, 2013; Carlos and Lewis, 2017), coordinated symbolic management support is typically not tethered to performance problems or crises, which should enhance its credibility with journalists.

Coordinated symbolic management support also conforms to the needs of journalists. The consistent, well-supported narrative provided by MSG members can be inserted into a story largely as is, along with quotations or references to multiple firm leaders, helping the journalist cope with time constraints and bolstering the credibility of the story with their superiors, peers, and ultimate "consumers." Thus, the rhetoric of coordinated symbolic management support is not only likely to be more persuasive to journalists than uncoordinated symbolic management, but it should also to be more useful to them. As a result, journalists are especially likely to incorporate the rhetoric of MSG members into their stories.

Our empirical analyses provided strong evidence for the relative efficacy of coordinated symbolic management support. Support by MSG members had a significantly more positive influence on the valence of journalists' reporting about firm leadership and strategy than the uncoordinated support of CEOs who were not MSG members. Moreover, there is suggestive evidence that coordinated support in MSGs entirely neutralized the bias in media coverage of firms with female or racial minority CEOs. While the valence of journalists' coverage of firms with minority CEOs is significantly more negative on average than comparable coverage of firms with white male leaders in industries that do not yet have an MSG, this difference is no longer statistically significant in industries that do have an MSG.

Although coordinated symbolic management support has diminished the social disadvantages faced by minority leaders in some industries, it has neutralized the effects of social discrimination rather than directly confronting and eliminating discrimination. The activities of MSGs require considerable investments of time and effort by minority leaders in order to achieve parity with white male leaders in media coverage. Moreover, MSGs have created a balkanized social structure, in at least two respects. First, members have elite social networks that are far superior on average to those of minority leaders who are not members, with respect to the number and strength of ties to fellow minority leaders, journalists, and other firm constituents. Second, MSGs have exacerbated the difference in social networks between white male leaders and racial minority leaders. MSG members have more strong ties to fellow leaders than white male leaders, but they have far fewer weak ties linking them to leaders outside their minority group. By extension, MSGs have not yet increased minority leaders' ties to white male leaders. Accordingly, coordinated symbolic management support has not necessarily reduced the separation or decoupling between appearance and reality of diversity and inclusion discussed above. Minority leaders are generally aware of this limitation to MSGs, and many are hopeful that it may be corrected over time.

As MSGs spread further and continue to bolster the reputations of minority leaders, however, it may become easier for minorities to form ties with members of the majority. The MSG members whom we interviewed generally agreed that a long-term goal of this movement is not only greater equality, but also greater social connectedness between minority and majority leaders. As one female member put it, "We are already separate, we don't want to be more separate... progress means going in the other direction... [toward] one group of leaders." However, there was disagreement over how and when such connections will be forged. While current norms within MSGs favor discretion and maintaining a low profile, with some leaders continuing to believe that publicity about the groups would damage their relationships with white male colleagues and firm constituents, others believe that the groups should be publicized to increase the leverage of minority leaders with the white male majority. As one minority member told us,

> Everyone agrees that the groups have accomplished a lot, but people disagree on how to take it to the next stage. Some say the groups should go public, coordinate [across groups] and organize, others think that would create backlash and [a negative reaction that results in] backsliding, and that more change will happen with an organic approach.

Similarly, while some believe that the groups should remain focused on bolstering the reputations of minority leaders, others feel that the groups should broaden their activities to counteract other kinds of discrimination. MSGs are similar in certain respects to African American groups studied by Davis and colleagues in their classic study of the social structure of the American Deep South in the 1930s (Davis et al., 1941). Those groups were strictly social, and were not intended to neutralize social discrimination, but they were similar in their tendency to maintain a low profile regarding the groups' activities. Some felt that African Americans missed an opportunity to formalize these groups and broaden their objectives to include reductions in various forms of social inequality. There would be value in future research that examines whether and how these groups evolve and change over time.

Symbolic Management Support and Institutional Change

Symbolic management support has not only bolstered the reputation of firm leadership and strategy, but it has also contributed to a gradual shift in the prevailing, institutional logic of governance. In particular, we suggest that symbolic management support has contributed to a shift in assumptions about firm governance among corporate stakeholders away from the "pure" agency logic described in Chapter 2, toward a new, hybrid logic that integrates assumptions of the traditional, corporate logic of governance with central prescriptions from agency theory. Our survey data indicated that, in making positive statements about the leadership and strategy of other firms, CEOs frequently suggest that the board of directors is independent of management, and that independence promotes the quality of strategic decision making (Westphal and Park, 2012). Moreover, while IM about governance previously highlighted independent board control over management (Westphal and Graebner, 2010), beginning in the early 2000s CEOs increasingly suggested that independent boards provide more "objective input" or "advice" on strategy, which enabled them to better "assist" or "help" management with strategy and policy issues facing the firm. Symbolic management support also commonly includes descriptions about individual leaders as "difficult to replace," "uniquely capable," and/or as possessing "rare" talent or ability.

Such rhetoric effectively integrates the agency and corporate logics of governance. In particular, it integrates the central prescription of the agency logic—board independence—with assumptions about firm leadership and governance contained in the corporate logic. Whereas the agency logic proceeds from the assumption that executives are self-interested and fungible agents of shareholders who are prone to creating "agency problems," as discussed in Chapter 2, in the corporate logic they are highly trained and experienced professionals who have risen to the top because they possess unique leader talents and strategic knowledge that is uniquely valuable for efficiently allocating corporate resources. Rather than a source of agency costs, firm leaders are well-intentioned and highly capable stewards of their firms (Davis et al., 1997; Moore and Kraatz, 2011). The rhetoric of symbolic management support uses a central policy prescription of the agency logic as a kind of Trojan horse to reinstate behavioral assumptions that are more favorable to managers.

We refer to this new hybridized logic of governance, which co-opts a key prescription of agency theory, as the neo-corporate logic of governance. The emergence of the neo-corporate logic was facilitated by the institutionalization of board independence from management as a central policy prescription for effective corporate governance. We suggest that as board independence became institutionalized, or taken for granted as a means of ensuring effective governance, there was less need for social actors to engage in dialogue or cognitive reflection about the function that it serves. As a result, the premises that originally supported the institutionalized policy became less salient to organizational stakeholders. In effect, as board independence became taken for granted as normatively appropriate, it was progressively decoupled from the agency theoretic assumptions that motivated the policy prescription in the first place. This decoupling of institutionalized prescriptions from agency assumptions afforded an opportunity for managers to reinterpret board independence in terms of the more salutary assumptions of the corporate logic. By this account of institutional change, firm leaders are "bricoleurs" who reconceive organizational practices by borrowing and recombining elements of different institutional logics (Rao et al., 2005: 971; Greenwood and Suddaby, 2006; Kisfalvi and Maguire, 2011). Our theory suggests how bricolage is facilitated by institutionalization.

The neo-corporate logic derives legitimacy in part from its connection to meritocratic values. In characterizing firm leaders as difficult to replace, uniquely capable, and possessing rare talent, the neo-corporate logic validates normative beliefs about equal opportunity and individual ability and hard work as drivers of success in America (Blasi and Jost, 2012). More generally, the neo-corporate logic appeals to American optimism (Du Bois, 1955; De Tocqueville, 2003). Whereas the agency logic is fundamentally pessimistic about human motives, portraying corporate leaders as self-interested and untrustworthy (Westphal and Zajac, 1994; Davis et al., 1997), the neo-corporate logic is optimistic about the intentions of firm leaders, as well as the governance system in which they operate.

Moreover, the rhetoric of symbolic management support often characterizes board involvement as "participative decision making" and/or "democratic governance," thus deriving legitimacy from the institutional logic of democratic process (DiMaggio, 1997; Friedland and Alford, 1991) (see Chapter 3). While some versions of the agency logic also embraced democratic governance, it was implicitly or explicitly characterized as board control over management on behalf of shareholders (i.e., based on the assumption that executives would otherwise pursue initiatives that satisfy their own preferences at the expense of shareholders) (Langevoort, 2006). The rhetoric of symbolic management support essentially reinterpreted democratic governance as participative decision making in which the CEO solicited input from the board rather than the board exercising control over management. Although the shift from "control" to "input and advice" is sufficiently subtle that it has gone unnoticed among many firm stakeholders and observers, it is fundamentally important because it implies a shift in final decision-making authority away from the board, and away from shareholders and other firm stakeholders represented by the board, and toward top executives. In effect, firm leaders reinterpreted the institutional logic of democratic process in ways that help to preserve managerial autonomy.

The rhetoric about board independence and involvement in episodes of symbolic management support is frequently decoupled from actual board behavior. There is considerable evidence not only that formal board independence is unrelated to board control over management (see Chapter 2), but also that independence is *negatively* associated with board input and advice to management (Westphal, 1999; for reviews, see Finkelstein et al., 2009; Hillman and Dalziel, 2003). Such decoupling can persist in part due to information asymmetry between firm leaders and their constituents, including journalists and analysts, and in part because persuasion attempts that are framed in terms of higher-order institutional logics tend to receive less critical scrutiny (Westphal and Graebner, 2010). Moreover, while journalists are motivated to uncover the truth, a more immediate motive is to tell a credible story (Schudson, 2003; Tuchman, 1978), and citing firm leaders about the quality of governance at another firm builds credibility with superiors, fellow reporters, and readers (or other "consumers").

Symbolic management support exerts social influence on multiple levels. Symbolic management about a particular firm increases the confidence of journalists and analysts about the quality of governance, leadership, and strategy at that firm, and supports external attributions for low performance at the firm. Such "first-order persuasion" has an immediate impact on constituents' beliefs about particular firms. In addition, cumulative exposure to symbolic management support across firms and over time should gradually influence the normative assumptions of journalists and analysts about governance, or the implicit or explicit criteria by which they evaluate the quality of governance. By virtue of such "second-order persuasion," the neo-corporate logic may have acquired cognitive legitimacy over time among the influential journalists and analysts who are commonly targeted for symbolic management support.

Our survey research indicated that journalists of leading publications with the largest circulation (more than one standard deviation above the mean) who reported regularly on firm leadership and performance at large companies were exposed to symbolic management support on a regular basis from 2001 to 2007 (Westphal and Park, 2012). Moreover, the average rate of exposure was high: approximately nineteen times per year on average. Journalists who were subjected to symbolic management support tended to interact with many different executives, and were therefore exposed to rhetoric of the neo-corporate logic from a variety of sources. Figure 4.1 details the exposure of one journalist from 2001 to 2007; this person was exposed to symbolic management support 137 times over this time period, or twenty times per year on average, which is approximately average for leading journalists. In this example, fifty-nine executives were implicated in episodes of symbolic management support over this period, either as providers of support, or as the subject of support. Repeated exposure to a

Figure 4.1 — A Leading Journalist's Exposure to IM support: 2001–2007

Year	Q1	Q2	Q3	Q4
2001	CEO 1 for CEO 2; CEO 3 for CEO 2; CEO 4 for CEO 2	CEO 5 for CEO 6; CEO 7 for CEO 6	CEO 8 for CEO 9; CEO 10 for CEO 9; CEO 11 for CEO 9; CEO 12 for CEO 9; CEO 13 for CEO 9; CEO 14 for CEO 15; CEO 16 for CEO 15	CEO 9 for CEO 17; CEO 10 for CEO 17; CEO 12 for CEO 17; CEO 18 for CEO 17
2002	CEO 9 for CEO 29; CEO 10 for CEO 29; CEO 12 for CEO 29; CEO 18 for CEO 29; CEO 30 for CEO 29	CEO 12 for CEO 19; CEO 17 for CEO 19; CEO 18 for CEO 19; CEO 20 for CEO 19	CEO 1 for CEO 3; CEO 4 for CEO 3; CEO 21 for CEO 3; CEO 22 for CEO 3; CEO 6 for CEO 5; CEO 23 for CEO 5; CEO 24 for CEO 5	CEO 25 for CEO 26; CEO 27 for CEO 26; CEO 28 for CEO 26
2003	CEO 2 for CEO 35; CEO 3 for CEO 35; CEO 4 for CEO 35; CEO 37 for CEO 35	CEO 25 for CEO 27; CEO 28 for CEO 27; CEO 31 for CEO 27	CEO 1 for CEO 2; CEO 4 for CEO 2; CEO 31 for CEO 2; CEO 6 for CEO 32; CEO 23 for CEO 32; CEO 33 for CEO 32	CEO 9 for CEO 12; CEO 34 for CEO 12
2004	CEO 15 for CEO 14; CEO 16 for CEO 14	CEO 1 for CEO 9; CEO 8 for CEO 9; CEO 10 for CEO 9; CEO 11 for CEO 9; CEO 29 for CEO 9; CEO 6 for CEO 4; CEO 13 for CEO 4	CEO 25 for CEO 38; CEO 26 for CEO 38; CEO 27 for CEO 38	
2005	CEO 8 for CEO 11; CEO 9 for CEO 11; CEO 10 for CEO 11; CEO 12 for CEO 11; CEO 12 for CEO 30; CEO 18 for CEO 30; CEO 29 for CEO 30	CEO 25 for CEO 26; CEO 27 for CEO 26; CEO 38 for CEO 26; CEO 39 for CEO 26; CEO 14 for CEO 16; CEO 15 for CEO 16	CEO 5 for CEO 40; CEO 6 for CEO 40; CEO 7 for CEO 40; CEO 41 for CEO 40; CEO 42 for CEO 40; CEO 43 for CEO 40; CEO 6 for CEO 3; CEO 36 for CEO 3; CEO 37 for CEO 3	
2006	CEO 1 for CEO 31; CEO 2 for CEO 31; CEO 4 for CEO 31; CEO 36 for CEO 31	CEO 5 for CEO 41; CEO 7 for CEO 41; CEO 42 for CEO 41; CEO 43 for CEO 41; CEO 44 for CEO 41	CEO 4 for CEO 13; CEO 6 for CEO 13; CEO 8 for CEO 13; CEO 9 for CEO 13; CEO 12 for CEO 13; CEO 5 for CEO 45; CEO 7 for CEO 45; CEO 41 for CEO 43; CEO 42 for CEO 43; CEO 44 for CEO 43	CEO 27 for CEO 46; CEO 28 for CEO 46; CEO 47 for CEO 46; CEO 48 for CEO 46; CEO 49 for CEO 46; CEO 6 for CEO 33; CEO 23 for CEO 33; CEO 32 for CEO 33
2007	CEO 2 for CEO 1; CEO 4 for CEO 1; CEO 31 for CEO 1	CEO 28 for CEO 47; CEO 48 for CEO 47; CEO 49 for CEO 47; CEO 25 for CEO 38; CEO 26 for CEO 38; CEO 27 for CEO 38; CEO 39 for CEO 38; CEO 16 for CEO 14; CEO 50 for CEO 14	CEO 51 for CEO 52; CEO 53 for CEO 52; CEO 54 for CEO 52; CEO 30 for CEO 55; CEO 4 for CEO 7	CEO 10 for CEO 56; CEO 18 for CEO 56; CEO 30 for CEO 56; CEO 57 for CEO 56; CEO 58 for CEO 56; CEO 59 for CEO 56

Figure 4.1 A Leading Journalist's Exposure to IM support: 2001–2007*

persuasive message tends to increase acceptance (Lee, 2001; Zajonc, 2001), especially when the message is conveyed by different individuals.

Moreover, the logic of a persuasive message is especially likely to be accepted when it appears to be pervasive and robust in its application across different contexts, and the leading journalists who are targeted for symbolic management support tend to cover a range of companies operating in different business environments. Thus, as leading journalists are subjected repeatedly over time to the neo-corporate logic through symbolic management support about the variety of firms that they cover, they will gradually come to accept this perspective on governance as normatively appropriate. We therefore expected that the neo-corporate logic would be increasingly reflected in the reporting of influential journalists. Since the reporting of these journalists exerts a disproportionate influence on the reporting of their peers (Schudson, 2003), symbolic management support also has a second-order effect on the reporting of journalists who were not directly targeted by CEOs.

Media coverage of corporate governance in turn influences the normative assumptions of other corporate stakeholders, including financial analysts, investors, and public policy makers. The media is a "propagator of legitimacy" whose coverage not only influences investor evaluations of individual firms, but also exerts a deeper influence on the implicit criteria by which firms are evaluated (Pollock and Rindova, 2003: 632; Pollock et al., 2008). Moreover, the same factors that make accounts of firm leadership and governance rooted in the neo-corporate logic persuasive to journalists, including the co-optation of agency theoretic prescriptions such as board independence, should also make these accounts persuasive to members of the financial community.

Although it is difficult to provide conclusive evidence for a causal relationship between exposure to symbolic management support and change in the prevailing, normative beliefs about corporate governance, our large-sample survey data do suggest that normative beliefs about governance among journalists and security analysts have shifted toward the neo-corporate logic since the early 2000s. Table 4.1 provides mean responses to a set of survey questions about governance practices for representative samples of journalists and analysts in 2001 and 2009–10 (see Table 4.1; Westphal and Park, 2012 for further information on these samples). The data show that while board independence from management is still accepted as a central prescription for effective governance in 2010, normative beliefs about the proper form of board involvement had changed significantly from ten years earlier. Whereas in 2001 journalists and analysts tended to disagree that "effective corporate governance depend[s] on the ability of the board to assist management with strategic decision making and/or policy matters facing the firm," by 2010 they tended to agree with that statement. And while in 2001 respondents tended to agree that "effective corporate governance depend[s] on the board exercising control over management," by 2010 they tended to disagree

Table 4.1. Normative beliefs about corporate governance among journalists and security analysts

Item	Journalists[1]		Security analysts[2]	
	2001	2010	2001	2009
To what extent does effective corporate governance depend on the board's independence from management (five-point scale: not at all... to some extent... very much so)?	4.52	4.48	4.59	4.46
To what extent does effective corporate governance depend on the board exercising control over management (five-point scale: not at all... to some extent... very much so)?	4.45	1.98	4.57	2.26
To what extent does effective corporate governance depend on the ability of the board to assist management with strategic decision making and/or policy matters facing the firm (five-point scale: not at all... to some extent... very much so)?	1.89	4.49	1.83	4.34
Democratic corporate governance means board of director participation in strategic decision making (seven-point scale: agree... disagree)	2.26	4.44	2.11	4.39
Democratic corporate governance means board control over management on behalf of shareholders (seven-point scale: agree... disagree)	4.48	1.80	4.52	2.01

[1] Sample frame included 600 journalists selected at random from journalists who participated in a larger study on executive–journalist relations (Westphal et al., 2012). The sample frame was randomly selected from all journalists who (1) had reported in the prior year on a firm with a CEO who participated in the study (participating CEOs were from public U.S. firms with more than $100 million in sales), and (2) were employed at major news and business publications in the U.S. (as listed in *Factiva* and *LexisNexis*) or daily newspapers in the city where the participating CEO's firm was headquartered. 255 participated in the 2001 survey and 251 participated in the 2010 survey. Respondents were representative of journalists in the larger sample frame with respect to circulation of their employers, years of experience working as a journalist, and negativity and frequency of coverage about firm leadership, strategy, governance, and performance.

[2] Sample frame included 500 sell-side analysts who covered at least one public U.S. firm with more than $100 million in sales. 199 participated in 2001, 196 participated in 2009. Respondents were representative of analysts in the larger sample frame with respect to size of the analyst's employer, "All-America status" of the analyst, and average (standardized) earnings forecasts and stock recommendations.

Source: Westphal and Park (2012: 37)

with this statement. As shown in Table 4.1, there was also a shift in the prevailing definition of "democratic corporate governance" among responding journalists and analysts. In 2001 respondents tended to agree that "democratic governance means board control over management on behalf of shareholders," and to disagree that it means "board... participation in strategic decision making." By

2010 these beliefs were completely reversed. A follow-up survey of journalists and analysts in 2015 fully replicated results of the 2010 survey. These data provide at least some indication that key normative beliefs about governance have become aligned with the neo-corporate logic, as represented in the rhetoric of symbolic management support.

Symbolic Management about the Social Structure of Corporate Leadership

Over the past decade firm leaders have increasingly engaged in symbolic management about the social structure of corporate leadership in their communications with external stakeholders. The growing cultural recognition of the social and professional importance of social network ties has provided top executives with an opportunity to enhance the reputation of corporate leadership.

The most visible indicator of social network ties between firm leaders is the board interlock network. The Clayton Act has long prohibited interlocking directorates among firms that compete in the same industry, under the presumption that such ties facilitate collusion (Buch-Hansen, 2014). Moreover, the density of the broader board interlock network has declined significantly since the late 2000s (Chu and Davis, 2016; Mizruchi, 2013). In recent years, firm leaders have increasingly referenced the sparsity of board interlock ties between firms in the same industry as evidence of competition in communicating with journalists at general media outlets. Analysis of our recent survey data indicated that top executives are three times more likely to mention the absence of board ties in their industry within six months of announcing a merger or acquisition among firms in the industry. As one journalist whom we interviewed told us,

> Executives are increasingly vocal about the absence of board connections [between leaders] in their industries. You especially hear this around the time of a merger that could raise anti-trust concerns. The larger claim is that regulation is already ensuring free market competition . . . the absence of board [interlock ties] being a prominent marker of that.

Our survey data also indicate that journalists tend to find this message persuasive. Among a representative sample of 106 journalists at general media outlets, 92 per cent agreed or strongly agreed that "the absence of board interlock ties [as defined in the survey] between top executives in the same industry promotes competition." Moreover, our analyses show that the frequency of references by top executives to the sparsity of board interlock ties between firms in the same industry in communicating with a journalist is positively associated with the valence of the journalist's subsequent reporting about firm products and services in the industry (controlling for the level of communication between top executives and journalists and other factors that have been shown to influence the valence of journalists' coverage (Bednar, 2012; Shani and Westphal, 2016)).

Yet, our research also shows that while board interlock ties between competitors are rare, top executives of competing firms are nonetheless often connected by a specific kind of two-step network tie, which we call "board friendship ties," in which the personal friends of a firm's CEO serve on the board of a competitor firm (Westphal and Zhu, 2019b). In our representative sample of 509 large and medium-sized public companies, the average number of board friendship ties to CEOs of competitors over the period 2007 to 2013 was 2.2. Our theoretical argument suggested how such ties may facilitate interfirm collusion and reduce competition. Directors who form board friendship ties are in a position to facilitate the mutual sharing of information about pricing, production, and other strategic plans, as well as information about common buyers and suppliers, enabling them to negotiate more favorable exchange terms. Our regression analysis indicated a strong, positive effect of board friendship ties to competitors on firm profitability: An increase of one such tie was associated with an average increase in return on assets of approximately 1.6 per cent, which corresponds to an average increase in net income of $134 million.

Moreover, our survey data corroborated our theoretical argument for the performance benefits of board friendship ties. The survey asked directors and CEOs and directors at potential suppliers of a focal firm, "To what extent has [the focal firm] been able to keep prices higher than might be expected, given economic conditions?" "To what extent is it difficult to negotiate favorable terms with [the focal firm]?" "To what extent has [the focal firm] been able to keep its terms with [buyers in respondent's industry], with respect to price or value-added services, more favorable than might be expected, given economic conditions?" "[over the past twelve months] To what extent has [the focal firm] seemed to be acting in concert with competitors, with respect to (1) price (2) production?" There was a parallel set of questions for directors and CEOs of potential buyer firms. The factor score for this measure partially mediated the hypothesized effect of board friendship ties to CEOs of competitor firms on performance (Westphal and Zhu, 2019b).

The separation between appearances and reality with respect to board ties between competitors parallels the decoupling between formal board independence from management and the board's (lack of) social independence (see Chapter 2). In both cases, moreover, verbal IM by firm leaders toward information intermediaries has exacerbated the separation between external perceptions and the reality inside corporate leadership. In Chapter 6 we discuss other kinds of direct and indirect social connections between firm leaders, including friendship ties between CEOs in different industries and common ties to headhunters and other consultants. All of these ties are invisible to stakeholders, or lie "below the radar." The picture that ultimately emerges from this analysis is a multi-faceted decoupling between appearances and reality with respect to the social structure of corporate leadership. What appears to be a lack of connectedness between leaders that should promote independence and competition in reality masks a persistently high level of relational and structural embeddedness that promotes collusive behavior. We propose an extension of Podolny's (2001) metaphor of networks as pipes or prisms, in which networks function as symbols rather than as signals. That is, rather than signaling underlying characteristics such as quality in ways that reduce information asymmetry, as Podolny suggests (also Stuart et al., 1999), networks are often social constructions that are decoupled from actual organizational behavior, due in part to the symbolic management activities of powerful actors (see Chapter 6).

The apparent decrease in social connectedness of corporate leadership is matched by the gradual increase in racial and gender diversity of top management and corporate boards over the past two decades. Both trends would appear to suggest a decline in cronyism and an increase in meritocracy within corporate leadership. Our surveys confirm that journalists and analysts generally perceive membership and success in corporate leadership to have become more merit-based over time, and they perceive prejudice and discrimination to have become much less common. Most journalists and analysts are unaware of the magnitude or the prevalence of the various forms of social discrimination described in Chapter 3. In a recent survey, we included a series of questions that listed the specific forms of discrimination identified in our research, and asked journalists and analysts whether they were surprised by each type (e.g., "Would you be surprised to learn that female and racial minority [first-time] directors have less access than white male [first-time] directors to mentoring from [incumbents on the board]?") More than 70 per cent of responding journalists and analysts were surprised or very surprised by each form of social discrimination that we described.

Conclusion

The effectiveness of the various cooperative and collectivistic forms of symbolic management described in this chapter can be attributed largely to their inconspicuous nature. IM is typically conceived as an individual or firm-level behavior, such that symbolic management support comes across as more sincere, apolitical, and credible than traditional forms of IM. The inconspicuous nature of symbolic management support not only increases the first-order persuasiveness of communication about the leadership, strategy, and governance of particular firms, but also enhances the second-order effect of repeatedly invoking normative assumptions of the neo-corporate logic of governance. Whereas institutional entrepreneurship is normally conceived as an overtly political process in which change agents highlight or even overstate the contrast between extant social prescriptions and the new goals and/or practices they seek to enact (Rao et al., 2003), firm leaders have instigated institutional change in corporate governance without overtly contesting the prevailing agency model. Accordingly, symbolic management support is a more subtle and insidious form of institutional entrepreneurship than previously examined in the institutional change literature. In fact, journalists appear to be largely unaware of its effects. Among journalists who responded to the 2010 survey described above, 86 per cent indicated that it was "unlikely" or "not at all likely" that journalists' responses to the survey questions in Table 4.1 have changed over the previous decade (Westphal and Park, 2012). It appears that journalists were unknowing carriers of the neo-corporate logic of governance.

PART II

THE SOCIAL AND PSYCHOLOGICAL DETERMINANTS OF SYMBOLIC MANAGEMENT

This section of the book examines the social and psychological determinants of various forms of symbolic management described in the prior section. In the first two chapters we discuss social mechanisms that have a relatively direct influence on symbolic decoupling. In Chapter 5 we begin by discussing the sources of CEOs' social influence over boards of directors. The board is a central control mechanism in the agency logic of governance, and thus CEO influence over the board must play a central role in the subversion of that logic. Boards approve incentive plans that have the potential to align executive and shareholder interests, and they are expected to monitor and control strategic decision making on behalf of shareholders. If boards appear capable of independent control, the perceived need for shareholder activism and other forms of external control is reduced. CEO influence over the board enables symbolic decoupling of executive incentive plans, and symbolic changes in board structure that give the appearance of independent board control, thus reducing the impetus for monitoring and control by institutional investors and other stakeholders.

We argue that CEOs exert influence over boards through a multi-stage process that begins with director selection, is strengthened by socialization of first-time directors into norms of director conduct that maintain CEO autonomy in strategic decision making, and is further reinforced by interpersonal influence behaviors in CEOs' social interactions with directors, and social control of directors who violate prevailing social norms. Moreover, we contend that there is a distinct separation of appearances and reality at each stage of the social influence process, and this decoupling is attributable in part to the rhetoric of corporate leaders. Top managers and directors put a positive spin on how director selection, mentoring, interpersonal interaction, and even social control promote board effectiveness, despite empirical evidence to the contrary. We also explain how CEO influence is amplified by ties among corporate leaders, and knowledge asymmetries between CEOs and outside directors. Moreover, we present descriptive evidence that the strategic experience of outside directors at large and medium-sized companies has declined in recent years, making it more difficult for boards to exercise control over strategy. The agency logic suggests that boards occupy a sweet spot in the governance system, close enough to firm operations to monitor management efficiently, but independent enough to exercise control objectively. The symbolic management perspective suggests that what appears to be a sweet spot is actually no man's land. Directors are too far removed from operations and strategic decision making, too inexperienced, and too psychologically and socially connected to management to render an expert, independent evaluation of management performance.

Chapter 6 describes how social network ties between firm leaders contribute directly to symbolic management. We explain how board interlock ties facilitated the diffusion of decoupled stock repurchase plans, and how informal friendship and advice ties between firm leaders facilitated the spread of coordinated impression management support and the decoupling of participative strategic decision making programs. We argue that scholars have underestimated the influence of social networks on symbolic management by focusing on board interlock ties to the exclusion of other kinds on social connections between firm leaders.

The next three chapters describe social and psychological processes at different levels of analysis that support and perpetuate symbolic action. In Chapter 7 we describe micro-level social influence processes in relations between firm leaders and external stakeholders. We explain how sophisticated forms of ingratiation, favor rendering, and negative reciprocity by firm leaders combine to exert a powerful and robust effect on the behavior of firm constituents. Moreover, we contend that the covert nature of these micro-level processes complements more public forms of symbolic action. In particular, these processes reduce the inclination of information intermediaries and powerful investors to validate policy implementation, or to verify the rhetoric of impression management, while maintaining the appearance of objective and independent evaluation and control by external stakeholders. In Chapter 8 we describe group-level social and psychological processes that support symbolic management, including social control and pluralistic ignorance. We explain how these processes reduce the effectiveness of groups at multiple levels of the governance system, ranging from small groups within the firm (i.e., top management teams and boards) to professional communities beyond the firm (i.e., communities of journalists and security analysts). In Chapter 9 we explore the individual-level, cognitive tendencies of corporate leaders that facilitate symbolic management. We describe different forms of self-regulated cognition by executives and directors that enhance the effectiveness of social influence processes such as ingratiation and impression management in leaders' communications with external constituents. Overall, this section reveals a web of subtle, inconspicuous, and mutually reinforcing social psychological processes, operating at different levels of analysis, that amplify the effectiveness of more public forms of symbolic action examined in prior research.

5

The Multi-Stage Social Influence Process in CEO–Board Relationships

As discussed in Chapter 2, the CEO's social influence over the board of directors is a primary determinant of symbolic action. CEO influence over the board has been implicated in the adoption and decoupling of CEO LTIPs and stock repurchase programs, and CEO influence over the board-nominating committee is a main determinant of symbolic increases in board independence from management. In this chapter we examine the multi-stage, multi-level process by which CEOs tend to exert influence over the board.

Director Selection

Demographic Similarity

This chapter details the multi-stage, self-reinforcing process by which CEOs tend to exert social influence over their boards of directors. The process begins with director selection, as CEOs normally have substantial input into the director-nomination process. Westphal and Zajac (1995) drew from the literature on similarity attraction and in-group bias in arguing that CEOs would tend to favor director candidates who were similar on salient demographic attributes, such as functional background. Their empirical analysis showed a strong association between the demographic characteristics of CEOs and the characteristics of new directors on their boards, and a weaker association between the characteristics of incumbent directors and those of new appointees. The results are especially strong for functional background: When CEOs have a finance (marketing) background, new directors are much more likely to have a finance (marketing) background, controlling for a host of firm-level, dyad-level, and individual-level characteristics. Moreover, these results have been replicated for more recent samples (Zhu and Westphal, 2014). Similarity attraction and in-group biases are preconscious, and consequently they are relatively robust to changes in economic conditions or firm reputation. There is little evidence that the association between CEO and new director characteristics is contingent on firm performance, the appraisals of security analysts, or the tenor of press coverage of firm leadership.

Symbolic Management: Governance, Strategy, and Institutions. James Westphal and Sun Hyun Park,
Oxford University Press (2020). © James Westphal and Sun Hyun Park.
DOI: 10.1093/oso/9780198792055.001.0001

Managers with similar functional backgrounds share the same biases: They favor similar approaches to strategic issue diagnosis, and they gravitate toward similar solutions to performance problems (Dearborn and Simon, 1958; Fligstein, 1990). There is longstanding evidence that greater similarity in salient demographic characteristics between superiors and subordinates is associated with more positive performance evaluations (Turban and Jones, 1988; Tsui and O'Reilly, 1989; Tsui et al., 2002). When superiors socially identify with subordinates, they tend to share their performance attribution biases: They blame poor firm performance on uncontrollable trends in the industry and macro-economic environment, and they credit the CEO's leadership and strategy for positive performance outcomes. Demographic similarity is also associated with interpersonal trust (Dovidio and Gaertner, 2010). Thus, outside directors are more likely to presume that similar CEOs can be trusted to prioritize shareholder interests and the interests of other stakeholders over their own personal agenda, reducing the perceived need for executive incentive alignment or vigilant monitoring of executive decision making. Multiple studies have shown that increases in demographic similarity are associated with lower subsequent levels of performance-contingent compensation for CEOs (Westphal and Zajac, 1995; Westphal, 1998; for a review, see O'Reilly and Main, 2010).

Friendship Ties

Although CEOs' friendship ties to outside directors may complement demographic similarity as another source of CEO influence over the board, there is mixed evidence that friendship ties directly reduce the vigilance of board-monitoring behavior (Westphal, 1999), perhaps because CEOs are personal friends with only a minority of outside directors at many large companies. However, there is evidence that CEO friendship ties to members of the board-nominating committee are especially common, and that this helps explain the typically high level of CEO influence over director selection at large firms (Westphal and Graebner, 2010). Such ties contribute to a separation of appearances and reality in director selection. The New York Stock Exchange and NASDAQ require that listed companies have board-nominating committees composed entirely of directors who are formally independent of management. Thus, decoupling between formal independence and the informal or social independence of directors is particularly acute on nominating committees.

This structural decoupling is also supported by a more micro-level, social psychological decoupling between the beliefs and behavior of corporate directors. Our interviews and surveys suggest that most corporate leaders ascribe to an implicit theory of professional friendship that contains seemingly opposing assumptions about friendship behavior. A core premise of social psychological perspectives on friendship is that friends feel socially obligated to care for each other's welfare (Krackhardt, 1992; Segal, 1979), and our research indicates that most corporate leaders share this assumption. At the same time, our interviews and surveys suggest that most firm leaders do not perceive a conflict between CEO–director friendship ties and board control. In a representative survey sample of 134 CEOs and 765 outside directors (Stern and Westphal, 2010), 95 per cent of respondents strongly agreed that "professional friends are obligated to support each other," while 86 per cent agreed or strongly agreed that "outside directors who are friends with the CEO are no less likely to oppose the CEO's proposals than outside directors who are not friends of the CEO." In fact, CEOs and directors often maintain that the CEO's friends on the board are *more* likely to disagree with them on strategic issues. In our interviews, one of the most common assertions about CEO–director relations is that, as one director put it, "it's the CEO's friends [on the board] who tell him what he really needs to hear." Another said, "if you don't want to have groupthink, make sure you have a friend on the board. Everyone [on the board] is accomplished, but it's still not always easy to disagree with the CEO. A friend feels more comfortable doing that." In response to such assertions, we asked interviewees whether a director-friend would feel comfortable firing the CEO. Although some did not have a clear answer to this question, many answered in the affirmative, sometimes citing a particular case in which the CEO's friend on the board purportedly volunteered to deliver the bad news to the CEO.

Yet, these beliefs about the behavior of CEO director-friends appear to be more myth than reality. There is large-sample evidence that the number of CEO friendship ties to outside directors is negatively associated with CEO dismissal in response to low firm performance (Park et al., 2011). Moreover, Westphal and Graebner (2010) found that friendship ties between the CEO and the nominating committee were negatively related to a reliable survey measure of board control that is based on the responses of both CEOs and outside directors. However, socially constructed myths about the implications of CEO–director friendship ties enable firm leaders to psychologically reconcile their normative beliefs about friendship with normative expectations about board behavior, reducing the likelihood of dissent among them about appointing the CEO's friends to important roles such as the board-nominating committee. Moreover, shared myths and stories about the behavior of CEO friends on the board also enable firm leaders to articulate a common narrative about director behavior, which makes them more persuasive in response to questions about board independence, as discussed in Chapter 4 in reference to cooperative IM.

Different myths about director selection prevail among external firm constituents. There is a widespread presumption among business journalists, security analysts, and other constituents that independence from management has become a more important criterion in selecting corporate directors. Yet, our surveys indicate that new outside directors are no less likely to be friends of the CEO in 2013 or 2015 than in 2003 or 2005. In fact, among firms with relatively low firm performance, or low consensus earnings forecasts by security analysts, new directors are significantly *more* likely to be friends of the CEO in the recent time periods than in the earlier time periods. Moreover, while the demographic diversity of boards has increased marginally on some dimensions, including race and gender, demographic similarity between CEOs and new directors remains high on work-related characteristics such as functional background (Zhu and Westphal, 2014).

Socialization

The second stage of the influence process involves the socialization of first-time corporate directors. In a survey of over 1,000 directors who acquired their first board seat at a U.S. public company between 1999 and 2006, McDonald and Westphal (2013) found that a majority of first-time directors were advised by incumbent board members about appropriate ways to contribute to board discussions about policy and strategy. Moreover, such "participation process mentoring" implicitly or explicitly conveys that outside directors should participate in board deliberations in ways that recognize that, except under unusual circumstances, top managers should exercise ultimate control over the formulation of firm strategy. For example, 74 per cent of first-time directors agreed that "another director [told them] that directors are expected to clear concerns about policy and strategy issues with the CEO informally in advance of formal meetings to make sure the CEO is OK with discussing the issue(s) in the meeting," and/or that they were advised by another director that "directors are expected to provide advice and information to the CEO on strategic issues rather than exercise control over policy and strategy" (McDonald and Westphal, 2013: 1178). In effect, participation process mentoring helps to socialize directors into the neo-corporate logic of governance.

Moreover, participation process mentoring is also supported by socially constructed beliefs about the relationship between mentoring and board effectiveness. Our interviews indicated that directors tend to frame such mentoring as an important prerequisite to director and board effectiveness. As one director who has served on multiple boards of large companies told us, "mentoring is a good thing, right? If a director doesn't understand the 'rules of the road' he can't contribute and won't add value." When asked if the mentoring socializes new directors into board norms of deferring to the CEO, he said: "I wouldn't put it that way. It's about learning. The director learns how he can contribute. The boards that have this kind of mentoring are the best boards." The consultants whom we interviewed tended to espouse a similar perspective. When asked about his opinion of participation process mentoring, the response of one consultant at a large management consulting firm was typical: "That's a best practice. Boards that get their new members up to speed on how to contribute are usually . . . better than ones that don't." Moreover, our interviews and surveys indicated that top managers and directors increasingly mention mentoring of new directors in communicating with external constituents about the board. In our surveys conducted in 2013, 61 per cent of journalists and 69 per cent of analysts who had recently communicated with top managers about a firm's governance reported that at least one top manager had mentioned the mentoring of new directors as evidence of their board's effectiveness in the prior twelve months.

Yet, our survey data and empirical analyses suggest a separation between rhetoric and reality with regard to director mentoring. Based on the survey responses of new directors and their fellow board members, new directors who received participation process mentoring are much less likely to engage in decision-control behaviors (McDonald and Westphal, 2013), and they are no more likely to provide strategic advice and input to the CEO. At the board level, participation process mentoring is negatively related to board control over strategy and unrelated to the provision of strategic advice and information. Thus, the overall effect of director mentoring on the board's contribution to strategic decision making is negative.

CEO Interpersonal Influence Behavior

The third stage of the influence process entails interpersonal influence behavior in relations between CEOs and outside directors. Westphal (1998) found that most CEOs in a representative sample of large U.S. corporations engaged in periodic social influence behavior toward outside directors, including ingratiatory behavior (e.g., flattery and "opinion conformity") and attempts to persuade directors about the merits of their strategies. Such behavior was related to more generous, subsequent compensation contracts for the CEO, as well as changes in firm strategy that appear to conform to the CEO's preferences. This stream of research also showed that changes in board structure that increased the board's power and independence from management, such as separation of the CEO and board chair positions, tended to prompt much higher levels of CEO ingratiation and persuasion attempts, and this social influence behavior tended to neutralize the effects of increased board power on CEO compensation and strategy (Westphal, 1998). Moreover, ingratiation and persuasion attempts were directed primarily at outside directors who had a different demographic profile from the CEO, and with whom the CEO lacked personal friendship ties. Ingratiatory behavior is a primary means of building social ties (Chapter 7). Flattery elicits positive affect and triggers norms of reciprocity, and opinion conformity also elicits similarity attraction

(Vonk, 2002; Cialdini and Goldstein, 2004). As discussed in Chapter 7, moreover, top managers tend to be relatively subtle and sophisticated in their flattery and opinion conformity in ways that increase the potency of ingratiatory behavior.

Ingratiation and persuasion are complementary strategies. Persuasion provides the ostensible rationale for informal interaction, while ingratiation during the interaction provides much of the interpersonal influence. CEOs approach outside directors informally with the stated purpose of explaining their point of view on a strategic issue, and then use the opportunity to engage in flattery and opinion conformity. While directors may or may not agree with the CEO's arguments, nearly everyone appreciates flattery. Ingratiation exerts influence on a preconscious and emotional level, and can bias directors' evaluation of the CEO's persuasive arguments.

In managing the impressions of security analysts about board control, CEOs and directors sometimes mention the need for CEOs to "explain" their positions on strategic issues to the board. As one director told us, "when I describe our [governance] to an analyst, I let them know that the board has an important role. The CEO has to explain his position and we have to all be convinced, or [a strategic proposal] is not going forward." Of course, no mention is made of the ingratiation that frequently goes along with persuasion.

Moreover, most directors believe that they are invulnerable to ingratiation. In fact, most believe that they are less influenced by ingratiation than their peers. In the representative survey sample of outside directors mentioned above (Stern and Westphal, 2010), 86 per cent agreed or strongly agreed that "flattery does not work on me," and 81 per cent agreed or strongly agreed that "I am less influenced by flattery than most firm leaders." Most directors believe that they are influenced *only* by rational persuasion. As one director whom we interviewed put it, "if you want me to support your strategy, then make a persuasive case. I don't mind flattery, I get it a lot, but it's not going to affect my evaluation of your strategy." In Anglo-Saxon cultures, rational persuasion is the *only* socially legitimate influence strategy among professionals. Thus, persuasion attempts effectively "cover" for ingratiatory behavior in professional interaction. This suggests a separation between appearances and reality at the micro-, dyad-level. CEO social influence attempts toward outside directors appear to rely solely on rational persuasion, but actually rely on an interaction between ingratiation and persuasion. This decoupling is supported by a self-serving bias of the "Lake Wobegon" variety, as most directors believe they are above average in their immunity to ingratiation.

Social Distancing

The fourth stage of the social influence process is the social control of "deviant," counter-normative behavior by outside directors. Drawing from the sociological and anthropological literatures on social control, Westphal and Khanna (2003) described social distancing as a set of behaviors, or the withdrawal of behaviors, toward deviant group members that together represent a relatively subtle form of social ostracism. Specific components of social distancing are neglecting to ask the opinion or advice of deviant individuals in the course of group decision making, not inviting them to informal meetings, ignoring their comments in formal meetings, and more subtle behaviors such as exclusionary gossip, in which group members gossip about third parties with whom the deviant individual is unfamiliar (Bogardus, 1959; Barkow, 1974). Using a reliable survey measure of social distancing adapted from prior research (Hollinger and Clark, 1982), Westphal and Khanna (2003) found that outside directors who violated the norms of director conduct described above (e.g., raising a concern about the CEO's strategy in a board meeting without clearing the issue with the CEO beforehand) were more likely to experience social distancing from other board members. Moreover, they also hypothesized and found that directors who participated in policy actions *on other boards* that threatened managerial control, such as separating the CEO and board chair positions (i.e., so that the CEO is no longer board chair), or repealing takeover defenses, were more likely to experience social distancing *on the focal board*.

Social distancing helps maintain social norms in two fundamental ways. It has the "sanitary function" of reducing social interaction with deviants (Gluckman, 1963: 48; Zippelius, 1986), thus minimizing the social influence of minority opinions or behavior. And it functions as negative reinforcement. The interdisciplinary literature on social control indicates that social distancing in which individuals who violate group norms experience the withdrawal of social support or affirmation from fellow group members is often more effective in deterring future deviance than sanctions which involve the loss of more tangible or material resources (Hollinger and Clark, 1982; Zippelius, 1986; Tittle, 1980, 1995). Theory and research in social psychology suggest that people are fundamentally and preconsciously motivated to avoid social exclusion from groups that are important to their self-identifies (James, 1890; Baumeister and Leary, 1995; Williams, 2009). In fact, there is strong evidence that self-esteem can be conceived as a regulatory system that continually monitors one's inclusionary status in social groups by attending to interpersonal cues that connote exclusion (Leary et al., 1995). Evolutionary psychologists have suggested that "humans have an evolved system for automatically detecting cues of [social] exclusion" (Wesselman et al., 2009: 1308). Recent studies even indicate that people experience social distancing as a kind of physical pain (DeWall and Richman, 2011). The pain induced by social distancing is a source of negative reinforcement that strongly motivates social conformity. Westphal and Khanna (2003) found that directors who experienced social distancing at particular boards were much less likely to participate subsequently in policy actions that threatened managerial control, such as separating the CEO and board chair positions or repealing takeover defenses on other boards.

Westphal and Khanna also measured the average level of social distancing at other boards where a focal director had an appointment. Participation in social distancing or exposure to distancing of deviant board members may further socialize directors into prevailing norms of director conduct. In addition, Westphal and Khanna measured *indirect* exposure to social distancing as the average level of distancing at other boards in the sample to which the focal director is connected by an indirect board tie. An indirect tie exists between focal director A and another board B if director A sits on a third board that includes one or more outside directors from B. Directors may be more likely to hear about cases of social distancing when they serve together on boards with directors who have participated in distancing at other firms. Gossip is a powerful social control mechanism (Gluckman, 1963; Coleman, 1994; Dunbar, 1998). Gossip about social distancing deters deviant behavior in two ways: by informing group members about the potential for exclusion in response to counter-normative behavior, and by making it salient to individuals that they will be the target of negative gossip if they violate group norms, which is itself an aversive prospect. The effect of social distancing is amplified by the "fear of gossip," or the fear that other group members are talking about one's loss in social status (Gluckman, 1963: 308). The results confirmed that both direct and indirect exposure to social distancing significantly reduced directors' subsequent participation in policy actions that threaten managerial control.

Consequently, while policies that protect or enhance managerial control tend to diffuse widely among large U.S. firms (Westphal and Zajac, 1994; Davis and Greve, 1997), social distancing has helped stem the diffusion of multiple policy changes that would align governance more closely with the agency logic. Participation in board reforms such as separation of the CEO and board chair positions triggered social controls that not only stemmed the diffusion of those particular reforms, but also the spread of other policy changes consistent with the agency logic, such as the repeal of takeover defenses.

Again, directors' socially constructed beliefs about board effectiveness serve to rationalize this form of social influence behavior. The directors whom we interviewed did not deny the existence of social distancing, but tended to justify such behavior as mitigating disruptive or obstructive behavior that would reduce the board's contribution to firm strategy and policy. As one director put it, "if a director doesn't follow standard procedure [for contributing to discussions about strategy] he'll get ignored. Why? Because it's disruptive. We all need to be on the same page about process or we get less done, we'll get less input to the CEO, and we'll be less valuable ultimately to the company." Another director expressed a common sentiment: "if you're suggesting we punish non-conformity, that's only non-conformity to the process [of board involvement in strategy and policy].

We *want* non-conformity on ideas." Moreover, much as directors perceive that they are unaffected by ingratiation, they also tended to dispute the proposition that social distancing would effectively deter individuals from disagreeing with the CEO or other board members, or otherwise challenging the status quo. Such notions challenged the prevailing, socially constructed identity of corporate directors as tough, hard-nosed leaders who have little need for social acceptance. As one director put it, "Most of us got to where we are by being very tough. We're battle tested. I know you're a psychologist [smiling] but you have to understand, most of us aren't afraid of getting our feelings hurt. We're not afraid to go against the group."

Yet, our empirical analyses strongly disconfirm these claims. Social distancing is negatively associated with (1) director-challenging behavior, or the propensity to disagree with the CEO or other directors in formal meetings, (2) the level of strategic advice and input provided by outside directors to the CEO and other top managers, and (3) measures of strategic change in response to low firm performance (Westphal and Khanna, 2003). As with mentoring of new directors, there is decoupling between rhetoric and reality with regard to the consequences of social distancing.

Recommendations for Board Appointments

A final phase of the social influence process by which CEOs tend to exert influence over their boards is director recommendations for board appointments. In an important extension of agency theory, Fama (1980) proposed that directors have an incentive to engage in decision control in order to develop a favorable reputation on the director labor market, with the corollary that directors who exercise control over management are more likely to be selected onto other boards. Zajac and Westphal (1996) proposed instead that the director labor market was effectively segmented: While directors who served on boards that exerted power over the CEO were more likely to be appointed to other, similarly powerful boards, directors who served on boards in which the CEO exerted power over the board were more likely to be appointed onto other boards with similarly powerful CEOs. A number of subsequent studies have provided empirical evidence in support of this proposition (Eminet and Guedri, 2010; Bouwman, 2011; Benton, 2016; Levit and Malenko, 2016; Li et al., 2018).

However, while studies have confirmed a segmented director labor market, they also indicate that, on balance, the reputational costs to directors of exercising decision control typically outweigh the reputational benefits. Westphal and Stern (2007) found that, all else equal, directors were less likely to gain additional board appointments to the extent that they engaged in monitoring and control behavior on the focal board, including such behaviors as (1) requesting information from the CEO or another inside director for the purpose of evaluating management's progress in implementing the firm's corporate strategy, and (2) constructively criticizing or suggesting revisions to a strategic proposal put forth by management. Further analysis indicated that directors who engaged in such behaviors were less likely to secure a colleague's recommendation for a board appointment at another firm (see also McDonald and Westphal, 2013). At the same time, directors were more likely to obtain their colleagues' recommendations for board appointments to the extent that they provided strategic input, advice, and information at the CEO's request (Westphal and Stern, 2007). Overall, the results indicated that directors derive the maximal reputational benefit by participating in strategic decision making in ways that conform to the neo-corporate logic of governance, as opposed to the agency logic.

There are several reasons why the neo-corporate logic predominates over the agency logic in determining director recommendations. First, independent board control over strategic decision making is the exception rather than the rule at large and mid-sized U.S. companies (e.g., firms above $100 million in annual revenue). Our representative, large-sample surveys have consistently shown that less than 20 per cent of boards in this population have multiple outside directors engaged in decision-control behaviors as described above; the percentage has ranged from 13 per cent to 19 per cent in annual surveys from 2002 to 2015, with no detectable long-term trend. Thus, the segment of the director labor market characterized by low board control over strategy is much larger than the high-control segment.

Second, CEOs and officers (i.e., inside directors) are also frequently asked for director recommendations, and they are much more likely to recommend directors whose behavior conforms to the neo-corporate logic, regardless of whether their boards engage in high or low levels of decision control. Third, on average, outside directors on high-control boards have far fewer social connections to directors on other boards in either segment (i.e., low-control *or* high-control boards), and consequently these directors provide far fewer recommendations for board appointments than outside directors on low-control boards (or inside directors on either kind of board). Benton (2016) has shown that directors affiliated with "managerialist firms," which tend to have relatively low board control, select into relatively dense subgroups of the board interlock network, and our data similarly suggest that these directors tend to be relatively central within networks of informal social ties. For example, outside directors on low-control boards report an average of approximately 6.3 friendship ties to directors on other boards, while outside directors on high-control boards report approximately 3.4 such ties on average. In effect, the existing social structure of the corporate elite enhances the reputational benefits of serving on low-control boards, and mitigates the benefits of serving on high-control boards, thus perpetuating the predominance of the low-control segment.

In addition, Westphal and Stern found that the strongest single determinant of gaining recommendations for board appointments is ingratiation. Just as CEOs can increase board support by engaging in ingratiatory behavior toward independent directors (Westphal, 1998), top managers significantly increase the likelihood of getting their CEO's recommendation for a board appointment by engaging in flattery and opinion conformity toward him or her (Westphal and Stern, 2006). For example, an increase in ingratiation from the mean level that involves (1) challenging the CEO's opinion on a strategic issue one less time during the past twelve months, (2) complimenting the CEO on his or her insight on a strategic issue two more times, and (3) doing one more personal favor for the CEO during that time increased the likelihood of receiving a board appointment where the CEO serves as a director by 64 per cent (Westphal and Stern, 2006: 186). Outside directors also greatly increase their chances of getting a fellow board member's recommendation by engaging in ingratiatory behavior. Ingratiation can be viewed as an act of submission or deference. It has the second-order effect of affirming the power of the influence target (i.e., the target of ingratiation), which is a deeper kind of flattery (Jones, 1964; Vonk, 1998). People are attracted to those who affirm their power (Sadler and Woody, 2003). Thus, an implication of Westphal and Stern's findings is that norms of director deference to CEOs in strategic decision making may persist in part because managers and directors who tend to be deferential or submissive toward CEOs are more likely to be recommended for board seats. In managing the impressions of information intermediaries about corporate governance, corporate leaders sometimes assert that the "best" directors, meaning directors who contribute the most to strategic decision making, garner the most board appointments. In effect, the rhetoric of corporate leaders tends to echo Fama's (1980) theory of director labor markets. Instead, the empirical evidence suggests that individuals are most likely to succeed on the director labor market by ingratiating the CEO and their peers, while avoiding involvement in board decision control.

The high-control segment of corporate boards, though small in comparison to the low-control segment, has symbolic value to corporate leaders because it furnishes anecdotal evidence to support claims that boards exercise control over top management. When directors are asked rhetorically whether boards are really likely to exercise control over strategy on a regular basis, they tend to cite the same, few examples of board control from the high-control segment. One frequently cited example was a board in our survey sample that was unrepresentative of boards at large or mid-sized U.S. firms on many dimensions: The CEO had no personal friends on the board; none of the outside directors had the same functional background as the CEO; and the firm had the worst performance of any firm in its industry by a considerable margin. The common account of board control at this firm was broadly accurate, if somewhat exaggerated, but it was highly unrepresentative of board behavior at firms in the larger population.

Nevertheless, in supporting a socially legitimate narrative about board behavior with the same, specific examples, directors are more persuasive in defending corporate boards from the criticism of external stakeholders.

The Lack of Strategic Decision-Making Experience among Outside Directors

An additional factor that has increasingly reinforced CEO influence over the board is the general lack of relevant strategic decision-making experience among outside directors at many large and mid-sized U.S. companies. There is growing empirical evidence that outside directors' strategic experience is an important determinant of their ability to monitor and control management decision making, and otherwise contribute to firm policy and strategy (Carpenter and Westphal, 2001; Kroll et al., 2008; McDonald et al., 2008; Barroso-Castro et al., 2017; Johnson et al., 2013). For example, Carpenter and Westphal (2001) found that directors were better able to contribute to board discussions on strategic issues, and engaged in higher levels of monitoring and advising activity, to the extent that they had recent board experience at companies with similar corporate strategies to the focal firm (e.g., similar levels of product-market diversification and internationalization). Moreover, in relatively unstable industry environments, the level of board monitoring and advising activity hinged on the extent to which directors had a diversity of strategic experience. Yet, there is little empirical evidence that prior experience with relevant corporate strategies is a significant factor in garnering recommendations for board appointments (Westphal and Stern, 2006, 2007). The determinants of director recommendations are fairly generic: Managers and directors who engage in ingratiatory behavior and conform to board norms are more likely to receive recommendations for board appointments at other companies, often with little regard to whether their management and board experience is a good fit with the particular strategic needs of those companies.

The conventional wisdom among most corporate stakeholders is that outside directors at U.S. companies tend to be better qualified for board service today than they were in previous decades. However, the data suggest otherwise. On average, outside directors at large and medium-sized U.S. companies had significantly less top management experience in 2015 than in the year 2000, and they had less management or prior board experience at firms with similar corporate strategies. For example, the number of outside directors who have at least one year of prior management or board experience at a firm operating in one or more of the same product markets as the focal firm declined by 83 per cent on average over this time period. There was a comparable decline in outside directors' prior experience in similar international markets (77 per cent). Consequently, there is now a grave shortage of relevant strategic decision-making experience among outside directors at large and mid-sized U.S. companies. In 2015, the average board of an S&P 1500 firm had fewer than two outside directors with any prior top management or board experience at another firm operating in one or more of the same product *or* geographic markets as the focal firm. This decline in outside directors' strategic experience appears to have resulted largely from the increased emphasis on formal director independence since the early 2000s. On average, outside directors who lack formal affiliations with a focal firm tend to possess significantly less top management or board experience at other companies.

Consequently, there is now a wide disparity between conventional wisdom and reality in regards to the general capability of boards to effectively monitor management decision making. In our large-sample surveys of directors conducted in 2001 and 2015, we included open-ended questions that asked directors to list the most important qualifications for board service. In 2001, prior management and/or strategic decision-making experience was the third most frequently listed qualification for board service, with a large majority (77 per cent) of respondents including prior experience in their list of important qualifications. In 2015, prior management and/or strategic decision-making experience was only the ninth most frequently listed qualification, mentioned by a minority of respondents (23 per cent). An even smaller portion of respondents mentioned strategic decision-making experience as an important qualification (11 per cent). We posed the same question to journalists and security analysts in 2014, and an even smaller portion of respondents mentioned prior management and/or strategic decision-making experience as an important qualification for board service (18 per cent of responding analysts and 14 per cent of responding journalists). In 2015, a large portion of responding directors mentioned *only* director independence from management as an important qualification, supporting our suggestion that the singular focus on (formal) independence as a determining factor in board effectiveness has eclipsed strategic experience or virtually any other factor as a salient qualification for board service.

The general lack of strategic experience among outside directors significantly reduces the board's credibility in monitoring and evaluating the strategic decision making of top management, further compromising the board's ability to exert influence over strategy on behalf of shareholders and other stakeholders. According to the agency logic, the board is a central player in firm governance because it compensates for knowledge asymmetries between management and shareholders. However, the severe lack of strategic experience within the population of outside directors has created significant knowledge asymmetries between most boards and their top managers, contributing to a void in the larger system of control. Moreover, the prevailing assumption that outside directors are much more qualified for board service than in prior years has made it difficult to gain traction in redressing the problem. Such assumptions are another example of how American optimism that socio-economic progress occurs naturally without state intervention (Jost et al., 2009; Blasi and Jost, 2012) can interfere with the identification and resolution of widespread organizational problems.

Conclusion

Overall, CEOs acquire social influence over the board of directors through a multi-stage process in which appearances are decoupled from actual behavior at each stage. The first stage is director selection, as CEOs favor the appointment of demographically similar individuals to the board, and the appointment of personal friends to the board-nominating committee, which perpetuates their influence over new appointments. The director selection process is insulated from pressures for reform by the widespread presumption among information intermediaries and other firm stakeholders that independence from management has become a more important criterion in selecting directors and making appointments to board committees, despite empirical evidence that demographic similarity between CEOs and new directors remains high, and that CEOs often have multiple friendship ties to members of the board-nominating committee.

The second stage of the influence process is socialization, as first-time directors receive mentoring from incumbent directors about how to participate in board decision making that reinforces norms of CEO control over firm strategy and policy. Moreover, there is decoupling between rhetoric and reality in regards to director mentoring, as top managers and directors have increasingly cited mentoring of new directors as a "best practice" that promotes board effectiveness, while empirical analyses indicate that such mentoring is negatively associated with board control over strategy.

The third stage involves interpersonal influence, as CEOs engage in ingratiation and persuasion toward demographically dissimilar directors, and directors with whom they lack personal friendship ties. While the rhetoric of corporate officers and directors about board involvement in strategy highlights the need for CEOs to explain their positions on strategic issues to the board, effectively framing CEO persuasion as indicative of board influence over strategy, the reality is that CEO persuasion interacts with ingratiatory behavior toward directors to further the CEO's preferences on a range of policy issues, including compensation and corporate strategy.

The fourth stage of the social influence process entails social control, as directors engage in social distancing toward members who violate prevailing norms of director conduct (e.g., by raising a concern about the CEO's strategy in board meetings without clearing the issue with the CEO beforehand). While the rhetoric of corporate directors suggests that social distancing promotes board effectiveness by reducing disruption in the policy-making process, the reality is that distancing deters directors from disagreeing with the CEO and reduces their influence over strategy and policy decisions.

Finally, CEO influence over the board is further reinforced by recommendations for board appointments. Although the rhetoric of corporate leaders suggests that the "best" directors receive the most invitations to serve on corporate boards, and corporate stakeholders tend to presume that independence from management has become an important criterion in director selection, the empirical evidence indicates instead that individuals are most likely to succeed on the director labor market by engaging in ingratiatory behavior toward CEOs and peers, while avoiding involvement in decision control. It appears that norms of director deference to CEOs in strategic decision making persist in part because relatively deferential or submissive individuals are more likely to be recommended for board seats.

Moreover, in recent years, the board's ability to exercise influence over strategy has been further compromised by a general and quite serious decline in strategic experience among outside directors at large and mid-sized U.S. companies. Due in part to the singular focus of board reform efforts on director independence from management, this trend has gone largely unnoticed by corporate stakeholders, and it stands in direct opposition to the conventional wisdom that outside directors have become *more* qualified for board service in recent years. Such misguided optimism is again reinforced by the rhetoric of corporate leaders, which emphasizes the formal independence of directors and implicitly downplays the importance of strategic experience.

The pervasive decoupling between directors' rhetoric about CEO–board relationships and the reality indicated by years of large-sample survey and archival data is reinforced by the socially constructed beliefs of directors themselves, and by self-serving biases that protect directors' personal and social identities. For example, most directors believe that they are immune to ingratiation and social distancing, and that their evaluations are unbiased by friendship ties, despite abundant evidence to the contrary. Moreover, most directors are loathe to admit that they or their colleagues lack the requisite strategic experience to effectively monitor and evaluate the strategic decision making of top managers.

Thus, CEO influence over the board is a multi-layered phenomenon, as well as a multi-stage process. It results not only from dyadic interaction in CEO–director relationships, but group-level influences (e.g., social distancing), social network effects (recommendations), the socially constructed beliefs of firm constituents, and individual-level biases of top managers and directors themselves. When these social and psychological factors are considered in their entirety, it becomes easy to see why substantive increases in board influence over strategy and policy have failed to occur over the past thirty years, and are unlikely to occur in the foreseeable future, at least without regulatory intervention.

6

Social Network Ties and Symbolic Management

In this chapter we examine social network ties among firm leaders as a second key determinant of symbolic management. The vast majority of studies on social network ties in firm leadership and strategy have examined board interlock ties between firms, where the CEO or other top manager of one firm serves on the board of another firm (referred to as "directional" interlock ties), or the same individual serves as outside director at multiple firms ("non-directional" interlocks). Although relatively few studies have examined the social network determinants of symbolic management, the limited research in this area has also focused almost entirely on board interlock ties. In addition, social network researchers have largely ignored firm leaders' indirect ties through third-party service providers, such as management consultants, lobbyists, or attorneys, as well as common ties to information intermediaries (e.g., analysts or journalists), shareholders, or other stakeholders.

We contend that the singular focus on board interlocks, and the limited attention to indirect ties through service organizations and other third parties in social network research on firm leadership, governance, and strategy has led scholars to greatly underestimate the relational and structural embeddedness of corporate leadership, and by extension to underestimate the influence of social networks on symbolic management. Moreover, the underestimation of social embeddedness has become more severe in recent years as board interlock ties between large and mid-sized U.S. companies have become ever more scarce (Mizruchi, 2013; Chu and Davis, 2016).

We begin by reviewing extant theory regarding the potential influence of board interlock ties on symbolic management, and then proceed to explain how other kinds of ties between corporate leaders facilitate the various forms of symbolic management described in previous sections. In particular, we detail how symbolic management is promoted by (1) director ties to informal groups of firm leaders, (2) social exchange ties between leaders, (3) personal friendship ties between leaders, and (4) mutual ties to management consultants. In considering the influence of these different kinds of social connections, we introduce theoretical mechanisms that have received little attention in the symbolic management literature. While extant theory has focused on how network ties promote awareness and social learning about symbolic management, we describe how different

Symbolic Management: Governance, Strategy, and Institutions. James Westphal and Sun Hyun Park,
Oxford University Press (2020). © James Westphal and Sun Hyun Park.
DOI: 10.1093/oso/9780198792055.001.0001

forms of reciprocity and personal and social identification influence IM and symbolic decoupling.

Moreover, in suggesting how social network ties facilitate decoupling, we also further reveal a separation between appearances and reality in regards to the social structure of corporate leadership. The ties that we examine are less visible to firm stakeholders than board interlocks, and yet they are more prevalent, especially when considered together (e.g., CEOs are connected to a large portion of CEOs at other, similarly sized firms by *at least one* kind of tie). As a result, many corporate stakeholders tend to underestimate the prevalence of social connections among firm leaders, and the resulting frequency of leader communication and cooperation, much as scholars have underestimated the level of social embeddedness in the corporate elite.

Board Interlock Ties and the Diffusion of Symbolic Decoupling

Early perspectives on the network diffusion of symbolic decoupling characterized board interlock ties as a means of vicarious learning. Interlock ties to firms that have adopted and decoupled a particular policy such as stock repurchase plans are thought to raise awareness about the symbolic and political benefits of ceremonial adoption, while also educating managers and directors about how to mitigate or avoid the risks and potential drawbacks of decoupling (Westphal and Zajac, 2001). Extant theory further suggests that decoupling can diffuse across firms either through direct interlock ties or certain kinds of indirect, or "two-step" ties. Mizruchi's (1996) classic study showed that board ties to the same financial institutions was a particularly strong predictor of similarity in political behavior between firms. Boards of financial institutions were thought to provide a clearing house for information on successful business practices, so that firms with mutual ties to the same financial institution were more likely to have exchanged information about their recent policy decisions, facilitating diffusion of successful practices (Useem, 1984; Palmer et al., 1986; Mizruchi, 1996). Moreover, social network theory would suggest that firms are prone to imitating the innovative policies of other organizations in similar structural positions (Burt, 1987), and common ties to financial institutions may be especially likely to promote imitation, as firms compete for capital from the same institutions.

Consistent with these theoretical arguments, Westphal and Zajac (2001) found that both direct interlock ties and two-step ties through financial institutions to firms that decoupled stock repurchase programs increased the rate of decoupling at the focal firm. They also found that interlock ties interacted with measures of CEO power, such that decoupling at tied-to firms was especially likely to increase decoupling at the focal firm to the extent that CEOs were in a position to exert power over the board of directors.

Westphal and Zajac (2001) also theorized that board interlock ties can facilitate vicarious learning about the potential for decoupling of corporate policies *in general*, such that interlock ties to firms that decoupled one kind of policy may increase the likelihood of decoupling a different policy at the focal firm. Consistent with this proposition, direct interlock ties to firms that had decoupled CEO LTIPs increased the likelihood of decoupling stock repurchase plans at the focal firm (the effect of two-step ties was not statistically significant).

The potency of board interlock ties as a determinant of symbolic decoupling has likely diminished somewhat in recent years. The density of the board interlock network has decreased substantially over the past fifteen years, with sharp declines in the number of direct interlock ties and indirect ties through financial institutions (Mizruchi, 2013; Chu and Davis, 2016). Moreover, there have been particularly large declines in "directional" interlock ties between firms, where the CEO or other top manager of one firm serves as outside director at another firm. Such ties may be especially potent vehicles of vicarious learning. The firm-specific and generalized strategic knowledge of top managers renders them better able to utilize the information gained from board service, and also makes them more persuasive advocates for policies that they have adopted or observed at other firms. As discussed in Chapter 5, moreover, the average levels of strategic experience among outside directors at large to mid-sized U.S. firms have declined over the past fifteen years, reducing boards' absorptive capacity, or their capacity to learn vicariously from the experience of tied-to firms with decoupled policies.

Nevertheless, board interlock ties likely remain significant channels for the diffusion of at least some kinds of symbolic action. Although the density of the board interlock network has declined, interlocks are hardly rare (e.g., see Benton, 2016), and the absorptive capacity required to learn vicariously about decoupled LTIPs or repurchase programs would seem to be minor in comparison to some other forms of symbolic action, such as decoupled PSDM programs or coordinated IM support. Moreover, recent empirical evidence suggests that firms' position in the network of interlocking directorates can still influence their propensity to engage in symbolic corporate governance practices (e.g., Markóczy et al., 2013).

Director Ties and the Diffusion of Coordinated Impression-Management Support

The board interlock ties examined in prior research may be insufficient to promote the spread of some forms of symbolic management described in Part I, including coordinated IM support. While decoupled governance policies such as LTIPs or repurchase plans are relatively generic and vary little across industries, the rhetorical content and targets of coordinated IM support must be adapted or customized to particular industry contexts. Vicarious learning through board interlock ties may often be inadequate to ensure the successful adaptation of coordinated IM support to new industries. The larger literature on collective action similarly suggests that social network ties between participants in one geographic location and potential organizers in another location are often insufficient to facilitate the diffusion of particular models of collective influence (Andrews and Biggs, 2006; McAdam et al., 2001; Tarrow, 2010). While social ties to members of existing groups can increase awareness of the general potential for collective influence, they are often inadequate to resolve subjective uncertainty among potential organizers and participants about whether or how a form of collective action that arose in another region, culture, and/or environment could be adapted successfully to the focal location (Klandermans, 1984, 2002; Brewer and Silver, 2000; Chabot, 2010).

Our research suggests how and why director ties to informal groups of firm leaders who engaged in coordinated IM support in another industry can facilitate IM support in the focal industry (Westphal et al., 2019). In Chapter 4 we described coordinated IM support by MSGs, which are informal groups of female or racial minority CEOs from the same industry, broadly defined (e.g., including competitors and their buyer and supplier firms). We described how IM support in these groups involves working together to develop a persuasive message about the quality of leadership and strategy at an individual member's firm, and then reaching out separately to relatively influential journalists to convey the message. In this chapter we develop theory suggesting how generalized reciprocity motivates directors who received help in organizing an MSG in another industry to proffer similar help to minority leaders in the focal industry, and we explain why the prospect of receiving such assistance resolves around subjective expected uncertainty among minority CEOs about the value of participating in coordinated IM.

In particular, we argue that a primary impetus for the network diffusion of coordinated IM support in MSGs is chain-generalized reciprocity, in which CEO-directors (i.e., directors at a particular firm who serve as CEO in another industry) who previously received help in organizing an MSG feel impelled to pay it forward by helping other corporate leaders in the same way that they were helped (Ekeh, 1974; Douglas, 1990; Mauss, 1990; Molm et al., 2007; Horne et al., 2013: 515). Chain-generalized reciprocity is one manifestation of the general norm of reciprocity, a nearly universal code of social behavior (Ekeh, 1974; Gintis, 2000). A multi-disciplinary literature on inequity aversion indicates that people are hardwired to feel psychological distress when they fail to reciprocate help (Cosmides and Tooby, 1992; Diekmann, 2004; Fehr and Schmidt, 2006; Dunn et al., 2012), and they tend to feel particularly distressed about failing to take the opportunity to assist others in the same way that they were helped (Gurven, 2004). Conversely, people are "genetically pre-programmed" to feel a deep sense of satisfaction from generalized reciprocity, despite substantial costs to the self (Cosmides and Tooby, 1992: 222; Hill, 2002; Gintis et al., 2008). As noted in our discussion of coordinated IM, leaders who help organize an MSG and assist with coordinated IM typically invest a considerable amount of their personal time in doing so, as they give advice to group members across multiple meetings. Thus, minority leaders who have received such guidance are likely to feel impelled to reciprocate, when given the opportunity.

The motivation to reciprocate is further strengthened by in-group identification. Minority race and gender are known to provide salient bases for social identification (Kinzler et al., 2010; Kosloff et al., 2010), particularly in contexts such as business leadership where white males form a very large majority (Brewer, 1979; Turner et al., 1987; Westphal and Milton, 2000). In-group identification is believed to bolster inequity aversion and strengthen chain-generalized reciprocity (Yamagishi and Kiyonari, 2000; Lawler et al., 2008). Minority status is especially salient to MSG members as a basis for in-group identification, because the explicit objective of these groups is to neutralize specific social inequities faced by minority leaders. Thus, minority leaders who have received help in organizing coordinated IM are likely to feel an especially strong motivation to pay it forward by helping fellow minorities in the same way that they were helped.

The prospect of receiving guidance on how to organize an MSG from a minority leader who has participated in such a group and who serves as a director in the focal industry should substantially reduce subjective uncertainty among potential members about the likely success of coordinated IM support in the focal industry. As current or former members of an MSG, these leaders can give specific and credible advice on how to recruit members, who to target for IM support, and how to approach them. They can also provide specific input regarding the content of IM, including first-hand accounts of which communication strategies were most effective in influencing journalists' reports. Calls to action are more persuasive in mobilizing participation in collective influence efforts when they are specific about the tactics required and include first-hand testimonials about how those tactics succeeded in improving outcomes for members (Alinsky, 1971; Kelly, 1993; Klandermans, 2002; Brewer and Silver, 2000).

As noted above, leaders who help organize an MSG typically provide advice to group members across multiple meetings, and the prospect of receiving ongoing help rather than one-shot advice should further reduce uncertainty about participating in coordinated IM support. Research on consulting services suggests that consultants are more likely to secure a client and the client is much more likely to adopt their recommendations if the consultant remains available to guide implementation (McKenna, 2006; Walker, 2014). In guaranteeing the client that they will remain accessible after the outcomes of their recommendations are known, a consultant creates the perception of accountability for their advice, increasing their credibility with the client and bolstering the client's confidence in their recommendations. Likewise, a minority leader who offers ongoing guidance on IM support signals their commitment and confidence, which should enhance the confidence of potential MSG members that the group can succeed.

In addition, a minority leader who has experience in an MSG and who is also a director in the focal industry is familiar with the particular strategic threats and opportunities in the industry environment, and the positions of firms in the industry, which renders them uniquely qualified to reduce uncertainty about the likely success of the group. Industry knowledge enables the director to articulate how the content of IM can be adapted to the focal industry environment. Persuasive IM support often requires explaining in a credible way how the relatively low performance of a member's firm can be attributed to challenging conditions in the industry environment, rather than to the firm's leadership or strategy, or vice versa in the case of high firm performance. As discussed above, subjective uncertainty about how a model of influence that worked in another location can be adapted or customized to the local environment is a primary barrier to the spread of collective action (Klandermans, 1984, 2002; Brewer and Silver, 2000; Chabot, 2010).

In summary, our theory suggests that (1) minority leaders who received guidance on how to organize an MSG will be impelled by generalized reciprocity to offer similar guidance to a fellow minority when given the opportunity, and (2) the prospect of receiving such help from a director in the focal industry who has participated in an MSG increases the likelihood of group formation in the focal industry by reducing subjective expected uncertainty about the benefits of participation. We specifically hypothesize that minority CEOs who have participated in an MSG and who serve as director on a board *with a minority CEO* have the potential to spur MSG formation in the focal industry. CEOs are prone to seeking advice and counsel from outside directors with whom they socially identify (Westphal, 1999; Zhu and Westphal, 2014). Because gender and racial minority status provide a highly salient basis for in-group identification in corporate leadership (Westphal and Milton, 2000), minority CEOs are especially prone to seeking advice and counsel from minority directors on their boards. Our data indicate that 86 per cent of female CEOs in our survey samples sought and received advice and counsel from a female outside director on their board (i.e., an individual director specified by name in the survey) outside formal meetings at least once in the prior six-month period. Eighty-two per cent sought advice and counsel from fellow women directors more than once during that period. The corresponding figures for racial minority CEOs are 81 per cent and 78 per cent, respectively. Thus, minority directors on a board with a minority CEO typically have multiple opportunities to proffer guidance on how to organize and operate an MSG, and our theory explains why this should facilitate the diffusion of these groups.

We tested the hypothesized effect of CEO-director ties on MSG formation using discrete-time event history analysis (see Westphal et al., 2019).[1] The results

---

[1] We used the complementary log-log function and estimated robust standard errors using the Huber/White sandwich estimator. The longitudinal samples included industries at risk of MSG

showed that the presence of a director tie to an MSG in another industry that received guidance in organizing the group had a strong, positive effect on the likelihood of MSG formation in the focal industry, where a director tie specifically indicates the presence of an outside director who received such guidance and who serves on a board with a minority CEO. The effects were strong in magnitude: The presence of a director tie to a racial minority (female) MSG in another industry that received guidance in organizing the group increased the hazard rate of forming a racial minority (female) MSG in the focal industry by 596 per cent and 528 per cent, respectively. Moreover, director ties to MSGs in another industry that did *not* receive guidance in organizing the group were unrelated to the likelihood of MSG formation. This pattern of results supported our argument that social network ties as conventionally defined (i.e., ties from minority leaders in the focal industry to MSGs in another industry) are insufficient to spur group formation, and that generalized reciprocity and uncertainty reduction that result from the guidance of an MSG member is necessary for the diffusion of this group-level form of IM.

We further corroborated our theory using multi-item survey scales that more directly measure generalized reciprocity and subjective uncertainty. Specific items in the reciprocity measure include the following five-point Likert-type scales: "I feel an obligation to help other [racial minority/women] leaders organize a group that can provide each other with support"; "It is incumbent on me to help other [minority/women] organize a group that can provide each other with support in communicating with the press"; "I feel an obligation to give advice to other [minority/women] leaders on how to communicate with the press." Items in the subjective uncertainty measure include the following five-point Likert-type scales: "I feel uncertain about the value of forming a group of minority leaders to communicate with the press"; "I feel uncertain about the benefits of participating in a group of [minority/women] leaders that communicates with the press"; "I feel confident about the likely success of organizing a group of [minority/women] leaders to communicate with the press"; "I feel uncertain about the likely success of organizing a group of minority leaders to communicate with the press." Confirmatory factor analysis showed that the items loaded onto two factors that correspond to generalized reciprocity or a felt obligation to help other minority leaders organize an MSG, and subjective uncertainty about the value of forming an MSG. Inter-item reliability of the two scales was high ($\alpha = 0.90$ and 0.89). We

---

formation from 2005 to 2011, defined as industries that included at least three firms with racial minority (female) CEOs, and which did not yet have a racial minority (female) MSG; N = 1510 (1807) industry quarters for the analysis of racial minority (female) MSGs. No industry had more than one racial minority or female MSG during the study period. None of the female or racial minority CEOs whom we interviewed or surveyed were aware of an MSG prior to 2005, and our subsequent surveys revealed no new groups formed after 2011, suggesting that left censoring and right censoring are likely to be minimal (see Westphal et al., 2019 for further detail).

conducted a mediation analysis to examine whether both measures mediated the hypothesized effects of director ties to an MSG that received guidance in organizing the group on MSG formation. This analysis was limited to the sub-sample of cases with a responding CEO. We first conducted Sobel tests, which showed statistically significant, indirect effects of the independent variable on MSG formation through (1) felt obligation to help ($z = 2.68$ for racial minority groups and $z = 2.87$ for female groups), and (2) reduced uncertainty about the value of forming a group, and through ($z = 2.76$ for racial minority groups and $z = 2.84$ for female groups).[2]

Coordinated IM in MSGs has the second-order effect of strengthening ties among minority leaders in an industry, which may lead to the exchange of other social and professional resources, including strategic advice, the exchange of competitor and other industry information, mentoring, and social support. Thus, in spreading coordinated IM, CEO-director ties to MSGs in other industries may ultimately have a significant influence on the social embeddedness of minority leaders. Such connections are not visible to external firm stakeholders, thus contributing to the separation between appearances and reality with respect to the social structure of corporate leadership.

Social Exchange Ties and Uncoordinated Impression-Management Support

While CEO-director ties have facilitated the diffusion of coordinated IM support among female and racial minority leaders, informal social exchange ties have facilitated the spread of uncoordinated IM support among the white male majority of corporate leaders. As discussed in Chapter 4, the verbal content of uncoordinated IM support is similar to the content of coordinated support. It includes positive statements by a CEO about the leadership and strategy of another CEO's firm, and/or external attributions for low performance at the CEO's firm in communications with journalists and security analysts. Uncoordinated IM support is not a rare event among CEOs at large and medium-sized U.S. corporations. On average, CEOs in our survey samples have received IM support from other CEOs approximately 3.6 times per year. Our analyses indicate that while uncoordinated IM support has less impact on the tenor of journalists' coverage of firm

---

[2] Further analysis showed that bootstrapped 95 per cent confidence intervals for the coefficients of the indirect effects excluded zero, which confirms that the indirect effects are significant at the .05 level (Hayes, 2013). This analysis helps rule out the alternative explanation that our independent variables indicate awareness of social disadvantage. Moreover, responses to separate survey questions indicated that female and racial minority leaders were generally aware that they were disadvantaged in accessing IM support (i.e., there was little variance in such awareness), and such awareness is not correlated with our independent variables.

leadership and strategy than coordinated support in MSGs, it has significantly more impact than IM by CEOs and other top managers about their *own* leadership and strategy (see Chapter 4).

Our research shows that uncoordinated IM support has diffused and intensified in large part through the combined effects of three distinct social exchange mechanisms. First, IM support is triggered and perpetuated at the dyad level through direct reciprocity. A CEO is much more likely to provide IM support for another CEO who has given them similar help in the past. Such direct reciprocation is psychologically and socially compelled by the norm of reciprocity (Gouldner, 1960). The literature on inequity aversion discussed above indicates that most people feel a pronounced, psychological aversion to overbenefitting from their social relationships, and will often invest considerable time and effort to mitigate or avoid social inequities (Fehr and Schmidt, 2006; Dunn et al., 2012). Although the norm of reciprocity is likely bolstered by instrumental motives to create social exchange ties with colleagues (Blau, 1964), experimental studies indicate that most people reciprocate helping behavior without any expectation of ongoing exchange, as in one-shot exchanges with strangers (Fehr et al., 2002).

Beyond direct reciprocity, two distinct forms of generalized reciprocity have contributed to the diffusion of uncoordinated IM support. First, chain-generalized reciprocity helped spread uncoordinated IM support in much the same way that it has contributed to the diffusion of MSGs. As discussed above, research on inequity aversion suggests that people who have received valuable assistance tend to feel distressed about failing to take the opportunity to "pay it forward" by helping others in the same way that they were helped (Fehr and Schmidt, 2006). Conversely, a growing literature in evolutionary psychology and anthropology reveals that most people are "pre-programmed" to feel emotional satisfaction from generalized reciprocity (Cosmides and Tooby, 1992: 222; Hill, 2002; Gurven, 2004; Gintis et al., 2008). Thus, inequity aversion is the cognitive mechanism by which generalized norms of reciprocity promote the diffusion of helping behavior at the community level. Inequity aversion is illustrated by the following quote from our interviews:

> I felt compelled to put in a good word for him with [a journalist]. Someone did that for me a couple years ago in the same situation, so I felt like I should do it for him.
>
> [When asked why he felt compelled:] Again, someone helped me in the same situation. It wouldn't feel right not to take the opportunity to help this guy. I'd feel guilty in a way. (Westphal et al., 2012: 224)

Although generalized reciprocity can occur among strangers, or when givers and receivers are anonymous (Gintis et al., 2003; Greiner and Levati, 2005; Stanca,

2009), the frequency of such reciprocity tends to be highest when there is a basis for social identification among actors, as noted above (Ekeh, 1974; Buchan et al., 2002). While the basis for social identification is likely to be strongest among female or racial minority CEOs, there is qualitative and large-sample survey evidence that CEOs of relatively large companies tend to socially identify with each other, at least to some significant degree, as fellow corporate leaders (Useem, 1984; O'Reilly et al., 1988; McDonald and Westphal, 2010). There is a pervasive belief among corporate leaders that CEOs tend to receive inordinate blame for low firm performance from the media and other firm stakeholders (Westphal and Park, 2012), and CEOs tend to sympathize with fellow leaders who are vulnerable to external criticism during a performance downturn. Thus, theory and research on social exchange, together with prior research on the social psychology of corporate leaders, suggests that IM support should tend to diffuse through generalized social exchange, as CEOs who have received IM support from a fellow corporate leader are more likely to provide similar support to another CEO when needed, e.g., following the disclosure of negative earnings at the CEO's firm. In effect, CEOs who have received IM support are motivated by inequity aversion to help a fellow leader, and firm performance determines the locus and timing of support giving.

Most people have a psychological aversion to social inequity, not only in their own relationships, but also in relationships among their peers (Camerer and Fehr, 2004). One such inequity is when a peer who has generously helped others in the past does not receive comparable help from his or her peers when in need. Most people feel cognitive dissonance or psychological distress at the prospect of such inequities, and conversely feel a deep-seated sense of satisfaction from resolving them (Walster et al., 1973; Johansson and Svedsäter, 2009), even when it requires an investment of material or other resources without any expectation of further benefits (Gintis et al., 2003; Seinen and Schram, 2006; Stanca, 2009). Again, such inequity aversion is heightened when there is a basis for social identification and sympathy among peers. Under such conditions, inequity aversion results in a second form of generalized reciprocity, sometimes described as fairness-based selective giving or social indirect reciprocity (Takahashi, 2000; Penner et al., 2005; Baker and Levine, 2013), in which individuals feel impelled to provide help to a peer who previously provided similar help to third parties. Thus, CEOs are more likely to provide IM support for fellow CEOs whom they believe have been generous in providing support in the past. The potential for inequity aversion to spur this form of reciprocity is illustrated by the following quote from our interviews: "I knew he had put in a good word for other CEOs a couple times in the past. I thought someone should put in a good word for him now. He came to others' defense. It just wouldn't seem right not to come to his defense now" (Westphal et al., 2012: 226). The three forms of reciprocity contributing to the diffusion of IM support are depicted in Figure 6.1. Empirical analyses showed that

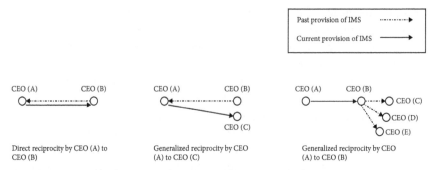

Figure 6.1. Social exchange mechanisms in the provision of impression-management support (IMS)

each form of reciprocity had a strong, independent effect on diffusion (Westphal et al., 2012). For example, an increase in the prior receipt of IM support from another CEO ("alter") of one standard deviation (from the mean level) increased the likelihood that the focal CEO would provide support for alter during the two-week period after a negative earnings surprise at alter's firm by 163 per cent (direct reciprocity). An increase of one standard deviation in the prior receipt of IM support *from other CEOs than alter* increased the chances that the focal CEO would provide support for alter by 102 per cent (indirect reciprocity or pay it forward). And an increase of one standard deviation in the prior provision of IM support *by alter for other CEOs* increased the likelihood of support by the focal CEO for alter by 87 per cent (generalized reciprocity).

Friendship Ties between Corporate Leaders and Symbolic Management

The influence of friendship ties on symbolic management has received very little theoretical or empirical attention in the organizational literature. The importance of friendship ties as a determinant of various forms of IM support is constrained by the relative scarcity of such ties among CEOs in the same industry (as discussed in Chapter 4, IM support is generally limited to CEOs in the same industry because they can speak most credibly about a focal CEO's leadership and the causes of firm performance). The average CEO in our 2013 survey had between one and two friendship ties to other CEOs in the same industry broadly defined, including competitors and current or potential buyer and supplier firms. Nevertheless, friendship ties were the strongest determinant of IM support in the dyad-level models, stronger even than the effect of low firm performance (Westphal et al., 2012). The personal identification, empathy and perspective taking, and first-hand knowledge of each other's strengths that goes along with friendship (Silver, 1990; Pahl, 2000; Penner et al., 2005; Swart et al., 2011) strongly motivates and facilitates the provision of IM support.

Friendship ties also facilitate the symbolic management of strategic decision-making processes. In particular, our research indicates that friendship ties between CEOs facilitate the spread of decoupled, PSDM programs, and the IM of such programs in communications with information intermediaries (Westphal and Zhu, 2019a; see Chapter 3 for a discussion of these forms of symbolic management). While board interlock ties promote the spread of relatively simple forms of decoupling that are publicly known, such as decoupled executive incentive plans or stock repurchase programs (Westphal and Zajac, 2001), and generalized social exchange ties promote the spread of IM support, neither kind of tie is likely to facilitate the symbolic decoupling of strategic decision-making processes such as PSDM programs. The decoupling of these programs is generally well concealed, and information about the decoupling is sensitive. Consequently, information about such decoupling is unlikely to spread through conventional board interlock ties, since communication in these ties generally occurs between weakly connected actors (e.g., acquaintances (Granovetter, 1973; Mizruchi, 1996)), and often in group settings (Westphal et al., 2001). It is also unlikely to diffuse through the kinds of CEO–board ties that helped spread coordinated IM support, as such ties rely on social identification from shared minority status. And, information about the decoupling of PSDM programs is also unlikely to diffuse through the kinds of social exchange ties that promoted the spread of uncoordinated IM support, as such ties only motivate CEOs to communicate with journalists and analysts on behalf of other CEOs, they do not facilitate direct communication between firm leaders.

However, friendship ties do facilitate the exchange of sensitive information between firm leaders. Friendship is based upon interpersonal trust (Chua et al., 2009), defined as "a state involving confident positive expectations about another's motives with respect to oneself in situations entailing risk" (Boon and Holmes, 1991: 194; Grosser et al., 2010: 4). Friends are normatively obligated to protect each other's interests and welfare (Silver, 1990; Krackhardt, 1992). Thus, a friend can be trusted not to reveal sensitive information to a third party. As one CEO whom we interviewed put it, "you don't have to say to a friend [who is a leader at another firm], 'let's keep this between you and me.' It's understood they'll be careful... you shouldn't have to worry." The decoupling of PSDM programs whereby CEOs and other top managers solicit input from lower-level managers on strategic options after they have decided on one, is very sensitive information that could damage the reputation of top managers if divulged to lower-level employees or other firm stakeholders. As discussed in Chapter 3, analysts generally assume that input solicited in PSDM programs is at least considered in the strategic decision-making process. The revelation that strategic decisions may have been made prior to seeking input from lower-level managers and staff would seriously undermine the credibility of firm leaders. Thus, CEOs are much more likely to discuss the potential for such decoupling, and to divulge information about which processes worked effectively and what could have been done differently, when communicating with a personal friend.

In addition, CEOs are more likely to trust the quality and reliability of information about PSDM programs that they hear from a personal friend (McAllister, 1995; Chua et al., 2009; Uzzi, 1996; Ingram and Lifschitz, 2006). Friendship relations are "temporally embedded" (Granovetter, 2017: 18) in ways that reinforce personal identification and mutual obligation (Heider, 1958; Fehr, 2004). In fact, friends may overestimate the reliability of each other's advice, leading to excessive risk raking. Thus, while the decoupling and IM of PSDM programs is an intricate process, and failed decoupling could harm the reputation of firm leaders with multiple stakeholder groups, CEOs are likely to perceive less risk in decoupling if they can access the tactical advice and first-hand experience of a personal friend. In effect, a CEO-friend who has direct experience with decoupling is a social resource that provides a perceived advantage in symbolic action.

Friendship ties to CEOs who have experience with PSDM programs also provide referrals to consultants who assist with program implementation. As discussed in Chapter 3, a small number of consulting firms advised firm leaders on the use of crowdsourcing technology in PSDM programs, and specifically on the use of such technology to solicit strategic input without sacrificing top managers' discretion over strategy. Given that the use of crowdsourcing technology is both integral to the decoupling of PSDM programs, and often leveraged in the IM of such programs, top managers must be very comfortable with their consultant's track record. To the extent that trust in a CEO-friend can be transferred to a third party (Coleman, 1990; McEvily et al., 2003; Brass et al., 2004; Burt, 2005; Grosser et al., 2010), the endorsement of a consultant from a CEO-friend should reduce ex ante uncertainty about decoupling a PSDM program in a way that preserves executive discretion. In addition, CEO friendship ties become a source of network power over the consultant, as friendship ties increase a third party's accountability (Uzzi, 1996; Krackhardt, 1998). As one CEO told us,

I let him know [the consultant who assisted with crowdsourcing technology on their PSDM program] he should assign his best people to [his CEO-friend's] project, and I told [the CEO-friend] about the conversation. Of course that made him more comfortable hiring the consultant, which made him more comfortable starting up [a PSDM program]. When [his CEO-friend] hired [the consultant], it benefitted both of us. You lose one [client], you lose the other, so you better put your best people on both. (Westphal and Zhu, 2019a: 15)

Friendship ties also increase the consultant's responsiveness to feedback. One CEO told us, "[the consultant] better heed my [performance] feedback. I'll be telling [his CEO-friend, who is planning to adopt a PSDM program] about it, so he [the CEO-friend] will be expecting the issue to be resolved" (from Westphal and Zhu, 2019a: 15). Friendship ties also increase the consultant's value added by transferring information about their strengths and weaknesses, and about how to best deploy them. For example, one CEO was advised by his friend to personally introduce the crowdsourcing platform to managers and staff in his own words, rather than relying on the consultant for this task.

Consultants who advise clients on crowdsourcing-enabled PSDM programs also typically advise them on communicating or "messaging" about the programs with information intermediaries (e.g., security analysts). While CEOs and their firms stand to gain substantial reputational and legitimacy benefits from their IM about PSDM programs (see Chapter 3), CEOs may be concerned about the risks of promoting a program despite decoupling. Friendship ties to a CEO who hired a consultant that advises on crowdsourcing-enabled PSDM programs should reduce a focal CEO's ex ante uncertainty about such IM, as well as their uncertainty about decoupling itself. In fact, our empirical analyses indicated that a CEO's friendship tie to another CEO who hired a consultant advising on crowdsourcing-enabled PSDM programs had a strong, positive effect on the (1) likelihood of adopting and decoupling a PSDM program at the focal firm, and (2) verbal IM by top managers at the focal firm about PSDM in communicating with security analysts (Westphal and Zhu, 2019a). These relationships were especially strong for firms that had relatively negative appraisals from security analysts in the prior period (e.g., the year prior to adoption).

The particular network tie that is responsible for the diffusion of a specific form of decoupling determines the pattern and magnitude of the reputational and legitimacy benefits that leaders and their firms derive from symbolic management. Communication about decoupled corporate policies such as LTIPs through board interlock ties was broadly dispersed, providing correspondingly widespread legitimacy benefits from symbolic management. However, the broad availability of information about the potential for decoupling through board ties also meant that firms derived few competitive benefits from symbolic management. That is, IM about these plans was generally not a source of differentiation from competitors in capital markets, constraining the reputational benefits from this form of symbolic management. While the board interlock network is relatively diffuse (Mizruchi, 1996; Davis et al., 2003), the network of CEO friendship ties is concentrated among a small portion of corporate leaders. For example, only approximately 39 per cent of CEOs in our sample had a friendship tie to another CEO of a large public company. Thus, social network access to information about the decoupling of PSDM programs, and to consultants who can assist with decoupling and verbal IM on relatively favorable terms, is restricted to a minority of corporate leaders.

Accordingly, the symbolic management of PSDM programs not only yields reputational and legitimacy benefits by conforming to prevailing institutional logics of good leadership and governance (see Chapter 3), but they also help differentiate the firm's leadership from competitors, engendering further reputational benefits. While some scholars have suggested that firms inevitably face a difficult tradeoff between differentiation and institutional conformity (e.g., Deephouse, 1999), firms can achieve both objectives by adopting policies that conform to prevailing institutional logics, or that can be persuasively framed in terms of such logics, but that are difficult for most of their competitors to replicate or imitate. The symbolic management of PSDM programs is one such policy, and the potential for differentiation derives from limited access to social capital that reduces ex ante uncertainty about the program's success.

Moreover, our interviews suggested that CEOs were cognizant that their friendship ties to fellow leaders were a valuable social resource in symbolic management, and they recognized the knowledge and influence benefits of friendship ties relative to weaker ties such as board interlocks. As one CEO told us, "talking to another director can tell you about common policies like anti-takeover measures, but there is insider knowledge that you only get from close connections." Moreover, a number of leaders suggested that board ties have become less useful as a vehicle for knowledge transfer over time, not only due to the general reduction in board appointments of top managers, but also due to a reduced willingness to share information and experience about policies and strategies with fellow board members. There is a need for large-sample research about whether such communication has in fact declined, and about the possible causes of this trend. One possibility is that increases in board diversity have reduced the willingness of top managers to share their experiences with policies and strategies in board meetings and the informal conversations that often occur outside formal meetings. If so, increases in board diversity may have ironically increased the exclusivity of information exchange networks among firm leaders.

There is also clearly a need for further research on exclusive forms of structural embeddedness that link a privileged subset of organizational leaders with consultants and other third-party service providers, such as lobbyists or attorneys. The limited research on inter-organizational ties that connect businesses and such third parties has focused mainly on board interlocks, and has examined the consequences of embeddedness at the sector level (e.g., see Hula's (1999) comparative analysis of board interlocks and common links to lobbyists and Washington attorneys). While this research has yielded valuable insights, it has given little attention to how informal, inter-organizational linkages such as CEO friendship ties contribute to structural embeddedness, or the organization-level benefits that accrue from such informal ties. Given the exclusive benefits available to leaders and their firms from friendship ties to other CEOs, it is also important to understand the antecedents of such ties. In Chapter 7, we examine the sophisticated interpersonal behaviors that enable some managers to build close ties to other corporate leaders.

Executive Search Firms and the Maintenance of Board Friendship Ties between Firms

In Chapter 3 we introduced a kind of separation between appearances and reality in the social network of corporate leaders, wherein the sparsity of board interlock ties between firms appears to indicate an atomistic social structure, when in fact leaders are commonly connected to each other by informal and less visible social network ties. We specifically explained that while the near absence of interlock ties between competitors helps to foster the impression of atomistic competition between firms, a perception which is reinforced by the IM of firm leaders with certain stakeholder groups, competitors are in fact commonly connected by a kind of two-step tie in which the personal friend of a firm's CEO serves on the board of a competitor firm, which we term "board friendship ties." We explained how board friendship ties may facilitate collusive behavior between rival firms. In this section we draw from recent research by Westphal and Zhu (2019b) to further explain how board friendship ties between firms are maintained with the assistance of executive search firms or "headhunters." We suggest that while boards hire headhunters in part to bolster the legitimacy of the director search process, headhunters broker network ties between competitors that would be viewed as illegitimate if not illicit by some firm stakeholders.

There is only limited theory or academic research on the role of consultants in the selection of firm leaders, and virtually none on the role of consultants in director selection. Yet, search firms are known to contribute to over 50 per cent of executive placements in the U.S. (AESC, 2011), and our surveys indicate that they contribute to a similarly large portion of director placements. Given the importance of top executive and director selection to strategic leadership and firm governance (Finkelstein et al., 2009), this is a critical gap in the literature.

We suggest that when a firm's board friendship tie to a competitor is broken (e.g., due to turnover of the rival's CEO), search firms help the board identify a new director who is a friend of the competitor's CEO. The limited academic research on executive search firms indicates that they often function as matchmakers who gather information from both parties to increase the efficiency and quality of executive placements (Bidwell, 2011; Khurana, 2002). Khurana (2002) suggested that headhunters are especially likely to be used for executive searches that involve sensitive or confidential selection criteria, because they lend normative legitimacy to the selection process. In hiring an established search firm, boards create the appearance of an objective, broad-based search for the most qualified candidates, while distancing themselves from the search process.

Thus, search firms are likely to be especially valuable to boards in reconstituting broken board friendship ties to competitors. By relying on a headhunter to identify director candidates who have the desired social connections, the board distances itself from selection criteria that would be considered illegitimate or illicit if discovered by customers, regulators, or certain other firm stakeholders. Moreover, headhunters at leading firms are perceived by corporate leaders to have special expertise in the "delicate social process" of obtaining sensitive information about external candidates for organizational leadership positions. Since the friendship ties of firm leaders are often not visible outside the firm, and external perceptions of friendship can be unreliable (Kilduff and Tsai, 2003; Keeves et al., 2017), information about a CEO's friendship ties must often be obtained directly from the CEO him or herself. The headhunters whom we interviewed consistently stated that if they were searching for outside executive or director candidates with strong ties to a particular leader, they would not rely on second-hand information, but would approach the leader directly to identify viable candidates. In communicating with the CEO of a competitor about possible candidates, the headhunter can also discretely signal the purpose of the director appointment. As one CEO told us, "If [a headhunter] asks you whether [a board candidate] is someone you know well and trust, and says this is important, and you say yes they're a friend and I trust them and recommend them, you're really saying 'signal received'" (Westphal and Zhu, 2019b: 12). Such indirect communication is a kind of "off-record indirect speech" (Lee and Pinker, 2010: 785), wherein the speaker solicits information and/or cooperation of a potentially illicit nature, without overtly describing the desired behavior (e.g., the exchange of strategic information between firms), thus maintaining "plausible deniability" for both the speaker and the interlocutor (Pinker et al., 2008: 834). Thus, a headhunter's solicitation of director candidates from a competitor's CEO is a key mechanism by which firms reconstitute broken board friendship ties.

Our analyses showed that firms were especially likely to reconstitute broken board friendship ties when the level of competitive uncertainty in their industry was relatively high (e.g., as indicated by a survey measure of competitive uncertainty, text analysis of analyst reports, and the mean-deviated concentration level of the firm's primary industry (Burt, 1983; Palmer and Barber, 2001)). Using a series of survey questions that prompted members of board-nominating committees in our sample to indicate whether and when a headhunter solicited director candidates from a competitor's CEO, we examined whether the positive relationship between competitive uncertainty and reconstitution of a broken board friendship tie to the CEO of a competitor was significantly mediated by a headhunter's solicitation of director candidates from the competitor's CEO (Westphal and Zhu, 2019b). The analyses provided consistent evidence for mediation, using either the product of coefficients method with Sobel-Goodman standard errors (MacKinnon et al., 2002) or the bootstrapping method with bias-corrected estimates (Preacher and Hayes, 2008).

Thus, while search consultants bolster the legitimacy of the director search process, they also broker social network ties between competitor firms that would be considered illegitimate, if not illicit, by some firm stakeholders. Accordingly, these consultants mediate decoupling between appearances and reality in the director search process, and thus also contribute to decoupling between the apparent function of corporate directors (i.e., independent monitoring) and their actual role in firm governance and strategy (i.e., brokering collusive behavior). At a higher level of analysis, consultants play a key role in the separation of appearances and reality with respect to the social structure of corporate leadership. They broker the appointment of seemingly independent directors who lack any apparent board ties to competitors, thus supporting the impression of an atomistic social structure of corporate leaders, while actually brokering informal ties that promote relational embeddedness between firm leaders.

The Moderating Effect of Prior Symbolic Management

Organizational scholars have long lamented the propensity for social network scholars to ignore historical factors at the organization and community level in theorizing and analyzing the effects of social network ties (Granovetter, 1985, 2017). In the governance and strategy literatures, scholars have given little consideration to how social network effects on the adoption of policies and practices may be conditioned by a firm's prior experience with similar practices. By extension, there has been little attention to how the influence of network ties on particular forms of symbolic management is moderated by prior experience. Westphal and Zajac (2001) examined repeated instances of symbolic management across multiple domains in their research on decoupled LTIPs and stock repurchase programs (see also Angst et al., 2017). They theorized that while leaders may learn about decoupling vicariously through board interlock ties, they may also learn from repeated, direct experience with decoupling at the focal firm. Behavioral decision theory indicates that actions which engender positive outcomes are more likely to be repeated, even after one instance of the behavior (March et al., 1991). Westphal and Zajac's studies showed that decoupled LTIPs and stock repurchase plans tended to engender positive, and often strong market reactions (1998; Zajac and Westphal, 2004). They therefore theorized that, due to such positive reinforcement, experience with decoupling will be encoded into organizational memory and routines and invoked in the process of adopting similar governance policies in the future (Westphal and Zajac, 2001). Empirical analyses showed that prior decoupling of LTIPs for CEOs was negatively associated with implementation of stock repurchase programs. They also found that this relationship was especially strong for firms in which the CEO was relatively powerful vis-à-vis the board of directors, suggesting that symbolic management routines may be invoked selectively to some degree, depending on the political interests of firm leaders.

However, Westphal and Zajac did not explore how direct experience with symbolic management interacts with vicarious learning through board interlock ties or other kinds of social network ties between firm leaders. One might expect that direct experience and vicarious learning could either substitute or complement one another. If firms have prior experience with a particular form of symbolic management and vicarious experience with the same or very similar form of symbolic management, the two kinds of experience may be substitutes, suggesting a negative interaction in predicting subsequent symbolic management. If firms have prior experience with one form of symbolic management and vicarious experience with a different but related form of symbolic management, there may be a positive interaction between them. The relationship would also likely depend on whether the symbolic management at tied-to firms is an elaboration or extension of the firm's prior symbolic management, such that the firm's prior experience provides a foundation for vicarious learning. Teasing out these relationships will require specifying the particular routines entailed in each kind of symbolic management, a topic which received very little theoretical or empirical attention in the literature. Although considerable progress has been made in defining and operationalizing decoupling and IM, and in developing broader theoretical models that address the antecedents and consequences of symbolic action, we still know very little about the micro-level behavioral processes of symbolic management (see Hallet, 2010; Tilcsik, 2010). Such research is a prerequisite for developing more sophisticated learning models of symbolic management, whether experiential learning, vicarious learning, or their interaction.

Conclusion

While the behavioral literature has focused on board interlock ties as a determinant of strategic action, including symbolic decoupling, it is necessary to consider the full variety of informal connections among corporate leaders in order to appreciate the influence of social networks on symbolic management. We have explained how ties to informal groups of firm leaders, personal friendship ties, social exchange ties of different kinds, and common ties to management consultants facilitate the diffusion of symbolic management across firms and industries. In comparison to board interlocks, these ties are relatively strong connections that facilitate diffusion through social identification, interpersonal trust, and/or reciprocity, rather than relying on the more impersonal mechanisms of awareness or "business scan" that drive network diffusion through board interlock ties (Useem,

1984). Moreover, the effects of common ties to consultants and two-step ties such as board friendship ties suggest the importance of examining relational embeddedness and structural embeddedness that result from informal ties between leaders and third parties in assessing the determinants of symbolic management.

Our analysis also suggests that the relevant source of network diffusion is contingent on the particular form of symbolic management. Board interlock ties can be effective in spreading forms of symbolic management that are relatively generic and straightforward to implement, such as decoupled LTIPs or buyback plans. More complex forms of symbolic management such as decoupled PSDM programs, or symbolic actions that must be customized to the particular industry environment such as coordinated IM support, require stronger social ties to stimulate their diffusion. In addition, whereas relatively diffuse networks of weak ties such as board interlocks can diffuse symbolic action widely, networks of strong ties have provided more exclusive access to forms of symbolic management that conform to prevailing institutional logics, while also differentiating the firm from competitors.

Further, our analysis suggests that social network ties lead to decoupling on multiple levels. They facilitate decoupling of firm-level policies, programs, and practices, such as LTIPs, PSDM programs, and director selection, and they create decoupling between appearances and reality with respect to the social structure of corporate leadership itself. Informal ties between leaders and third-party ties to many service providers are less visible to firm stakeholders than formal ties such as board interlocks, but they are more pervasive when considered together. Moreover, while board interlocks have become more sparse, some kinds of informal ties between leaders, such as board friendship ties, have become more prevalent. Network theorists have increasingly highlighted the importance of modeling the multiplexity of ties, or the variety of different social mechanisms by which actors and firms can be directly or indirectly connected (Lavie and Singh, 2012; Shipilov, 2012). In the context of firm leadership, consideration of tie multiplexity, together with the external visibility of ties reveals a growing decoupling in which corporate leadership appears increasingly atomistic, but has actually become more structurally embedded. As discussed in Chapter 4, board friendship ties are inconspicuous to external stakeholders, not only because they include informal, social mechanisms (e.g., friendship), but also because the links that make up the indirect tie between CEOs take different forms (i.e., friendship and board appointment). While most people, including firm stakeholders, tend to underappreciate the multiplexity of ties, they are even less sensitive to the potential for these mixed, multiplex ties. When prompted to consider possible indirect or third-party ties between CEOs (e.g., in open-ended survey questions), journalists and analysts rarely mention mixed ties of this kind. Moreover, such ties are inconspicuous even to social network scholars. It seems highly likely that there are other important mixed, multiplex ties linking firm leaders that have not yet been discovered by researchers or firm stakeholders, and which contribute to the decoupling between appearances and reality with respect to the social structure of corporate leadership.

Social network theory also suggests that network ties can function as pipes or prisms, meaning channels of communication or signals of quality (Podolny, 2001). Our theory and research indicates that the visible network ties of firm leaders may be conceived as prisms, but they may also be better conceived as symbols, rather than signals. That is, rather than signaling underlying attributes such as quality, networks convey the impression that firm leaders are increasingly independent of each other (Chapter 4), when they are actually embedded in a web of informal ties. Thus, rather than reducing information asymmetry between managers and constituents, as suggested by signaling theories of social structure, in a sense formal network ties can exacerbate information asymmetry. In widening the gap between external perceptions of social ties and the actual social connectedness of firm leaders, moreover, board interlocks create a more serious problem. Not only do constituents have a less accurate picture of corporate leadership, but they are unaware of the inaccuracy. In fact, they have become *more* confident in firm leadership, and thus less likely to monitor leader behavior and decision making in ways that would ameliorate information asymmetry. In addition, whereas network ties are usually assumed to convey the same signal of quality to various stakeholders, firms' IM about leader ties conveys a different message to different stakeholder groups; firms can highlight the lack of board interlock ties in communicating with the general media, customers, regulators, and others who would benefit from inter-firm competition, and they can highlight their ties to other firms in communicating with security analysts and shareholders, who would benefit from the absence of competition. Thus, networks of firm leaders are prismatic in the true sense that their characteristics are refracted differently through symbolic management to different audiences.

Our research has only begun to examine the relational and structural embeddedness of firm leadership. There is a clear need for further research on leaders' common ties to (1) service providers, such as lobbyists and attorneys; (2) information intermediaries, such as different kinds of journalists and analysts; and (3) firm stakeholders, such as regulators, institutional investors, and protest groups, and how these various ties influence symbolic management at different levels of analysis. Such research is critical to developing a comprehensive social theory of governance that integrates social structural and institutional perspectives, with symbolic management as the linchpin mechanism.

7

Social Influence Processes in Leader–Stakeholder Relations

In this chapter we describe common social influence processes in relations between firm leaders and external stakeholders. We focus particular attention on ingratiation, favor rendering, and negative reciprocity, as our research indicates that these social influence processes are perhaps the most impactful in leader–constituent relations. We begin by explaining why ingratiatory behavior by firm leaders is a relatively efficient, effective, and robust form of social influence. We describe especially sophisticated forms of ingratiation, and reveal the background characteristics of firm leaders that predict their deployment of these tactics. We go on to discuss the social and psychological side effects of ingratiation on firm leaders and strategic decision making, and explain how the backgrounds of firm leaders predict their vulnerability to these unfortunate effects. We then describe favor rendering and negative reciprocity as powerful but resource-intensive social influence processes in leader–stakeholder relations. We conclude that these micro-level social influence processes play an important role in the larger governance system, as they help perpetuate the ceremonial inspection by external stakeholders that facilitates symbolic decoupling and preserves the power of corporate elites. Moreover, the social processes described in this chapter are properly conceived as mechanisms of symbolic management, because they leverage generalized cultural norms in order to exercise social influence, including the generalized norms of reciprocity.

Ingratiation as a Primary Means of Social Influence

Ingratiation is a primary interpersonal mechanism by which organizational actors build social capital. It is defined as a pattern of interpersonal behavior that serves to enhance interpersonal attractiveness and gain favor with an influence "target" (Jones, 1964; Kumar and Beyerlein, 1991; Cialdini and Goldstein, 2004). Ingratiatory behavior includes flattery and "opinion conformity," or verbal statements that validate an opinion held by another person (Gordon, 1996). Ingratiation is a relatively efficient, effective, and robust social influence tactic. It is a relatively efficient tactic because it requires few social or material resources. One does not necessarily need social capital, status, or financial resources to ingratiate

Symbolic Management: Governance, Strategy, and Institutions. James Westphal and Sun Hyun Park,
Oxford University Press (2020). © James Westphal and Sun Hyun Park.
DOI: 10.1093/oso/9780198792055.001.0001

successfully. In fact, ingratiation can partially substitute for the lack of resources in developing or maintaining a social exchange relationship.

Ingratiation is a relatively *effective* tactic, in part because it exerts influence through multiple social and psychological mechanisms. Flattery elicits liking through reciprocal attraction, which is a kind of social exchange. A person who is "paid" a compliment feels socially and psychologically impelled to return the "favor" (Vonk, 2002). Opinion conformity triggers similarity attraction bias, as people feel positive affect toward others who they think share their beliefs or attitudes (Byrne, 1971; Wayne and Liden, 1995). Similarity attraction bias, in turn, is associated with more positive evaluations of an individual's competence and performance (Wayne and Liden, 1995; Montoya and Horton, 2004).

Ingratiation is also a relatively robust social influence tactic, in the sense that it can help actors secure a wide variety of outcomes. While the benefits of persuasion are limited to support for particular proposals or requests, ingratiation, by eliciting positive affect and triggering norms of reciprocity, leads to a more flexible kind of support. As discussed in Chapter 5, CEO ingratiation toward outside directors is associated with more favorable compensation contracts for the CEO on multiple dimensions, as well as more support for corporate strategies that would tend to benefit the CEO (Westphal, 1998). Ingratiation toward the CEO or an outside director also increases the likelihood of receiving that colleague's recommendation for a board appointment (Westphal and Stern, 2006, 2007).

Ingratiation is also robust in the sense that it "works" in a wide variety of organizational, social, and cultural contexts, and it works "on" a wide variety of different kinds of people. While the efficacy of persuasion is contingent on the inherent quality of the proposal or request, and the expertise of the influence target, among other factors, nearly everyone appreciates flattery and opinion conformity. Ingratiation exploits the self-enhancement bias, which is a systematic tendency to overestimate one's own abilities (Kwan et al., 2008; Sedikides and Gregg, 2008), as well as the nearly universal drive for social affirmation (Baumeister, 1998). The social and psychological mechanisms by which ingratiation engenders social influence are especially potent in corporate leadership. There is empirical evidence that the self-enhancement bias is pervasive and pronounced among corporate leaders (Park et al., 2011). As discussed in Chapter 5, there is also evidence that most corporate directors believe they are immune to ingratiation, which may reduce their vigilance for it.

The efficiency and robust effectiveness of ingratiation make it especially valuable to CEOs, as they seek to build and maintain social capital with a diverse set of firm stakeholders. Westphal and Bednar (2008) found that high levels of institutional ownership increased the frequency with which CEOs engaged in ingratiatory behavior toward institutional fund managers. Ingratiation in this context included flattering remarks, such as complimenting a fund manager on his or her investment performance or noting the manager's excellent professional reputation, and opinion conformity, such as expressing agreement with the fund manager's opinion(s) on a corporate governance issue, or expressing agreement with the fund manager's investment philosophy or approach. Results indicated that CEO ingratiation of this kind exerted significant influence on institutional owners across multiple dimensions of corporate policy. For example, although at low levels of CEO ingratiation the level of institutional ownership was positively related to the adoption of board reforms that are thought to reduce CEOs' discretion over strategy and policy outcomes (e.g., separation of the CEO and board chair positions), at relatively high levels of ingratiatory behavior institutional ownership had no significant effect on board reforms. Ingratiation had a similar, moderating influence on the relationship between high levels of institutional ownership and the level of CEO compensation, CEO compensation risk, and corporate diversification. Analyses also indicated that the moderating effects of CEO ingratiation were stronger for so-called pressure-resistant institutional investors, such as public pension funds, mutual funds, endowments, and foundations (Ryan and Schneider, 2002) than for pressure-sensitive institutional investors, such as banks and insurance companies. The findings ultimately suggested that CEOs' interpersonal influence behavior in the form of ingratiation toward fund managers helps explain why increased ownership by institutional investors may have failed to yield widespread changes in the governance and corporate strategy of U.S. companies.

Other research indicates that CEO ingratiation is similarly effective in exerting influence over information intermediaries. Westphal and Deephouse (2011) found that negative corporate earnings surprises (i.e., low reported earnings relative to the "consensus" forecasts of security analysts) was associated with a significant increase in CEO ingratiation toward journalists who cover their firm following the earnings announcement. Moreover, the level of CEO ingratiation toward a journalist significantly dampened the effect of negative earnings surprises on subsequent negative reporting by the journalist about the focal CEO's firm. It reduced negative references about the firm's performance, and it reduced negative statements about the firm's leadership or strategy. These effects were strong in magnitude: For example, an increase in ingratiation from the mean level that involved (1) complimenting the journalist about his or her work two more times since the announcement, and (2) expressing agreement with the journalist's view on a business issue one more time since the announcement, reduced the number of negative statements made by the journalist over the subsequent three-month period by 51 per cent. Journalists' reports can influence the perceptions of a wide array of corporate stakeholders, including customers, suppliers, and public policy makers (Tuchman, 1978; Deephouse, 2000; Fiss and Hirsch, 2005; Bednar, 2012; Wiersema and Zhang, 2013), and there is growing evidence that the tenor of media coverage can influence investor behavior (Pollock and Rindova, 2003; Johnson et al., 2005). Moreover, CEOs can focus their ingratiatory behavior on the most influential journalists, whose coverage influences other journalists, as well as firm stakeholders. Thus, CEO ingratiation toward journalists is efficient in multiple respects: It can be deployed selectively, requires few social or material resources, influences the valence of media coverage on multiple topics (e.g., firm performance, leadership, and strategy), and affects leader and firm reputation among a broad array of stakeholders.

While our research indicates that ingratiatory behavior by actors with lower status toward actors with higher status is generally effective (Westphal and Stern, 2006), it appears to be especially effective when initiated by high-status actors such as CEOs toward lower-status actors such as journalists. Compliments and expressions of agreement from a high-status source are more esteem enhancing (Vonk, 1998), and they are likely to be especially memorable. Whereas the reliability of most social influence measures declines after a year (i.e., if more than twelve months have elapsed since the time of the behavior being measured), one exception is the reliability of CEO ingratiation measures based on reports of the target (e.g., reports of journalists or fund managers about CEO compliments and expressions of agreement). Our interviews suggested that flattery by CEOs is highly memorable to journalists; they were able to quote or paraphrase CEO compliments that they received more than twelve months previously. By contrast, the reliability of CEO persuasion measures declines after a comparable time interval. Fund managers had more difficulty recalling the specifics of CEO persuasion attempts that occurred more than twelve months ago. Accordingly, the social influence benefits of CEO ingratiation toward information intermediaries and financial market actors also tend to be relatively long lasting.

Sophisticated Social Influence Behavior

While there are several advantages to ingratiation as a social influence tactic, and as a means of building social capital, there is also a seemingly fundamental limitation to ingratiation that has long been acknowledged in the social influence literature. In particular, flattery and opinion conformity is less effective if the influence target recognizes or interprets the communication as an insincere attempt to curry favor. Moreover, the influence target is most likely to make such an interpretation when the ingratiation would be especially valuable to the focal actor (e.g., after a negative earnings surprise, or if the journalist is relatively prominent or influential). This fundamental paradox facing social actors in exerting interpersonal influence is known as the "ingratiator's dilemma" (Jones and Pittman, 1982; Leary, 1995; Schlenker, 2003). Flattery and opinion conformity can still have some influence, even when interpreted as an attempt to curry favor, because it affirms the power or status of the influence target (Jones, 1964; Park et al., 2011). However, most people have a negative view of ingratiation and impute negative attributes to those who ingratiate. Individuals who are perceived to ingratiate themselves are more likely to be seen as self-interested and untrustworthy. Thus, when flattery and opinion conformity is interpreted as ingratiation, it is less likely to trigger similarity attraction or liking, and should therefore engender less interpersonal influence. Yet, while some experimental evidence suggests that ingratiation is less effective when it is most needed (Jones and Pittman, 1982), consistent with the ingratiator's dilemma, our research on social influence in corporate leadership suggests that, on average, ingratiation remains highly effective under such conditions. This raises an interesting and important theoretical and practical question: How is it that many corporate leaders are able to circumvent the ingratiator's dilemma?

Our theory and research has identified two factors that help explain how corporate leaders resolve the ingratiator's dilemma. The first factor relates to the types of social influence behavior employed by many corporate leaders, and the second relates to the cognitive tendencies of corporate leaders. We discuss the first factor here, and the second factor in Chapter 9 in our discussion of self-regulated cognition.

One effective "solution" to the ingratiator's dilemma is to engage in relatively subtle and sophisticated forms of flattery and opinion conformity that are unlikely to be interpreted by the influence target as attempts to curry favor. We conducted extensive interviews with corporate leaders to identify the various ways that top managers and directors engage in social influence, including more and less effective approaches (see Stern and Westphal, 2010). These interviews revealed seven forms of sophisticated flattery and opinion conformity: (1) framing flattery as likely to make alter (i.e., the influence target) uncomfortable; (2) framing flattery as advice seeking; (3) arguing prior to conforming; (4) conforming to opinions expressed by alter to a third party; (5) complimenting alter to alter's friend; (6) engaging in value conformity prior to flattery or opinion conformity; and (7) referencing social affiliations held in common with alter prior to flattery or opinion conformity. The social psychological basis of each tactic, along with illustrative quotes from our interviews, is provided in Table 7.1. As described in the table, there are several, more fundamental themes or principles of social influence that underlie the effectiveness of multiple, sophisticated forms of ingratiation. First, multiple tactics frame flattery or opinion conformity in ways that implicitly disavow ingratiatory intent (e.g., tactics 1–3), and/or that contradict stereotypic conceptions of ingratiation or the type of person who ingratiates (all tactics, but especially 5 and 6). Second, multiple tactics bias the influence target's interpretation of flattery or opinion conformity by triggering similarity—attraction bias ex ante (tactics 6 and 7). And third, multiple tactics leverage social network ties to increase the apparent sincerity of flattery and opinion conformity. Tactic 5 (complimenting alter to alter's friend) involves "sending" flattering comments to alter indirectly through mutual, third-party ties, and tactic 4 involves

Table 7.1. Sophisticated forms of flattery and opinion conformity

Social influence tactic	Illustrative quotes from interviews with top managers and directors	Social psychological basis
1. Framing flattery as likely to make alter uncomfortable.	One manager noted that he commonly prefaces flattering remarks with such phrases as "I don't want to embarrass you but...," or "I know you won't want me to say this but...," or "You're going to hate me for saying this but..."	The focal actor subtly disavows ingratiatory intent, and portrays the influence target as modest, a subtle and indirect form of flattery.
2. Framing flattery as advice seeking.	"if I wanted someone else to know that I admire him, rather than saying 'I really admire you,' I would be more likely to ask him for advice: 'How were you able to pull off that strategy so successfully?' Something like that... the basic question is, how can I replicate your success?"	Frames flattery as an attempt to learn from alter rather as an attempt to curry favor. Posing a question that requires cognitive reflection distracts the influence target from critically assessing the stated motive of the ingratiator.
3. Arguing prior to conforming.	"if you keep saying 'yes boss I agree boss' it looks like sucking up. If you appear to challenge the boss a bit before yielding—'OK you've convinced me, good point'— the agreement seems more genuine."	The expression of agreement is more likely to be interpreted as a genuine affirmation of alter's opinion rather than as an attempt to curry favor. Because alter's opinion appears to stand up to critical scrutiny, opinion conformity is likely to be viewed as a stronger and more meaningful validation of alter's judgment, and powers of persuasion.
4. Conforming to opinions expressed by alter to a third party.	"if you just keep agreeing with the boss it might seem like you're sucking up... but if you find out the boss' opinion on a policy from talking to his friend and then later in talking to the boss you raise the same opinion... it would come across as more sincere."	The agreement is unlikely to be recognized as opinion conformity by alter. It is also especially likely to trigger similarity attraction bias, because the focal actor appears to generate the opinion autonomously, and should thus receive more credit for the opinion than if simply agreeing with alter.

5. Complimenting alter to alter's friend.	"word gets around... complimenting someone to his face is kind of obvious brown-nosing, or at least suspect. If you regularly say nice things about him to his friend though, he [the influence target] will almost always find out about it eventually, and it will mean a lot more when he does."Another manager noted, "a friend recently told me 'You know, he [a colleague] sure thinks highly of you'... it was nice to hear that frankly—it seemed sincere because [the colleague] was complimenting me to someone else."	Does not fit with the prevailing schema or stereotypic conception of ingratiation, which is direct, face-to-face flattery, so it is less likely to be interpreted as an attempt to curry favor.
6. Engaging in value conformity prior to flattery or opinion conformity.	"I've found that a good way to begin a discussion is to make some reference to something that's important to me personally and that I have reason to believe is important to the other person—sometimes it's my religious conviction, sometimes it's my commitment to environmental protection, sometimes it's my family... [when asked why:] they're more likely to trust whatever I say afterward."	Triggers similarity attraction bias: Expression of similar values induces positive affect and liking, which reduces the likelihood of cynical or otherwise negative interpretations of an actor's behavior. The stereotypic ingratiator is coldly calculating and chameleon-like, not someone committed to a higher cause, institution, or code of conduct.
7. Referencing social affiliations held in common with alter prior to flattery or opinion conformity.	"If I'm trying to influence someone I might start the conversation by mentioning a group or organization that I know we both belong to... [when asked what sort of group:] might be a political party, a religious organization... [when asked why:] I think it helps build trust so you can be more convincing."	Reduces the likelihood of cynical interpretations of subsequentflattery and opinion conformity by triggering in-group bias, as a kind of similarity attraction (positive affect, liking, and presumptive trust between in-group members). Given some uncertainty about their motives, people are prone to giving in-group members the benefit of the doubt (Kramer, 2001; Hewstone

Continued

Table 7.1. *Continued*

Social influence tactic	Illustrative quotes from interviews with top managers and directors	Social psychological basis
		et al., 2002). In-group bias is preconscious and occurs even when the basis for group categorization is trivial and not necessarily linked to underlying values or opinions.

Source: Quotes from Stern and Westphal (2010: 282–4)

using information *from* mutual ties to agree with alter without the appearance of conformity.

Our analyses indicate that the use of these sophisticated tactics are especially likely to engender interpersonal influence in corporate leadership. *Flattery* by a top manager toward the CEO had a more positive influence on the likelihood of gaining a board appointment where the CEO served on the board-nominating committee to the extent that the focal manager (1) frames flattery as likely to make the CEO uncomfortable, (2) frames flattery as advice seeking, (3) compliments the CEO to the CEO's friend, (4) engages in value conformity prior to flattery; and/or (5) references social affiliations held in common with the CEO prior to flattery. *Opinion conformity* by a top manager toward the CEO had a more positive influence on board appointments where the CEO served on the nominating committee to the extent that the focal manager (1) conforms to opinions expressed by the CEO to a third party, (2) engages in value conformity prior to opinion conformity; or (3) references social affiliations held in common with the CEO prior to opinion conformity. We obtained similar results for a large sample of outside directors. In particular, outside directors who engaged in flattery and opinion conformity toward fellow board members were also more likely to gain board appointments where the colleague serves on the nominating committee to the extent that they employed these sophisticated interpersonal influence tactics.

Our survey data indicate that these sophisticated tactics are as common in relations between corporate officers and influential journalists, or in relations between officers and powerful ("pressure-resistant") institutional fund managers, as they are in relations between top managers and CEOs. Taken together, our theoretical arguments, data, and empirical analyses suggest that the use of relatively subtle and sophisticated forms of interpersonal influence is one way corporate leaders resolve the ingratiator's dilemma to gain influence with information intermediaries and powerful investors.

Sophisticated ingratiation is effective in part because it creates a separation of appearances and reality at the level of dyadic social interaction. The various sophisticated tactics that we have described effectively disguise ingratiatory intent, either behind the façade of a substantive, normatively acceptable interaction (e.g., framing flattery as advice seeking, or arguing prior to conforming), or by biasing the target's interpretation of the flattery and opinion conformity (e.g., prefacing flattery with value conformity, or referencing social affiliations held in common). As discussed above, successful ingratiation toward information intermediaries and investors amplifies the effectiveness of firm-level symbolic management, by reducing the inclination of these external parties to validate policy implementation, or to verify the rhetoric of IM. In effect, successful ingratiation reinforces the tendency toward ceremonial inspection, and the "logic of confidence and good faith" among organizational stakeholders, which undergirds the success of symbolic action (Meyer and Rowan, 1977: 357). Thus, to the extent that sophisticated ingratiation involves a kind of decoupling, or separation of appearances and reality in social interaction, our theory suggests how decoupling at dyad level contributes to the success of symbolic management at the firm level.

The Determinants of Sophisticated Ingratiation

The effectiveness of these tactics raises the question of who among corporate leaders is most capable of engaging in sophisticated ingratiation. Our research suggests that the vocational and socio-economic backgrounds of corporate leaders strongly predict the use of these sophisticated tactics. Top managers and directors with a background in sales, marketing, politics, or law are much more likely to use these tactics than managers and directors with a background in finance, accounting, or engineering. Qualitative evidence from our interviews corroborated the results of our large-sample regression analyses. Managers and directors with backgrounds in finance, accounting, or engineering often had difficulty answering an open-ended question that prodded them to consider more or less effective ways to flatter someone. For example, one director with an accounting background replied, "I'm not sure what you mean. I would just tell them 'you're the greatest.' What other way is there?" When asked for specific examples of bad ingratiation, ten of twelve managers and directors with backgrounds in sales, politics, or law provided at least one example (most provided a number of examples), and 82 per cent of the examples involved behavior by someone with a background in accounting, finance, or engineering. Again, most interviewees with a background in accounting, finance, or engineering had difficulty answering this question. One director with a background in engineering replied, "I'm not sure I follow you... I didn't know there was good or bad ingratiation. I guess it's all bad, or maybe it's all good. I don't know."

Another strong predictor of sophisticated ingratiation was socio-economic background. In particular, a common measure of upper-class background—whether the individual is listed in the Social Register or attended an exclusive preparatory ("prep") school—was strongly related to the frequency with which managers and directors engaged in six of the eight sophisticated forms of ingratiation, and it was also strongly related to a meta factor for sophisticated ingratiation derived from second-order factor analysis of the survey measures of all eight tactics. There is extensive qualitative and descriptive research in sociology validating this measure as an indicator of upper-class status (Baltzell, 1958; Levine, 1980; Useem, 1984; Palmer and Barber, 2001; Domhoff, 2002). Our survey also included a question about class background that promoted respondents to indicate whether they considered themselves to have a middle- or working-class background (with upper class as the omitted category), and this measure was strongly related to the second-order factor for sophisticated ingratiation. Separate analyses showed that the survey indicator of working-class background interacted with flattery and opinion conformity to *reduce* the likelihood of gaining a board appointment where the influence target (i.e., the CEO or fellow director) served on the board-nominating committee.

A distinctive characteristic of upper-class society is a cultural preference for subtlety in interpersonal communication and a distaste for blunt or especially direct forms of discourse (Baltzell, 1958; Burt, 1963; Jaher, 1982; Birmingham, 1987). Elites signal their upper-class status by displaying a subtle or refined interpersonal manner; a blunt manner of speaking betrays one's working-class origins. Subtlety in upper-class society, as in common parlance, is characterized by "non-obviousness," "refinement," and "skillfulness" in communication (*Webster's Unabridged Dictionary*, 1996: 1898). It may also involve interpersonal behavior that "operates insidiously," in the sense that the motive or purpose of the interaction is disguised (Baltzell, 1958; Jaher, 1982; Quinn, 1996; Wharton, 1996). The different forms of sophisticated flattery and opinion conformity described above are characterized by subtlety in each of these senses of the word. As one manager put it, "where I come from [an upper-class family in Boston] if you want someone to know you like them you wouldn't just come out and say 'I really like you,' that would be considered boorish or crude... unrefined. You'd find a more subtle, less obvious way to communicate that feeling" (Stern and Westphal, 2010: 289). Upper-class society has been described as a "powerful learning environment" that inculcates strong norms of interpersonal behavior through "an intricate web of exclusive associations" (Baltzell, 1958: 49; Domhoff, 2002). Thus, having been socialized from birth into a subculture that favors subtle forms of interpersonal behavior, corporate managers and directors with an upper-class background are more likely to have acquired a sophisticated style of flattery and opinion conformity through social learning.

Given that ingratiation is a primary interpersonal means of building social capital, which in turn amplifies the benefits of leaders' IM activity as discussed above, individual corporate leaders who are capable of engaging in sophisticated forms of ingratiation should be especially effective in managing the impressions of journalists, institutional investors, and firm stakeholders. Our research begins to address the question of which characteristics of corporate leaders make them effective symbolic managers. While decades of research in the upper echelon literature has examined how the backgrounds of corporate leaders affect their strategic choices (Finkelstein et al., 2009), very little research has examined the influence of executives' backgrounds on their social and interpersonal influence behavior, including their IM behavior. In effect, top management research has focused on how executive characteristics explain the substance of strategic decision making, and devoted little attention to how leader attributes explain the symbolic management of strategy. Our research suggests that firm leaders who have privileged socio-economic backgrounds, and/or vocational backgrounds in sales, marketing, politics, or law, tend to be relatively effective symbolic managers of governance and strategy.

The Side Effects of Ingratiation

Ingratiation, Self-Enhancement, and Strategic Persistence

While sophisticated social influence behavior by CEOs toward information intermediaries and other firm stakeholders can bolster the reputation of firms' leadership, strategy, and governance, research also suggests that ingratiation directed *at* CEOs can have adverse side effects on firm leadership and strategy. Park et al. (2011) suggested that CEOs who have acquired relatively high-status positions in the corporate elite tend to be an especially attractive target of ingratiation from other managers and directors, and that high levels of ingratiation toward the CEO can lead to biased strategic decision making. Leaders who have relatively high social status from elite affiliations and credentials, such as board appointments at prominent firms and non-profits, or degrees from prestigious schools (Finkelstein, 1992; Belliveau et al., 1996; Fiss, 2006), tend to exert disproportionate influence over decision making on a range of policy issues that affect interests of other top managers. They are more likely to be asked to recommend candidates for board and top management positions, as well as for prestigious positions outside the corporate sphere, and their recommendations tend to carry more weight in decision making (Allen, 1974; Useem, 1984; Gersh, 1987). High-status CEOs are also in a position to exert greater influence over the compensation of top managers and directors (Belliveau et al., 1996; Graffin et al., 2008). Thus, managers and directors can advance their professional interests in a variety of ways by engaging in flattery and opinion conformity toward CEOs who have relatively high status in the corporate elite.

Our analyses indicated that CEOs who have relatively high social status in the corporate elite, as indicated by measures of status such as elite education credentials or the number of board invitations that have been validated in prior research (D'Aveni, 1990; Finkelstein, 1992; Westphal and Khanna, 2003), do in fact receive higher levels of flattery and opinion conformity from top managers and outside directors at their firms, as well as from managers and directors at other firms. Further analyses showed that high-status CEOs also receive more flattery and opinion conformity from journalists and security analysts. More generally, our data and analyses indicated that when top managers are first appointed to the CEO position, they experience a tremendous increase in ingratiation from a variety of different actors inside and outside the organization, and the level of ingratiation continues to increase further if and when they rise to positions of higher status in the corporate elite. We suggest that when CEOs experience high levels of flattery and opinion conformity from a variety of different social actors, they become vulnerable to self-enhancement bias, or overconfidence in their strategic judgment and leadership capability. Research on the social psychology of persuasion indicates that most people rely on a consensus heuristic in processing persuasive messages, wherein they devote less critical scrutiny to messages that they have heard previously from different sources (Harkins and Petty, 1981; Chaiken and Stangor, 1987), especially when the message reflects well on the self (Weisbuch et al., 2003). When exposed to such messages, people engage in a biased search through memory for information that validates the message content, including similar statements made by other people (Sanitioso et al., 1990; Liberman and Chaiken, 2003). Jones (1964) suggested that flattery and opinion conformity is especially likely to be exaggerated when individuals are competing for the attention of a high-status actor, and our studies indicate that ingratiating managers and directors tend to exaggerate their opinions of CEOs' strategic judgment and leadership capability (Westphal and Stern, 2006; Stern and Westphal, 2010). For example, managers may overstate the extent to which they agree with the CEO's opinion on a strategic issue, or they may overstate their certainty about whether a firm's high performance can be attributed to the CEO's strategic judgment or leadership.

As a result, we should expect that high levels of flattery and opinion conformity directed at high-status CEOs will amplify the CEOs' self-enhancement or overconfidence in their strategic judgment and leadership capability. We tested this hypothesis with survey data from 451 CEOs and a large sample of potential ingratiators, i.e., outside directors at firms where a responding CEO served on the board, and top managers with whom a responding CEO reported having communicated during the prior year. We measured self-enhancement as the difference between CEOs' responses to a five-item scale about their strategic judgment and leadership capability (e.g., "How would you assess your strategic judgment compared to other CEOs of large U.S. companies? Well below average...somewhat below average...about average...somewhat above average...well above average...perhaps the best") and the average responses of potential ingratiators to a parallel set of questions (e.g., "How would you assess [the CEO's] strategic judgment compared to other CEOs of large U.S. companies? Well below average...somewhat below average...about average...somewhat above average...well above average...perhaps the best"). Our analyses showed that higher levels of flattery and opinion conformity directed at a CEO are strongly and positively associated with our survey measure of CEO self-enhancement.

Heightened self-enhancement resulting from high levels of flattery and opinion conformity can have a variety of adverse consequences for the CEO's strategic decision making. Structural equation models showed that high levels of CEO self-enhancement resulting from ingratiation reduced the likelihood and extent of strategic change following low firm performance, with strategic change measured both in terms of the pattern of business-level investments, and the level of corporate diversification (Park et al., 2011). Self-enhancement from ingratiation also reduced the CEO's propensity to solicit strategic advice from top managers at other firms in response to poor firm performance, which is also known to reduce the likelihood of needed strategic change (McDonald and Westphal, 2003). Moreover, additional analyses provided evidence that strategic persistence resulting from high levels of ingratiation directed at the CEO significantly contributed to further, subsequent declines in firm performance, which ultimately resulted in a higher likelihood of the CEO's dismissal. Taken together, these analyses suggested that ingratiation directed at high-status CEOs contributes to downward performance spirals. In an important study, Shi et al. (2019) provided evidence that chief financial officers tend to engage in a kind of preconscious mimicry of powerful CEOs referred to as "language style matching," and that this subtle form of ingratiation contributes to higher levels of merger and acquisition activity with lower announcement returns. This research extends our understanding of the sources, forms, and consequences of sophisticated ingratiation.

Ingratiation and Social Undermining

While ingratiation is a fundamental, interpersonal mechanism of building and repairing social capital, as discussed above, it may also damage the social capital of the influence target. Social capital includes goodwill and social support from an individual's social connections (Portes, 1998). While ingratiation elicits feelings of goodwill and social support from the influence target(s), it can also elicit negative affect toward the target, and social undermining behavior that damages the social capital of the target with third-party actors. In particular, we have argued that the act of ingratiation poses a threat to the ingratiator's self-regard, which elicits negative affect in the form of resentment toward the influence target (Keeves et al., 2017). Ingratiation threatens self-regard for three interrelated reasons. First, most people in Western cultures have a strong preference for authenticity and genuineness in themselves and in others (Sheldon et al., 1997; Cross et al., 2003; Heppner et al., 2008), and as noted above, ingratiation often entails some degree of disingenuousness or dissimulation. Second, ingratiation is an act of submission or deference that compromises the focal actor's interpersonal autonomy, and implicitly acknowledges dependence on a higher-status person. And third, ingratiation threatens positive self-regard by violating the meritocratic ideal that one should succeed on the basis of talent and hard work. We suggest that the tendency for ingratiation to threaten self-regard prompts feelings of resentment toward the influence target. Research on the self-serving attribution bias suggests that people tend to externalize blame for their own esteem-threatening behavior, including behavior that falls short of their ideals (Baumeister et al., 1996: 10). A salient object of blame for one's ingratiatory behavior is the recipient. Since most people respond positively to flattery and opinion conformity (Gordon, 1996; Vonk, 2002), the ingratiator can easily attribute his or her behavior to the preferences of the interlocutor, thus triggering resentment.

In fact, our empirical analyses confirmed a significant, positive relationship between the level of ingratiation by a top manager toward the CEO, as reported by the CEO or the top manager, and the manager's self-reported level of resentment toward the CEO. We also found that ingratiation by *other* top managers toward the CEO is associated with the focal manager's feelings of resentment toward the CEO. Resentment is enhanced by feelings of envy (Schoeck, 1969; Ferro, 2010), and since nearly everyone appears to appreciate flattery (Jones, 1964; Stevens and Kristof, 1995), top managers may feel envious of the CEO for the flattery he or she receives from other managers. Moreover, envy is amplified by self-enhancement bias, and most top managers believe their strategic judgment and leadership capabilities are better than average (Park et al., 2011). Thus, many top managers may feel that they deserve the flattery enjoyed by the CEO, exacerbating envious resentment. Separate analyses showed that ingratiation by other managers triggered higher levels of resentment among officers and inside directors than among lower-level top managers, which seems consistent with the view that envy amplifies resentment for flattery received by the CEO. Given their proximity to the CEO in the formal and status hierarchy, self-enhancing officers and inside directors are especially likely to feel "that should be me" when they observe flattery directed at the CEO.

Our analyses further indicated that feelings of resentment from ingratiation toward the CEO is associated with top managers' propensity to engage in negative commentary about the CEO's leadership in communicating with journalists. In particular, self-reported resentment mediated the effects of ingratiation by the focal manager and ingratiation by other managers toward the CEO on three different forms of negative commentary about the CEO's leadership: faint praise of the CEO's leadership; statements about other persons or firm characteristics that reflect negatively on the CEO's leadership (e.g., references to greater monitoring or control of the CEO by the board or other actors, implicitly in response to concerns about the CEO's leadership, or greater reliance on other managers, the board chair, or other directors in strategic decision making, implicitly in the absence of leadership by the CEO); and relatively direct, negative statements about the CEO's leadership. The emotion of resentment has a distinctive profile of negative thoughts, feelings, and action tendencies (Frijda, 1986). These include ruminations about ways in which the resented person might lose benefits that are envied, or perceived to be undeserved, and a kind of anticipatory schadenfreude, defined as pleasurable feelings at the thought of hard luck to the other person (Smith and Kim, 2007; Smith, 2013). The prospect of negative outcomes for a resented person has been shown to activate regions of the brain associated with "valuation," or "pleasure" in response to the negative outcomes, and "motivation (e.g., urges to inflict harm)" (Cikara et al., 2011: 307). In the context of firm leadership, it appears that feelings of resentment toward the CEO motivate interpersonal harm doing in the form of social undermining of the CEO in communications with journalists.

The magnitude of the effects of ingratiation on resentment, and the effects of resentment on social undermining, are quite strong. For example, an increase in compliments to the CEO by the focal manager of one standard deviation is associated with an average increase in resentment of between about 1.5 and 2 points on the five-point survey scale, depending on the item (e.g., from disagreeing with the statement "I can't help but feel some resentment toward [the CEO]," or neither agreeing nor disagreeing with the statement, to agreeing with the statement). Similarly, an increase in compliments to the CEO by other managers of one standard deviation is associated with an average increase in resentment of between about 1.7 and 2.1 points on the scale, depending on the item. Moreover, an increase in resentment from a 2 to a 4 on a five-point scale (i.e., from disagreeing with the statement "I can't help but feel some resentment toward [the CEO]" to agreeing with that statement) increases the likelihood that the focal manager will issue faint praise about the CEO's leadership in communicating with a journalist by about 98 per cent. The same increase in resentment increases the likelihood that the manager will make indirect or relatively direct negative statements about the CEO's leadership by 115 per cent and 93 per cent, respectively. In addition, these results understate the total effects on ingratiation at the level of the top management team. There is a kind of "social multiplier effect" of ingratiation on resentment and social undermining, in that ingratiation by an individual manager triggers resentment and undermining by that manager and other top managers on the team. Given that journalists are likely to be especially influenced by negative information about firm leaders that they receive from multiple sources, the overall effect on journalists' coverage of a CEO's leadership could be significant. In fact, separate analyses indicated a significant, total effect of ingratiation by top managers on negative commentary about a CEO's leadership that was attributed to a company insider in articles about the focal firm. Given that the CEO's reputation can have significant spillover effects on other aspects of corporate reputation (Love et al., 2017), and can influence stakeholder reactions to a variety of corporate policies, these side effects of ingratiation have adverse, firm-level implications.

Harnessing the Benefits and Mitigating the Side Effects of Dyadic Social Influence

Overall, while sophisticated social influence behavior by top managers is beneficial when directed externally at information intermediaries and firm constituents, it has significant, adverse side effects for strategic decision making, firm leadership, and reputation when directed at the CEO. This raises the question of how and when firm leaders are able to harness the benefits of sophisticated social influence behavior, while mitigating the side effects. We might expect that top managers who are capable of engaging in sophisticated social influence behavior, and who are cognizant of its potential benefits, might also be wary of becoming the target of sophisticated ingratiation. As discussed above, our analyses showed that top managers' vocational and socio-economic backgrounds predicted the sophistica-tion of their social influence behavior; managers with backgrounds in sales, marketing, politics, or law, and managers with an upper-class background were more sophisticated and effective ingratiators than top managers with other voca-tional or socio-economic backgrounds. Thus, we conducted separate analyses of our survey data that examined whether CEOs who had such backgrounds (1) discouraged flattery and opinion conformity from top managers, without discouraging social influence behavior directed at external parties, and/or (2) were less affected by the ingratiatory behavior of top managers. These analyses showed that CEOs with vocational backgrounds in sales, marketing, politics, and/ or law were significantly more likely than CEOs with backgrounds in finance, engineering, or accounting to report that they actively discouraged flattery from their top managers, or signaled that such behavior was unwanted, but they were more likely to encourage top managers to build relationships with journalists, security analysts, or other important firm stakeholders.

In addition, the positive relationship between flattery and opinion conformity directed at the CEO and our survey measure of CEO self-enhancement was significantly weaker for CEOs with backgrounds in sales, marketing, politics, and/or law. While most corporate leaders believe that they are unaffected by ingratiation, our survey data indicate that CEOs with a background in finance, accounting, or engineering are especially likely to agree or strongly agree that "flattery does not work on me." CEOs with these backgrounds not only tend to be less skilled at the art of social influence, but they tend to be less *aware* of the potential for sophisticated social influence. As a result, they are especially vulnerable to the adverse side effects of ingratiation. The relationship between ingratiation toward the CEO and negative commentary about the CEO's leadership in communicating with journalists was also weaker for CEOs with backgrounds in sales, marketing, politics, and/or law. Further analysis indicated that CEOs with these backgrounds are more likely to reciprocate the flattery that they receive from lower-level managers, and this appears to partially neutralize the effect of ingratiation on resentment.

CEOs with sales, marketing, politics, or law backgrounds are not only more sophisticated in their own social influence behavior, but they are more likely to enlist the participation of their team in external social influence, while mitigating the side effects of social influence behavior internally. Our analyses also indicated that CEOs with an upper-class background were *not* significantly more likely to discourage flattery from their top managers. Moreover, the positive relationship between ingratiation directed at the CEO and our measure of CEO self-enhancement was not significantly weaker for CEOs with a privileged background. Our survey data indicated that CEOs with backgrounds in sales, marketing, politics, or law were more likely to be cognizant of the benefits and dangers of sophisticated social influence behavior, and they were more likely to be strategic in deploying or discouraging sophisticated influence tactics, depending on the context. By comparison, CEOs with an upper-class background were less strategic, and more reflexive in their use of sophisticated social influence tactics, and they were less mindful of the potential side effects.

Reciprocity and Deterrence in Relations between Top Executives and Security Analysts

Our research indicates that, in addition to engaging in flattery and opinion conformity, top executives sometimes render personal and professional favors for security analysts who cover their firms (Westphal and Clement, 2008). For example, CEOs and chief financial officers sometimes help analysts acquire critical information about recent developments in an industry environment by putting them in contact with knowledgeable parties at buyer and supplier firms, or by personally disclosing valuable information gleaned from their industry contacts. Such information is often conveyed in private phone calls with individual analysts (see Soltes, 2014; Brown et al., 2015). They may also offer to meet or speak with an analyst's clients, since such contacts are highly valued by institutional investors, and reflect positively on the analyst (Brown et al., 2016). Top executives may also perform a range of personal favors for analysts, such as recommending them for job positions, helping them gain entry to an exclusive club, or giving them career advice. We found that top executives were especially likely to perform such favors for security analysts following the disclosure of relatively low corporate earnings or the announcement of diversifying corporate acquisitions. While favor rendering directed at powerful actors can lead to a wide range of beneficial outcomes, it is particularly effective in avoiding harmful actions (Cialdini, 2008). The norm of reciprocity dictates not only that people look for opportunities to help those who have benefitted them, but also that they should be especially motivated to avoid taking actions that would actually harm their benefactors, when given the opportunity to do so (Gouldner, 1960; Molm, 2003). Thus, an analyst who has received favors from an executive may be particularly averse to taking actions that would materially harm the executive's interests, such as downgrading the executive's firm.

In fact, our empirical analyses showed that analysts were significantly less likely to downgrade a firm following the disclosure of low corporate earnings or the announcement of a diversifying corporate acquisition, to the extent that executives of the firm rendered personal and professional favors for the analyst. The effects were particularly strong for the announcement of diversifying acquisitions. Such announcements were strongly associated with an increase in favor rendering, and favor rendering had a strong, moderating effect on the likelihood of downgrades following the announcement. For example, rendering two favors for an analyst after the announcement of a diversifying acquisition reduces the likelihood that the analyst will downgrade the firm by 65 per cent. In the absence of favor rendering, diversifying acquisitions tend to elicit a negative reaction from security analysts. Negative sentiment regarding diversification has been attributed to the predominance of an agency or shareholder-value conception of corporate strategy in the financial community (Zajac and Westphal, 2004; Zorn, 2004; Fligstein and Shin, 2007). According to the agency logic, diversification is an inefficient risk-reduction strategy that often fails to leverage a firm's core competencies; unrelated or diversifying acquisitions are often assumed to benefit executives more than shareholders, who can diversify firm-specific risk more efficiently through portfolio diversification. As the agency logic became well entrenched in the financial community, IM about diversifying acquisitions was no longer sufficient to avoid negative reactions from analysts. A stronger, more personal form of social influence was required. Our findings suggest that the norm of reciprocity can trump ideology in determining how analysts react to corporate strategies.

In addition, our research indicates that security analysts are influenced by negative reciprocity or retaliation by top executives. Our analyses provided evidence that executives sometimes retaliate against analysts who downgrade their firm's stock by limiting or cutting off personal communication with the analyst, making it more difficult for the analyst to obtain timely and relevant information about the firm (see also Chen and Matsumoto, 2006). Timely, personal access to top executives is valuable to analysts in generating insightful and accurate company reports, and enhances an analyst's stature with his or her clients (Kuperman, 2003; Mayew, 2008). Thus, the withdrawal of such access is costly and highly aversive to most analysts, and is therefore a meaningful form of punishment for issuing a downgrade. Experimental research on negative reciprocity indicates that most people evince a "punitive sentiment" in response to defection from social exchange relations (Carpenter and Matthews, 2004: 415). The inclination to punish defection may be stronger than the motivation to reciprocate helpful behavior (Fehr and Gächter, 2002).

Moreover, negative reciprocity can have deterrent value, as individuals cultivate a reputation for retaliating against non-cooperation by exchange partners (Ekeh, 1974; Axelrod, 1984; Friedman and Singh, 2004). The reputational benefit of negative reciprocity helps explain the evolutionary success of "tit for tat" as a strategy for social behavior (Axelrod, 1984; Fehr et al., 2002). Thus, in the context of executive–analyst relations, by cutting off personal access to an analyst who downgrades their firm, an executive may deter other analysts who witness the punishment or become aware of it through another means from downgrading the focal firm's stock in response to the disclosure of negative information about the firm. In fact, our analysis showed that analysts were less likely to downgrade a firm's stock in response to (1) relatively low corporate earnings, or (2) the announcement of a diversifying acquisition, to the extent that they were aware of another analyst's loss of favors or personal access to executives at the firm after issuing a downgrade (based on survey data from analysts).

In comparison to flattery and opinion conformity, favor rendering has a relatively strong influence on analyst behavior, but it is also resource-intensive, as it usually requires a significant investment of time, information, and/or social capital. As a result, top executives normally limit their use of favor rendering to relatively threatening circumstances, such as the disclosure of significant performance declines or relatively controversial corporate strategies. Negative reciprocity is naturally used much less frequently than ingratiation, and it has less influence on individual analyst behavior than favor rendering. However, it has a larger "total" effect on analyst behavior by deterring negative assessments by other analysts, and its effects appear to be very long lasting. Analysis of our survey data indicated that awareness of another analyst's loss of personal access to executives continued to influence analyst behavior for up to three years afterward. In that sense, negative reciprocity is a relatively efficient form of social influence. An advantage of sophisticated ingratiation over both favor rendering and negative reciprocity is its subtlety. Media disclosure of our findings and evidence of other, related studies, together with legal changes that discourage private communication between executives and analysts such as Regulation Fair Disclosure, may have inhibited some managers from engaging in favor rendering toward analysts. Our analyses of more recent survey data, while replicating the hypothesized results of Westphal and Clement (2008), showed a generally lower level of top executive favor rendering toward analysts, and a weaker—though still statistically significant—effect of negative earnings surprises on favor rendering (the other hypothesized effects were virtually unchanged). Our recent survey data have not shown a decline in sophisticated ingratiation by top managers toward external firm constituents.

Conclusion

While behavioral research has focused mainly on how social influence processes compromise internal corporate governance mechanisms (Aguilera et al., 2015), the micro-level social influence processes described in this chapter have powerful and robust effects on relations between firm leaders and external stakeholders. Aside from their direct effects on evaluations by financial market actors, they are likely to have important indirect effects on the behavior of other firm stakeholders that have not yet been demonstrated empirically. The social influence processes that we have described are largely invisible to non-financial stakeholders, including regulators and the general public. Complete information on these processes cannot be found in the text of conference calls or other public sources. The inconspicuous nature of these processes complements the more public forms of symbolic action described in Part I. While the adoption of policies and structures that conform to prevailing institutional logics of governance bolsters the legitimacy of individual firms and the larger governance system through overt symbolic action, the micro-level influence processes that we have described bolster legitimacy through largely covert means. By increasing the support of information intermediaries and pacifying institutional investors who are in a position to exert external control over firm governance, and doing so in a covert way, these social influence processes maintain the appearance of objective evaluation and control by financial market actors, while protecting managerial discretion over firm strategy and governance. In effect, they support the ceremonial inspection and evaluation (Meyer and Rowan, 1977) that make symbolic decoupling possible, and which preserve the dominance of corporate elites. They also derive symbolic value by leveraging generalized cultural norms in order to exercise social influence, especially the norm of reciprocity. Accordingly, the dyadic social influence processes that we have described are integral to symbolic management at multiple levels of the governance system.

8

Group-Level Social and Psychological Processes that Support Symbolic Management

In this chapter we examine group-level social and psychological processes that support symbolic management. Group-level processes are a longstanding lacuna in the corporate governance literature. Behavioral researchers have focused primarily on dyadic processes in CEO–board relationships and in relationships between firm leaders and external stakeholders (Finkelstein et al., 2009), and to a lesser extent social and cultural processes at the organization and field levels (Thornton and Ocasio, 1999). Examination of group-level factors has been limited primarily to research on board structure and composition. In this chapter we examine social and psychological *processes* at the group level that reinforce symbolic management. In particular, we describe how social distancing, a group-level form of social influence in which groups isolate individual members who deviate from group norms, can operate at multiple levels of the governance system: within boards of directors, in relations between firm leaders and information intermediaries (e.g., journalists), and within the professional community of information intermediaries. We then describe how pluralistic ignorance, a group-level social psychological bias, also occurs at multiple levels of the governance system. Pluralistic ignorance is a systematic tendency for group members to underestimate the extent to which their concerns about a policy or practice are shared by other group members. We explain how and why this group-level bias occurs in small groups within the firm, including top management teams and boards of directors, and among professional communities outside the firm, including sell-side security analysts. We go on to explain how social distancing and pluralistic ignorance contribute to the persistence of a wide range of suboptimal firm strategies, policies, and practices, including the various forms of symbolic decoupling described in Part I.

Symbolic Management: Governance, Strategy, and Institutions. James Westphal and Sun Hyun Park,
Oxford University Press (2020). © James Westphal and Sun Hyun Park.
DOI: 10.1093/oso/9780198792055.001.0001

Social Distancing as a Pervasive, Powerful, and Efficient Social Control Mechanism

Social Distancing on Boards

Social distancing is a powerful form of social control that operates at multiple levels within the corporate governance system. In Chapter 5, we described how social distancing among corporate directors helps to maintain CEOs' social influence over their boards. Social distancing is a subtle and informal kind of ostracism directed at individuals who deviate from group norms. It involves a set of social behaviors, or the withdrawal of behaviors, that serve to socially and psychologically isolate a deviant individual, such as not soliciting the input of the deviant in the course of group decision making, not inviting them to informal meetings, ignoring their comments in formal meetings, and exclusionary gossip, wherein group members talk about third parties with whom the deviant individual is unfamiliar, or gossip in ways that are difficult for the deviant to understand or participate (Bogardus, 1959; Barkow, 1974; Westphal and Khanna, 2003). Our more recent survey data indicate that social distancing also now involves exclusion from other important subgroup activities, such as collective IM of security analysts, or informal social activities (e.g., golf outings). As noted previously, Westphal and Khanna's (2003) analyses of large-sample survey data indicated that outside directors who violated prevailing norms of director conduct, for example by raising a criticism or concern about the CEO's strategy in a formal board meeting without clearing the issue with the CEO first, was strongly associated with social distancing from other members of the board. They also found that directors who participated in the adoption of corporate governance policies at other firms that were assumed to threaten managerial control were more likely to experience social distancing from directors on the focal board. Moreover, Westphal and Khanna showed that directors who experienced social distancing, or who were exposed directly or indirectly to the social distancing of deviant board members (i.e., directors who witnessed distancing or who had a board tie to a director who observed or experienced distancing), were less likely to participate subsequently in the adoption of governance policies that threatened managerial control. More generally, directors who experienced or witnessed social distancing, or who were exposed to information about distancing, were less likely to engage in behavior that violated norms of director conduct.

The effects of social distancing on subsequent participation in elite-threatening actions are also strong in magnitude. On average, a director who experiences an increase in social distancing on multiple dimensions (e.g., invited to fewer informal meetings, less input sought in formal board meetings, comments ignored in meetings, and so on) is less than 25 per cent as likely to participate subsequently in one or more governance policies that threaten managerial control (e.g., separation of the CEO and board chair positions or repeal of a takeover defense). Although the effects of witnessing social distancing or having board ties to instances of distancing are weaker in magnitude than actually experiencing distancing, they are still appreciable. As a result, the combined effects of experiencing or being exposed to social distancing on subsequent director behavior are extremely strong. They are also stronger in magnitude than several other factors that are believed by agency theorists to motivate or pressure directors to support governance reforms. Neither the level of ownership by institutional investors nor the level of director stock ownership is associated with director participation in governance reforms (Westphal and Khanna, 2003). The recent introduction of a shareholder resolution related to one or more of the specific reforms examined in our research also had no discernable effect on director participation in the reforms.

Further analysis indicated that social distancing is a provisional form of social control, in that it is typically lifted over time in response to "good" (i.e., normatively acceptable) behavior. Social distancing of a director in response to one or two instances of deviant conduct (e.g., raising a concern about the CEO's strategy in a board meeting without clearing the issue with the CEO first) is normally lifted within twelve months of the last violation. However, most boards appear to follow an implicit policy of "three strikes and you're out" in exercising social control of deviance; social distancing of a director in response to more than two instances of deviant conduct usually continued until the end of the study period, or until the director departed from the board.

Aside from deterring counter-normative behavior on boards, social distancing likely deters directors from "breaking ranks" and communicating with information intermediaries and other firm stakeholders in ways that might threaten managerial control. When a director whom we interviewed acknowledged that he would like to see widespread adoption of reforms that would make top executives more accountable to their boards and to various firm stakeholders, we asked whether he had expressed these opinions to members of the press. He responded, "certainly not, no opinion." When asked why not: "If I was quoted, officially or unofficially [i.e., in an article, or in communications by a journalist with another director] I would be ostracized, very probably. Professional suicide is a little strong, but it's not far off." We were unable to examine empirically whether exposure to social distancing reduces the likelihood of making statements to journalists that advocate or support corporate governance reform, because such statements were too rare to analyze.

By extension, social distancing among corporate leaders supports the persistence of symbolic decoupling. While the experienced corporate directors whom we have interviewed are well aware of the main forms of symbolic decoupling in governance and strategy identified in our research, they also consistently stated that they would be loath to acknowledge the potential for decoupling in communications with information intermediaries or other powerful stakeholders. For example, when we asked one director whether he would acknowledge to a reporter that firms might increase board independence to signal board control over management, but appoint directors who had ties to the CEO, or confirm such decoupling at a particular firm, he replied, "if word got out that [I said that] I would get treated differently [by other directors] . . . I would lose trust, I expect I'd get shut out to some degree." When asked whether he could simply take a position on another board, he replied, "I think word would get around. There would be no escape in terms of my reputation." The directors whom we interviewed perceived that there would be broad, reputational risks from disclosing the potential for decoupling in communicating with journalists or other information intermediaries.

Thus, social distancing is a powerful, norm-enforcement mechanism that deters corporate directors from engaging in communications with external parties that would threaten managerial control. It is also an efficient form of group-level influence. While other forms of social influence require the allocation of time and/ or resources, social distancing involves the *withdrawal* of interaction. Coleman (1990) characterized social distancing as an incremental social sanction, as the required contribution of each group member to social control is small, but the total effect on the sanctioned individual can be large, both socially and psychologically (also Goffman, 1963). Moreover, social distancing in the board setting creates social pressure on directors to participate, thus mitigating what Coleman called the second-order public goods problem of sanctioning. In addition, a single instance of social distancing can influence many corporate directors through direct and indirect exposure; as discussed above, while distancing has a very strong deterrent effect on the behavior of directors who experience it, it also has appreciable effects on the subsequent behavior of directors who witness it, or who are connected to it through board ties. Thus, the "total" effect of social distancing on the collective behavior of corporate directors dwarfs other forms of social influence, and considering the small contributions of time and other resources that are required of participating directors, the relative efficiency of distancing as a form of social control is even greater.

Social distancing is also an inconspicuous form of social influence. To the layperson, social influence connotes active behavior. One "exerts" or "exercises" social influence over another. Similarly, when managers, directors, and firm stakeholders are asked to consider how boards influence individual members, they typically describe active behaviors such as persuasion, cajoling, or pressure tactics. Social distancing is rarely mentioned or considered as a possible control mechanism. The inconspicuous nature of social distancing makes it especially powerful and insidious as a mechanism for enforcing social norms.

Social Distancing in Relations between Firm Leaders and Information Intermediaries

Social distancing also occurs in relations between firm leaders and information intermediaries, including journalists and security analysts. Social distancing in leader–constituent relations is unique among the forms of social influence we have described thus far, in that it involves collective behavior toward an individual constituent that can affect the behavior of that individual *and other constituents* toward leaders *as a group* (Shani and Westphal, 2016). Whereas corporate governance research has tended to focus on how social influence affects constituent behavior toward individual leaders or their firms (Westphal et al., 2012), social distancing can function as a group-to-group form of social influence behavior. Moreover, while scholars have focused on social ties among leaders as a basis for collective influence (Mizruchi, 2013), especially board interlock ties, and recently reciprocity (see Chapter 4), social distancing is based on multiple sources of social identification between corporate leaders. Our theory and research on social distancing suggests that a social psychological perspective on leader–constituent relations helps to explain a higher level of collective influence over information intermediaries than would be predicted by a traditional, sociological perspective.

In the context of relations between CEOs and journalists, social distancing is manifested as a lack of response from multiple CEOs to a journalist's requests for an interview or meeting (e.g., not returning the journalist's phone calls, or indications that the CEO is not available). In relations with security analysts, social distancing includes a reduced willingness by top executives of multiple firms to have private communications with an analyst after public earnings conference calls (see Brown et al. 2015 on the importance of these communications to analysts). We suggest that, due to the multiple potential bases of social identification among firm leaders, journalists who engage in negative coverage of firm leadership tend to experience social distancing from multiple CEOs, which in turn has a strong influence on the valence of journalists' subsequent reporting about firm leaders as a group.

Our theory suggests three bases of social identification that motivate social distancing: demographic similarity, social identification with the corporate elite, and friendship ties. Demographic similarity on salient dimensions such as functional background, race, gender, and age provides a basis for in-group categorization, and there is considerable evidence that people exaggerate their attitudinal and behavioral similarity to in-group members (Hewstone et al., 2002). Perceived similarity, in turn, increases positive affect and empathy toward in-group members (Penner et al., 2005; Stürmer et al., 2005). Therefore, corporate leaders are particularly likely to empathize with a CEO's negative affect toward journalists who have issued negative statements about the CEO's leadership and strategy, to the extent that they are similar on salient demographic characteristics. In-group categorization also leads to performance attribution bias, wherein people over-attribute the low performance of in-group members to extraneous factors over which they have little control (Crandall et al., 2007). Thus, corporate leaders are particularly likely to view a journalist's negative statements about a CEO's leadership and strategy as inaccurate and unfair to the extent that they are similar on salient attributes.

Such negative sentiments motivate corporate leaders to distance themselves from the journalist. Most people are preconsciously inclined to avoid interaction with persons for whom they feel negative affect, even when such interaction has professional benefits (Labianca and Brass, 2006). Relations between CEOs and journalists can be viewed as a social exchange relationship: CEOs provide credible information and commentary about firm practices and industry conditions, as well as industry contacts who can provide further information. In return, journalists are expected to provide good publicity, or coverage that is at least fair and accurate. If CEOs have concerns about the journalist's inclination to reciprocate in this way, they are less willing to invest in the social exchange relationship. As one CEO whom we interviewed stated, when asked how he would interact with a journalist whom he believed had provided inaccurate or unfair coverage of another firm:

> I wouldn't interact with him. If he calls me, it's to get my comments or use my contacts. Why would I give him that? I'd be afraid of getting quoted out of context, or getting quoted in a bad story that [annoys] someone else, or annoying my contact [to whom he referred the journalist] when he gets quoted out of context. I'll answer another journalist's call [whom] I can trust instead.
>
> (Shani and Westphal, 2016: 305)

Another social psychological connection between firm leaders that could provide the basis for social distancing is CEOs' social identification with the corporate elite. There is longstanding qualitative evidence and recent survey evidence that corporate executives implicitly recognize the corporate elite as a distinct social category (McDonald and Westphal, 2010; Useem, 1984). CEOs vary in the extent to which they socially identify with the corporate elite, and there is evidence that the level of such identification influences social behavior toward fellow CEOs. In particular, McDonald and Westphal (2010) showed that CEOs who identify more strongly with the corporate elite are more likely to provide strategic advice and information to other CEOs. We also suggest that social identification with the corporate elite may predict social distancing toward journalists who engage in negative coverage of fellow corporate leaders. CEOs who identify more strongly with the corporate elite should exhibit in-group biases about fellow corporate leaders, including external attributions for low firm performance, and they should be particularly likely to empathize with leaders who receive negative coverage of their leadership and strategy. Consequently, they should be especially likely to view negative statements about a fellow elite's leadership and strategy as inaccurate and unfair, and to feel negative affect for a journalist who issues such negative coverage. Our theoretical argument suggests that such negative sentiments should prompt CEOs to distance themselves from the offending journalist.

For similar reasons, CEOs should also be especially likely to distance themselves from journalists who engage in negative coverage about the leadership and strategy of another firm when the firm's CEO is a personal friend. Personal identification between friends is associated with performance attribution bias, empathic responding, and perspective taking (Heider, 1958; Fehr, 2004; Penner et al., 2005; Swart et al., 2011), which should increase the tendency to view negative coverage of a friend's leadership and strategy as unwarranted and unfair, leading to social distancing of the offending journalist.

The aggregate effects of these social and psychological connections between leaders on social distancing were quite strong in magnitude. For example, journalists who had issued at least one negative statement about firm leadership and strategy during the prior twelve months experienced social distancing from 5.8 CEOs on average during the subsequent twelve months, with distancing of a journalist by a CEO coded as 1 if the journalist disagreed or strongly disagreed that "over [the prior twelve months], [the CEO] has been willing to spend time with me." As an alternative, archival measure of distancing, we measured the number of times an individual CEO was quoted or cited by an individual journalist over the relevant time period. Our analyses showed that when journalists had issued at least one negative statement about firm leadership and strategy during the prior twelve months, on average their articles contained 81 per cent fewer quotations to CEOs during the following twelve months. Thus, it appears that journalists who engaged in negative coverage of firm leadership and strategy had substantially more difficulty obtaining quotations from CEOs for an extended period of time afterward.

Social Distancing and Subsequent Coverage

A growing body of social psychological research would suggest that social distancing may have a substantial influence on journalists' subsequent coverage. Several studies indicate that most people are preconsciously attuned to even subtle cues that others are avoiding or ignoring them (MacDonald and Leary, 2005; Wesselman et al., 2009). There is even evidence that people experience social distancing as a type of physical pain (DeWall and Richman, 2011), which MacDonald and Leary (2005: 202) describe as "social pain." Such a reaction is most likely when people detect a pattern of social distancing that spans multiple actors (Williams, 2007). The social pain induced by distancing is a source of "negative reinforcement" that exerts a strong, motivating pressure on the ostracized person to restore their social connections (MacDonald and Leary, 2005: 204). There is also evidence that social distancing makes the value of social ties more cognitively salient, and induces a cognitive and behavioral process called "affiliative social tuning" (Sinclair et al., 2005: 151), in which the ostracized person "form[s] attitudes and make[s] judgments that [conform] to the views of [valued] affiliates" (DeWall and Richman, 2011: 927), and becomes more "helpful, cooperative, and positive" about them (Williams, 2007: 435). Affiliative social tuning is also manifested as heightened "social caution," wherein the ostracized person becomes preoccupied with not offending those who can provide the informational and social benefits that are jeopardized by social distancing (MacDonald and Leary, 2005: 206).

The tendency toward affiliative social tuning in response to social distancing would suggest that journalists may respond to social distancing from CEOs by providing coverage that reflects more positively on firm leaders. In fact, our analyses showed that the higher the level of social distancing from CEOs experienced by a focal journalist, the fewer negative statements about firm leadership and strategy issued by the journalist over the subsequent twelve-month period, and the more positive such statements issued by the journalist over that period. The magnitude of these effects again suggests that social distancing is a powerful mechanism of social control. For example, an increase in distancing experienced by a focal journalist of one standard deviation from the mean reduced the number of negative statements about firm leadership and strategy over the subsequent twelve months by six on average, and it increased the number of positive statements by sixteen on average.

Moreover, further analysis of our survey data indicated that journalists who were *aware* of the social distancing experienced by *another* journalist engaged in more positive subsequent coverage of firm leadership and strategy. The effect of such awareness was weaker than the effect of actually experiencing social distancing, but it was still substantial. For example, on average a journalist who became aware of the social distancing experienced by another journalist during the previous twelve months issued three fewer negative statements about firm leadership and strategy over the subsequent twelve months, and seven more positive statements. Accordingly, the direct and indirect effects of social distancing on the valence of journalist coverage are very strong.

We also find evidence that social distancing "cascades" across communities. Our journalist surveys included a multi-item measure of distancing by a journalist's colleagues, which gauges whether colleagues take longer to return phone calls, texts, or emails, and are otherwise less willing to communicate with the journalist, or to provide the journalist with information. Social distancing of a journalist by

CEOs was significantly related to subsequent social distancing of the journalist by their colleagues. Moreover, the effects of social distancing by CEOs on a journalist's subsequent coverage of firm leadership and strategy were partially mediated by social distancing of the journalist by colleagues. That is, social distancing by CEOs had a positive, indirect effect on the valence of a focal journalist's subsequent reporting on firm leadership and strategy through social distancing by other journalists, as well as a strong, direct effect on the valence of coverage. Thus, social distancing cascades from the community of corporate leaders to the community of journalists, and this helps explain the power of distancing as a social control mechanism.

While it might be supposed that CEOs would be less likely to distance themselves from journalists who render negative coverage of competitors, each of our independent variables strongly predicted social distancing toward journalists who rendered such coverage. Moreover, these results held even for the subset of firms in relatively unconcentrated industries. The effects of different sources of social identification between CEOs fully neutralized the effects of competition on social distancing toward journalists who engaged in negative coverage of firm leadership and strategy.

One significant moderator of social distancing was journalists' career stage. In particular, our results indicated that journalists in the late phase of their career were least influenced by social distancing, while journalists in the middle stage of their career were most susceptible to its influence (i.e., in comparison to journalists in the early or late career stage). The results were consistent with our ex ante theoretical argument, which drew from the literature on professional careers to suggest that journalists' motivation to adhere to professional ideals changes over the course of their career. While the seasoned journalists whom we interviewed described the propensity to render positive coverage in order to retain access to high-status contacts as "playing the game," we expected that journalists would tend to derive some intrinsic satisfaction from adhering to the "ideal of journalistic objectivity" (Tuchman, 1978: 160; Schudson, 2003; Boudana, 2011) by resisting social pressure from CEOs to engage in more positive coverage of firm leadership and strategy in order to retain valuable contacts. We expected that journalists would tend to manifest heightened idealism and a reluctance to contradict the ideal of objectivity during the earliest phase of their career, then adopt a more pragmatic orientation during the middle or "advancement" stage, and then often manifest a "return to idealism" during the late career stage (Hall, 2002: 124). Most people exhibit a heightened concern for "solidarity with group ideals" in late adulthood (Erikson, 1994: 109; Sheldon and Kasser, 2001). As professionals near retirement, they increasingly engage in "projected cognitions," wherein they consider how they will feel about themselves and their actions when looking back on their career (Hall, 2002: 125). In addition, as journalists approach the end of their careers, the relative costs of adhering more closely to the ideal of objectivity also diminish. As one journalist told us, "losing a [top executive] contact without worrying too much about it... that's a luxury of being at a very senior stage of your career" (Shani and Westphal, 2016: 309). Thus, we expected that journalists would be more intrinsically motivated to adhere to the ideal of objectivity in journalism during the early and late stages of their careers, while perceiving fewer costs to such objectivity late in their careers. Supplemental analysis of our large-sample survey data from journalists provided relatively direct, corroborating evidence for our theoretical argument. Survey measures of personal satisfaction from reporting objectively about the role of firm leadership in performance and the perceived costs of engaging in negative coverage of firm leadership (and the instrumental benefits of engaging in positive coverage) significantly mediated the moderating effects of career stage on the relationship between social distancing and journalist coverage as predicted by our theory. Although social distancing is a weaker deterrent for journalists at the late career stage, it still reduces the influence of journalists who engage in negative coverage of firm leadership and strategy. As discussed above, social distancing of a journalist by CEOs is associated with distancing of the journalist by their colleagues, and a decline in the influence of the journalist's coverage on the reporting of their peers. In this sense, social distancing serves a kind of "sanitary function," which is characteristic of effective social control mechanisms (Gluckman, 1963: 48), in that it mitigates the social influence of deviant behavior on the larger professional community of journalists.

Social distancing can be described as a kind of bounded solidarity, which Portes (1998) suggests is an important form of social capital at the community level. Bounded solidarity does not involve unified actions among all members of the community on every issue, and it does not generally result from explicit coordination among actors. Instead, solidarity involves a shifting subset of leaders whose level of mutual involvement varies from case to case, depending on their social and psychological connections to the individual leaders who experience negative coverage. Moreover, it reflects a kind of structural equivalence among leaders, in the sense that CEOs who engage in distancing (1) share a connection to the leader who experienced negative coverage, (2) share a solicited tie from the journalist who rendered the negative coverage, and (3) jointly reject the solicited tie, but it does not result from coordination among leaders. Further, bounded solidarity in this context extends to information intermediaries, most of whom are complicit in the social control of deviant behavior.

Again social distancing is an inconspicuous form of influence in relations between leaders and information intermediaries, not only because it goes against the connotations of social influence behavior as active and assertive, but also because laypersons rarely consider the potential for second-order effects of influence behavior toward an individual (e.g., a journalist) on the behavior of other group members (e.g., the journalist's colleagues). Consequently, the potential for social distancing in leader–constituent relations is seldom considered, and if it is considered, its influence on constituents is underestimated.

Social distancing on boards and in relations between CEOs and information intermediaries supports the effectiveness of symbolic management, because it deters directors, journalists, and analysts from fully investigating and objectively evaluating and reporting on the quality of policy implementation. Accordingly, social distancing motivates a ceremonial form of monitoring and evaluation by boards and information intermediaries that helps to maintain the symbolic decoupling of governance policies, strategies, and strategic decision-making processes. Social distancing reduces the likelihood that these actors will become fully aware of decoupling, and to the extent that they do have concerns or reservations about the implementation of organizational policies or practices, they are less likely to raise them. Thus, by contributing to a ceremonial form of monitoring and evaluation by boards and information intermediaries, social distancing ultimately promotes decoupling between appearances and reality in the exercise of control at multiple levels of the governance system.

Pluralistic Ignorance at Different Levels of the Governance System

Another group-level, social, and psychological dynamic that supports symbolic management is pluralistic ignorance. Whereas social distancing is known to occur at different levels of analysis, pluralistic ignorance is a kind of social and psychological dysfunction that normally occurs *within* a small group or larger community. As defined in Chapter 2, pluralistic ignorance is "a situation in which [most] members of a group privately reject group norms, [policies or practices, or have concerns about them] but believe that virtually all other group members accept them" (Miller et al., 2000: 103). It has also been characterized as mismanaged or uncoordinated agreement, in that most group members share common concerns about the group's direction, but they fail to recognize that their concerns are shared, and thus fail to act on them (Miller and Nelson, 2002). Pluralistic ignorance is related to, but distinct from groupthink, which has received more theoretical and empirical attention in the group decision-making literature. Like groupthink, pluralistic ignorance is a group-level social psychological bias. Unlike groupthink, however, pluralistic ignorance involves an "attitude-behavior disjunction," in which groups or communities continue to follow or approve normative procedures, policies, or practices that most individual members have reservations about (Miller et al., 2000: 103). In groupthink, most group members become biased in favor of the group's strategy through social interaction, weak leadership, and the absence of outside input (Esser, 1998). In pluralistic ignorance, group members are not biased about the group's strategy, they are biased *about the beliefs of other group members* regarding the strategy. Thus, whereas groupthink is a bias about policy, pluralistic ignorance is a bias in social perception.

A key precursor to pluralistic ignorance is the hesitancy to voice minority opinions or to express concerns about policies or practices that are perceived to be supported by most group members. An extensive body of research in group decision making indicates that individuals tend to be evaluated more negatively after voicing a minority opinion on an important issue (Moscovici and Doise, 1994). Group members who express minority opinions may be categorized as out-group members by those who favor the majority position, resulting in a variety of out-group biases that compromise their social standing and influence in the group (Islam and Hewstone, 1993; Westphal and Milton, 2000). In the presence of such risks, individuals tend to look to the behavior of other group members for evidence that their opinion is shared before taking a public position on an important policy issue (Prentice and Miller, 1996; Bassili, 2003; Suls and Green, 2004). When they receive performance information that causes them to question the efficacy of a group policy or practice, group members will tend to hesitate in expressing concerns until at least some other group members voice similar concerns. At the group level, this behavioral tendency causes group members to systematically underestimate the extent to which their concerns are shared by others. Research by Miller and colleagues suggests that group members tend to perceive a lack of expressed concern about group norms or practices by others as agreement, even as they attribute their own reticence to socially induced inhibition. This kind of attribution bias appears to reflect a general lay dispositionalism in interpreting social behavior. That is, people tend to overattribute the behavior of others to internal beliefs and preferences, or approach motivation, while attributing their own behavior to situational constraints, or avoidance motivation (Miller and Nelson, 2002).

Pluralistic ignorance is also amplified in many contexts by a baseline tendency toward egocentric bias: Individuals tend to assume that they are more perceptive than most of their fellow group members, and therefore better able to discern problems with the group's policies and practices. Thus, systematic attribution and egocentric biases tend to produce a spiral of silence (Noelle-Neumann, 1993), in which group members who have private concerns about a group policy or practice assume from the silence of others that they are in the minority, inhibiting them from voicing their concerns, which makes others more reluctant to voice their concerns, and so on.

In the following section we describe how and when pluralist ignorance can occur in boards of directors and top management groups. We then extend the theory to consider how pluralistic ignorance occurs among information intermediaries. Finally, we discuss how these different forms of pluralistic ignorance combine to support the efficacy of symbolic management and the persistence of symbolic decoupling in corporate governance and strategy.

Pluralistic Ignorance in Boards and Top Management

Our theory and empirical research suggest that pluralistic ignorance is common on corporate boards of directors, and among outside directors in particular. While the perceived risk of expressing minority opinions is a nearly universal feature of group decision making (Moscovici and Doise, 1994), the risks of voicing minority opinions that challenge the preferences of powerful top executives are perceived to be especially high. These risks include the threat of social distancing from other board members, as discussed above, and negative referrals from other board members. If directors express concerns about the CEO's preferred strategy, or about the (non-)implementation of policies that would threaten top executives' interests (e.g., increases in the board's structural independence from management, or policies that increase executives' compensation risk), and most outside direct-ors do not share their concerns, they risk social exclusion from affairs of the board, and negative referrals from fellow directors that reduce their chances of securing board appointments and executive positions at other firms (Westphal and Khanna, 2003; Westphal and Stern, 2007).

Our interviews and surveys have revealed subtleties in how group decision-making processes can generate or sustain pluralistic ignorance. Directors may raise concerns about the CEO's preferred strategy, but frame them as others' concerns, or as concerns that could be raised by others (e.g., external stakeholders such as analysts, shareholders, or customers, or lower-level employees). In doing so, directors may appear to support the strategy personally, while still prompting a substantive discussion about how potential concerns about the strategy might be addressed. As one director put it, in describing a discussion about strategy in a board meeting several years earlier,

> [A fellow board member] came out with a criticism of the strategy, while still seeming to be on board with [the strategy]. The message seemed to be "there's this criticism [of the strategy] out there, we should find a way to defuse it." It led to a useful discussion and some refinements to how we executed [the strategy], and how we could explain it better to [stakeholders]. I only found out much later that [the fellow board member himself] had real problems with the strategy.

Another director told us,

> I've only rarely heard a director say "I have a major concern about our strategy," or something to that effect, in a board meeting. They'll often present themselves as the messenger for others [who have the concerns]. They won't take ownership, so the strategy might be tweaked, but it probably won't be fundamentally changed.

Thus, while board norms may allow directors to express concerns about top executives' preferred strategy, they seem to discourage directors from taking ownership of their concerns. As a result, boards can have meaningful discussions about how to improve the implementation of executives' strategies, or how to better articulate or explain their strategies, but directors' fundamental support for the strategy is typically taken for granted. Consequently, board-level discussions about strategy seldom reduce pluralistic ignorance, and may even exacerbate this group-level bias. In fact, our analyses revealed a small but positive and statistically significant correlation between the amount of time spent discussing corporate strategy in board meetings over the prior year (based on directors' estimates) and our measure of pluralistic ignorance (i.e., average the difference between directors' reported concerns about strategy and their perceptions of others' concerns).

An important moderator of pluralistic ignorance is the level of social cohesion among group members, especially cohesion that results from personal friendship ties. Such ties reduce the perceived risk of voicing a minority opinion. Personal friendship ties also increase the frequency of informal communication among group members outside of formal meetings. Thus, when group members are well connected to each other by friendship ties, they are not only less reluctant to express their concerns about group policies and practices, but they also have more opportunities to do so; friendship ties among group members facilitate the discovery of shared concerns. Conversely, sparse friendship ties among group members tends to increase pluralistic ignorance.

A related, moderating factor is the level of demographic homogeneity in the group. Similarity on salient demographic characteristics tends to increase inter-personal trust, and the openness of communication among group members (O'Reilly et al., 1989; Smith et al., 1994), and should therefore tend to reduce the misperceptions that underlie pluralistic ignorance. Demographic similarity on multiple, salient dimensions also tends to promote psychological projection: Group members are prone to assuming that colleagues who are very similar to them will share their reservations. Conversely, increases in demographic hetero-geneity tend to amplify this group-level bias, as preconscious biases cause indi-viduals to overestimate the differences between their own views and the beliefs of other group members (Hewstone et al., 2002). Moreover, demographic differences tend to be more noticeable and salient than similarities (Park and Westphal, 2013), such that increases in group heterogeneity on only one or two dimensions can more than offset the effects of similarity on multiple other dimensions.

These moderating factors would lead us to expect relatively high, average levels of pluralistic ignorance among outside directors on corporate boards. The average density of personal friendship ties among outside directors on corporate boards is relatively low (Westphal and Bednar, 2005), and has declined further over the past decade. Moreover, outside directors are part-time employees and most have extremely busy schedules (Jiraporn et al., 2009). As a result, the frequency of social interaction outside formal board meetings tends to be quite low, reducing opportunities for directors to discover shared concerns about strategy. Demographic heterogeneity has also increased across multiple dimensions since the early 2000s; outside directors of large and mid-sized firms have become more diverse with respect to their professional background, age, gender, and ethnicity (Westphal and Park, 2012; Zhu and Westphal, 2014). Westphal and Bednar (2005) showed a general tendency toward pluralistic ignorance among outside directors at mid-sized companies. After controlling for a variety of factors that could influence the level of directors' concern about corporate strategy, there was a statistically significant, positive difference between participating directors' reported concern about strategy and their perception that other board members were concerned about strategy, and this difference was especially large at companies with relatively low firm performance (i.e., below the firm's historical average and below the average performance of competitors (Greve, 1998; Arrfelt et al., 2013)).

There was also evidence that friendship ties and demographic differences moderated pluralistic ignorance as expected by our theory. The difference between directors' reported concern about strategy and directors' perception of others' concern became significantly more pronounced as the density of friendship ties among outside directors diminished. There was a similar moderating effect of demographic heterogeneity for three of the four characteristics that we examined (educational affiliation, gender, and functional background). There was also evidence that a survey measure which gauged the extent to which directors had recently expressed concern about strategy in board meetings was negatively related to the difference between directors' reported concern about strategy and their perception of others' concerns. These results provided relatively direct evidence for our theoretical argument that a key mechanism underlying pluralistic ignorance is the failure of directors to express their concerns about strategy.

Our survey data also indicated a significant difference on average between the level of concern about strategy among outside directors and the level of concern among inside directors, including the CEO. Again this difference was most pronounced at firms with relatively low performance. Inside directors at these firms rarely exhibit signs of pluralistic ignorance, but instead are much more likely to exhibit overconfidence in the firm's strategy (Park et al., 2011). Moreover, the very factors that reduce pluralistic ignorance on boards tend to increase overconfidence in strategy among inside directors. Personal friendship ties among the CEO and other corporate officers on the board increase the gap between outside directors' average level of concern about the current strategy and insiders' average level of concern. Similarity on some demographic characteristics, including organizational tenure and age, also tends to reduce the level of concern about strategy reported by insiders below the level of concern reported by outside directors. Demographic differences among inside directors with respect to gender and ethnicity also increased the alignment between the average level of concern about strategy reported by insiders and the average level of concern reported by outside directors. For example, among top management teams of low-performing firms in which the CEO or the chief financial officer was a woman or a racial minority, the level of concern about strategy reported by inside directors was significantly higher than in teams composed entirely of white males, and it was not significantly different from the level of concern reported by outside directors.

The perceptions of top managers at lower levels of the hierarchy, on the other hand, tend to resemble the perceptions of outside directors. On average, among top managers below the officer level, there was a statistically significant, positive difference between their reported concern about strategy and their perception that other top managers were concerned about strategy, and again this difference was especially large at companies with relatively low firm performance. As with outside directors, personal friendship ties and similarity on salient demographic dimensions among managers are negatively correlated with differences between their self-reported concerns about strategy and their perception of others' concerns.

Overall, the survey data suggest a common, social psychological profile for the leadership of relatively low-performing firms in our sample: pluralistic ignorance among outside directors and top managers below the officer level, and symptoms of groupthink among the inside directors. Stated differently, the social psychological profile of leadership in low-performing firms tends to exhibit a kind of core-periphery structure: There is often some degree of groupthink among the inner core of corporate officers, and pluralistic among lower-level executives and outside directors who tend to play a more peripheral role in strategic decision making. This tendency was only absent for a minority of low-performing firms with (1) a high density of friendship ties and high levels of demographic similarity among outside directors and top managers below the officer level, and (2) very few friendship ties and low levels of demographic similarity among inside directors.

The Interplay of Social Influence and Pluralistic Ignorance

As discussed above, pluralistic ignorance is underpinned by the perceived risk of expressing a minority point of view. Not surprisingly, our interviews and surveys indicate that senior top executives perceive significantly lower risks to outside directors and lower-level managers from expressing minority views on strategy and governance policies than managers and directors themselves perceive. Moreover, while the CEOs whom we have interviewed often claim that they encourage dissenting views, our director surveys indicate that a large majority of directors either disagree that their CEO encourages dissent, or agree that their CEO "does not necessarily want to hear dissenting views" or "views that challenge their preferred course of action [with regard to a strategy or policy issue]."

Our interviews and surveys also indicate that a common persuasion tactic among CEOs and other top executives in our samples involves characterizing the executive's preferred strategy as widely supported and/or influenced by communication with other firm stakeholders. To a greater degree than outside directors or lower-level managers, CEOs and a few other corporate officers (e.g., the chief financial officer) play a central role in the firm's informal communications with various stakeholder groups, affording them the unique opportunity to reference their communications with external stakeholders in making persuasive arguments about strategy to directors and lower-level managers. This tactic can be characterized as a kind of "social proof" (Rao et al., 2001; Cialdini, 2008) that is available only to the CEO and other top executives who play central and wide-ranging boundary-spanning roles. In fact, our research specifically indicates that CEOs and other top executives sometimes characterize their preferred strategy as supported or influenced by one stakeholder group in communicating with a second group, while also conveying that the strategy is supported by the second group in communicating with the first. Such tactics are akin to the symbolic management and decoupling of PSDM programs described in Chapter 3, but are more informal and routine in nature. They likely reflect some combination of self-serving biases and strategic intent. For example, as a retired chief financial officer from a Fortune 500 firm told us, in describing how the firm's CEO communicated with the board,

> When he was trying to build support for [a strategic option] with directors, he would make it sound like customers, analysts and others were pushing for it, or enthusiastic about it. But I know multiple times [when] he did the same thing with analysts...told them directors were on board [with his strategy]. Each group went along partly because they thought the other group was on board, if not pushing for it. [When asked why the CEO communicates in this way:] I think it's a little bit wishful thinking: there was some blurring between what [the CEO] thought the analysts *should* say and what they did say. And a little bit tactical...of course it's persuasive.

By highlighting and potentially exaggerating the support for a strategy among one stakeholder group in communicating with another, the CEO may reinforce pluralistic ignorance among both groups. As a result of such communications, outside directors may tend to underestimate the extent to which their reservations about the CEO's preferred strategy are shared, not only among fellow directors, but also among external constituents. Consequently, they may be particularly reluctant to express their concerns about the CEO's preferred strategy in board meetings.

While social influence behavior by the CEO and the threat of social distancing can reinforce pluralistic ignorance, there may also be pluralistic ignorance about social influence behavior on the board. In one of our recent surveys, 71 per cent of retired outside directors agreed or strongly agreed that "I have some misgivings about the way the CEO managed the board [at the firm where they served as director]," and 74 per cent of such directors agreed or strongly agreed that "other outside directors seemed unconcerned about the way the CEO managed the board [at that company]." Such pluralistic ignorance may help perpetuate suboptimal CEO–board relationships.

Firm-Level Consequences of Pluralistic Ignorance

Westphal and Bednar (2005) found that pluralistic ignorance among outside directors was a significant determinant of strategic inertia. Directors' concerns about corporate strategy were less likely to prompt subsequent strategic change to the extent that directors perceived that fellow board members did not share their concerns. This relationship was mediated by a reduced propensity for directors to voice their concerns about strategy in board meetings. These results held for multiple dimensions of strategic change, including change in product market diversification and geographic diversification.

Pluralistic ignorance among executives below the officer level is also negatively associated with the propensity for managers to express concern about corporate strategy in communications with the CEO or other corporate officers. Although research has not yet examined the influence of pluralistic ignorance among top managers on strategic decisions, it seems likely to impede strategic change in response to poor firm performance.

Our findings also indicate that pluralistic ignorance among outside directors is associated with the persistence of several forms of decoupling described in Part I. For example, among firms that adopted a stock repurchase plan within the past three years but have not yet made a repurchase under the plan, outside directors systematically underestimated the extent to which other responding directors shared their concerns about the firm's stock repurchase plan. This misperception reduced the tendency for outside directors to voice their concerns about the plan, which in turn reduced the likelihood of subsequent stock repurchases at the firm. We found analogous results for the persistence of decoupling of board independence from management. For example, among firms that increased the board's formal independence from management within the past two years while reducing the board's social independence (e.g., by adding outside directors who are friends of the CEO), and without increasing board control over management (as reported by directors themselves), outside directors systematically underestimated the extent to which other responding directors shared their concerns about the board's level of independence from management. Again, this misperception reduced the tendency for directors to express concerns about board independence or the board's role in strategy and policy, which reduced the likelihood of subsequent increases in multiple measures of board control.

Pluralistic ignorance in regards to board independence is an interesting case, because it often involves some level of hypocrisy: Directors may report concerns about the board's independence or lack of control over management, even though they appear to lack independence and fail to exercise control themselves. When asked about this in interviews, some directors acknowledged the contradiction, and others characterized themselves as exceptions to the rule. In either case, however, they tended to attribute their failure to voice concern about board independence to the lack of apparent concern among fellow directors. For example, one director who told us he was concerned about the independence of his board, even though he was a personal friend of the CEO, remarked:

> Yes it's a contradiction. I'm part of the problem, I realize that. I hope I still add value, just not in the way a truly independent director would. The problem is no one else is truly independent either—almost no one. But others aren't as concerned about it as I am.

Another director who expressed concern to us about his board's independence from management and its willingness to "stand up to the CEO," even though he was a personal friend of the CEO and had been characterized by other directors as consistently supportive of the CEO's initiatives, stated: "Actually I do think I take an independent view [of the CEO's initiatives]. Do I stand up to [the CEO]? Yeah I think so. Sometimes in subtle ways. Others seem to think they're independent enough, but that's not what I see." While the first director acknowledged his role in the board's lack of independence, the second viewed himself as the only independent director on the board. In effect, directors in the second category exhibit a kind of egocentric bias: They assume that while social ties to the CEO may compromise the independence of other directors, it does not affect their objectivity. This is a second-order bias, in that the director recognizes egocentric biases in others, but mistakenly believes that he is invulnerable to bias himself. As another director told us,

> You're correct that I'm friends with the CEO, but I'm still independent. Why? I think about it [i.e., the importance of being independent]. I work hard at it. I don't think my colleagues work as hard [at being independent]. They're good, they have a lot to contribute, but I don't think they're consciously trying to be objective like I am.

In general, our interviews suggest that many directors are aware of decoupling between appearances and reality on corporate boards, but fewer are aware of their role in decoupling. The decoupling persists in part due to pluralistic ignorance, a group-level bias that results from the social attribution biases and egocentric biases of the individual directors themselves.

Pluralistic Ignorance among Information Intermediaries

Pluralistic ignorance occurs not only in small groups such as top management teams and boards, but also in large groups and communities. In Schank's (1932) classic study of a neighborhood community in Pennsylvania, individuals expressed private concerns about social norms prohibiting drinking and gambling but presumed most of their neighbors supported them. In surveys of racial attitudes and preferences, O'Gorman and colleagues found that white survey respondents tended to systematically underestimate the degree to which other whites shared their reservations about segregation (O'Gorman, 1975; O'Gorman and Garry, 1976; Shelton and Richeson, 2005). We suggest that pluralistic ignorance can occur in organizational groups of various types and sizes, and it can occur in extra-organizational groups and communities, such as professions, stakeholder groups, and social movements. In fact, pluralistic ignorance can occur among members of virtually any salient social category. Our research has examined pluralistic ignorance among information intermediaries, including security analysts and journalists. Our findings from this stream of research ultimately suggest that pluralistic ignorance among information intermediaries can compromise external control of firm governance and strategy in ways that facilitate and perpetuate symbolic decoupling.

In one study we investigated the potential for pluralistic ignorance among security analysts in their reactions to a specific corporate policy, namely stock repurchase plans (Zhu and Westphal, 2011). As discussed in Chapter 2, our previous research indicated that many firms adopted stock repurchase plans in part to demonstrate their commitment to shareholder value, but failed to implement the plan (i.e., they did not make repurchases), providing an instance of symbolic decoupling. Moreover, we found that stock market reactions to repurchase plan adoptions became increasingly positive over time, even though the rate of decoupling increased in tandem. In a subsequent study, we examined whether pluralistic ignorance among security analysts may have contributed to the increasingly positive reactions to these plans, despite the increase in decoupling. Our theoretical arguments proceeded from the premise that analysts, like most critics, face some level of risk in rendering minority opinions. Evidence suggests that analysts who deviate from the consensus opinion with respect to their recommendations or forecasts tend to be evaluated especially negatively if their judgments prove to be inaccurate (Daniel et al., 1998; Zwiebel, 1995). Keynes (1936: 158) observed that in financial markets "it is better for reputation to fail conventionally than to succeed unconventionally" (also Zuckerman, 2000).

In the presence of such risks, as discussed above, individuals will tend to look to the behavior of others for an indication that their opinion is shared (Prentice and Miller, 1996; Westphal and Bednar, 2005). In this context, while accumulated evidence of decoupling may raise private concerns about the benefits of repurchase plans, in deciding how to react publicly to such plans analysts are likely to consider the recent reactions of other analysts to similar plans in order to discern whether their reservations are shared. In doing so, they will observe that fellow analysts generally reacted favorably to stock repurchase plans, despite evidence of decoupling. Such observations provide the basis for pluralistic ignorance, as attribution biases lead analysts to interpret public support of repurchase plans by fellow analysts as reflecting a prevailing belief or assumption that the plans have economic value. In fact, our analyses revealed a pronounced, systematic tendency for analysts to underestimate the extent to which fellow analysts shared their reservations about stock repurchase plans: After controlling for factors that could be associated with analysts' reservations about stock repurchase plans, there was a large, statistically significant (and positive) difference between analysts' own reservations about repurchase plans and their perception that other analysts have reservations about the plans. The average difference was nearly two points on a five-point, Likert-type scale. Pluralistic ignorance may be especially pronounced in this context, in part due to the material risks to analysts from rendering minority opinions about organizational policies and practices, as noted above. It may also be heightened by a generally low level of social cohesion within the community of security analysts, which reduces the frequency with which analysts discover shared concerns about a policy.

In fact, further analyses indicated that social network ties to other analysts tended to reduce pluralistic ignorance: Analysts were less likely to underestimate the extent to which others shared their reservations about repurchase plans to the extent that they had frequent communication ties to fellow analysts. These results extended the moderating effect of social network ties on pluralistic ignorance that we observed in corporate boards to a very different context (i.e., from a small decision-making group within the firm to a professional community). They also suggest that network connections have very different effects on symbolic management at different levels of the governance system. As discussed in Chapter 6, network connections between firm leaders such as friendship ties and board interlock ties between CEOs have been important factors in the diffusion of some forms of symbolic management. Moreover, Westphal et al. (1997) showed that inter-firm networks accelerated the legitimation of total quality management programs as a kind of symbolic action. Yet, social connections between outside directors and information intermediaries appear to dampen the symbolic value of some corporate policies. In effect, the social embeddedness of managers and practitioners facilitate symbolic management, while the social embeddedness of actors who occupy evaluative roles in the system serve to constrain symbolic action.

Nevertheless, our survey data indicated that there was still pluralistic ignorance among analysts who engaged in relatively frequent communication with other analysts, in part because even the best connected analysts have ties to only a small part of the analyst community, and in part because pluralistic ignorance extends across communities. For example, our surveys indicate that security analysts systematically underestimated the extent to which their concerns about the value of repurchase plans were shared by outside directors. As discussed above, CEOs and other corporate officers appear to fuel such misperceptions by some-times exaggerating the level of support for their policies among outside directors when they communicate with security analysts. In effect, symbolic management contributes to pluralistic ignorance at the system level, as actors who occupy one role in the system (information intermediary) underestimate the extent to which actors in a different role (outside director) share their concerns about a particular corporate policy.

As with pluralistic ignorance among board members, our evidence indicates that pluralistic ignorance among security analysts has a strong effect on decision making. We found an interaction between analysts' own reservations about repurchase plans and their perception of others' reservations, such that analysts were especially likely to issue more positive earnings forecasts and upgrade a firm's stock following a repurchase plan adoption despite their reservations about such plans to the extent that they believed other analysts did not share their concerns. Analyses also showed that the same independent variables underlying pluralistic ignorance.

Our surveys have provided evidence of pluralistic ignorance regarding other corporate policies as well. For example, among the security analysts surveyed in Westphal and Graebner's (2010) study, there was a systematic ten-dency for analysts to underestimate the extent to which fellow analysts shared their reservations about the value of (formal) board independence from management.

Further, survey evidence suggests that there may also be a core-periphery structure to beliefs about some corporate governance policies among information intermediaries, which parallels the core-periphery structure of beliefs among top managers described above. Our surveys indicated that security analysts who communicate with top executives most frequently (e.g., in private conversations outside conference calls (Brown et al., 2015)) tend to express significantly more confidence in the corporate governance practices of firms that they cover, in comparison to the majority of analysts who obtain information more from conference calls and other public sources. For example, among the security analysts surveyed in Westphal and Graebner's (2010) study who were in the top decile of dyadic communication with top executives (i.e., communication outside conference calls), 86 per cent agreed or strongly agreed that "for the most part boards of directors at [companies covered by the analyst] make valuable contributions to strategic decision making." Similarly, 84 per cent agreed or strongly agreed that "for the most part top executive incentives at [companies covered by the analyst] align the interests of executives with the interests of stakeholders."

As discussed in Chapter 2, analysts who have the most frequent dyadic communication with top executives naturally tend to have the highest status in their profession; they are more likely to have been selected as members of the "All-America Research Team" by *Institutional Investor* magazine, and they are more likely to work at the largest, most prestigious brokerage firms. This high-status minority of analysts exhibits bias about certain governance policies *and* they exhibit bias about the beliefs of fellow analysts. Whereas most analysts underestimated the extent to which fellow analysts shared their reservations about the value of (formal) board independence from management, it seems that a minority of high-status analysts exhibited a reverse kind of ignorance: They *over*estimated the extent to which their *confidence* in the value of board independence was shared by other analysts.

Moreover, this bias appears to have increased over time. Our 2016 survey indicated that pluralistic ignorance among security analysts about the value of (formal) board independence and the contributions of boards to strategic decision making had increased since 2003. On average, analysts expressed more private reservations about the value of board independence in 2016 than in 2003, and yet they also perceived more strongly that other analysts had few reservations about the value of board independence in the recent time period. The reverse form of ignorance exhibited by analysts who have the most private access to top executives was also greater on some dimensions in 2016 than in 2003. On average, analysts who were in the top decile of dyadic communication with top executives continued to express a generally high level of confidence in (1) the value of board independence, (2) the contributions of boards to strategic decision making, and (3) executive incentive alignment in the 2013 survey, and they continued to perceive that their confidence was shared by most other analysts. Since private reservations about boards increased over time among most of the analysts whom we surveyed, the tendency for analysts with the greatest private access to top executives to overestimate the extent to which their confidence in governance policies was shared by other analysts also increased for two of the three dimensions that we examined.

These data indicate that some learning did occur over time, but it was limited to the private beliefs about particular policies among analysts who lacked the highest levels of access to top management. There was no evidence that such learning occurred among analysts with the highest status, whose assessments should ironically suffer from the least information asymmetry. And critically, there was also no evidence of learning in analysts' *social* cognitions (i.e., their beliefs about the perceptions of other analysts), regardless of status.

Resolving Group-Level Biases

Given the pervasiveness of group-level biases such as pluralistic ignorance and groupthink, and their demonstrated impact on firm governance and strategy, it is important to consider how these biases might be prevented or mitigated. The dangers of groupthink are well known, if not fully understood, among firm leaders and educated stakeholders, as well as among psychologists and organizational scholars. There is an extensive scholarly and managerial literature on groupthink, some of which suggests prescriptions that may mitigate the risk of groupthink in certain contexts (for a review, see Esser, 1998; Camillus, 2008; O'Toole and Bennis, 2009). Most of these prescriptions involve decision-making aids or techniques that broaden input into the decision-making process, or reduce the perceived risk of voicing minority opinions, such as the nominal group technique, anonymous surveys, or various kinds of crowdsourcing. However, very little research has directly and systematically examined the effects of these techniques on symptoms of groupthink. Partly for this reason, such techniques are seldom used in strategic decision-making processes. Groupthink is a notoriously difficult bias to avoid or correct, in part because many managers believe or assume that they are invulnerable to its effects. Top managers in particular are motivated to believe that they are open to criticism of their strategies and proposals, and that they are capable of providing objective, critical feedback on the proposals of their colleagues. As a result, most top executives and top management teams are prone to underestimating the value of anonymous feedback and outside input on their strategies. There are also social barriers to revealing the symptoms of groupthink. While our surveys demonstrate a systematic tendency for outside directors of low-performing firms to report higher levels of concern about the firm's current strategy than inside directors, they also reveal a systematic reluctance among outside directors to express their concerns to top executives. This not only allows groupthink to persist, but may even amplify executives' overconfidence in the firm's strategy, as they interpret outside directors' silence as an implicit acceptance of the current strategy.

While groupthink is well known but difficult to correct, pluralistic ignorance is little known but potentially easier to avoid. Much like social distancing, pluralistic ignorance is a common but inconspicuous influence on decision making. Group-level biases such as pluralistic ignorance are typically difficult to detect, because they result from preconscious biases (e.g., social attribution biases), and they are often not apparent to any one individual in the group. Without outside intervention, pluralistic ignorance may only be discovered through informal communication that involves a large portion of group members. Most boards lack the requisite density of informal ties to reliably discover pluralistic ignorance. Moreover, outside observers such as consultants may not notice pluralistic ignorance, unless they are specifically looking for it. Whereas groupthink can reveal itself through the overly confident assessments of group members, or through an overly insular decision-making process, there are often no clear behavioral indicators of pluralistic ignorance. On the other hand, once pluralistic ignorance is detected, it may be easier to reduce. While most firm leaders are reluctant to accept that they are vulnerable to the egocentric biases that contribute to groupthink, pluralistic ignorance is less ego threatening, since it results only from misperceiving the concerns of others. Consequently, it may be possible for an outside party such as a consultant who is educated about the potential for pluralistic ignorance to reduce or avoid it, by making outside directors aware of their shared concerns about strategy or corporate governance, or by increasing awareness of pluralistic ignorance as a common phenomenon on corporate boards ex ante. Our research suggests that when outside directors discover that their concerns are shared, they are significantly more willing to express their concerns in board and committee meetings, and the expression of concern about the firm's corporate strategy by multiple outside directors is significantly associated with strategic change during a period of low firm performance (Westphal and Bednar, 2005). In the last iteration of our surveys for this project, we included a brief description of pluralistic ignorance in half of the questionnaires, which were randomly assigned to study participants. Our subsequent analyses showed that there was a significantly stronger relationship between (low) firm performance and multiple measures of subsequent change in corporate strategy for the subsample of firms that received information on pluralistic ignorance than for firms that did not receive this information.

However, the tendency for analysts with special access to top executives to overestimate the extent to which their confidence in policies such as (formal) board independence is shared by other analysts may be more difficult to correct. Reducing this bias requires that analysts acknowledge the possibility that they have been unduly influenced by their communication with top management. Our interviews would suggest that while lower-status analysts who have relatively limited access to top executives may acknowledge the potential for bias, analysts with the highest status are much more reluctant to accept this possibility. For example, when we described the potential for bias from communication with top management, an analyst from a smaller brokerage firm responded, "That doesn't surprise me. A small number of analysts get targeted for the biggest sell job. [Top executives] wouldn't do it if it didn't work." By contrast, an analyst with "All-America" status who was in the top decile of dyadic communication with top executives told us,

Influence is the wrong word. It's information, confidence from information. [When told that he overestimated the extent to which his confidence in the value of formal board independence was shared by other analysts:] I'm a little surprised but I guess I shouldn't be. I have more direct information [from top executives] than most other analysts have. They have less information, so they have more uncertainty. [When we described the pervasive decoupling between increases in formal board independence and actual board control over management:] I can see how this can happen in some industries, but I don't think in [the industry he covers].

The analyst had difficulty accepting the possibility that he had overestimated independent board control among the firms that he covered, especially those at which he had regular, private communication with top executives. He also seemed unprepared to accept that his perceptions of board independence and control were less accurate than those of analysts who had less private access to top executives. In general, our interviews suggested that analysts who occupied the highest status positions in their profession may be the most defensive about the potential for social influence and bias to affect their evaluations. Although these interviews are not necessarily representative, they are supported by evidence from the management decision-making literature that cognitive biases may be especially difficult to correct in populations of experts (Bazerman and Moore, 2013). Of course, it is possible that analysts who are informed about the potential for social influence and bias, while initially defensive, would nonetheless become more alert to this possibility in their future assessments. The potential to correct for the biases discussed in this chapter is clearly an important topic for future research.

Conclusion

In many ways, group-level social and psychological processes are the missing link in corporate governance research. Scholars have extensively examined social processes in dyadic relationships, including relations between CEOs and boards, and relations between firm leaders and external stakeholders, but they have devoted little attention to social and psychological processes at the group level, whether in small groups such as corporate boards, or in large groups and communities, such as communities of information intermediaries. We have explained how two key group-level processes—social distancing and pluralistic ignorance—operate at multiple levels of the governance system, and how they contribute to the persistence of firm strategies, policies, and practices that do not necessarily advance the interests of firm shareholders and other stakeholders, including different forms of symbolic decoupling. Social distancing and pluralistic ignorance play key roles in supporting symbolic management, because they reduce the propensity for directors, information intermediaries, and other stakeholders who are influenced by information intermediaries to raise questions and concerns about the quality of policy implementation. They perpetuate myth and ceremony in monitoring and evaluation by boards, analysts, journalists, and other external actors who are in a position to exercise control over firm leadership and governance. Their effects are strong in magnitude and broad in scope, as they contribute directly or indirectly to virtually all the forms of decoupling that we have described. They are also subtle and inconspicuous to firm stakeholders, and even to corporate leaders themselves. In general, institutional investors, regulators, and other firm stakeholders are well aware of how formal policies, structures, and procedures can compromise the effectiveness of corporate control mechanisms, and they are partially aware of how informal, dyadic processes such as reciprocity can compromise control, but they are largely unaware of how these group-level processes reinforce managerial control. Corporate leaders themselves lack awareness of these processes, or underestimate their influence, which allows them to speak with greater conviction about the independence and support of their boards and top management teams in communicating with external stakeholders. Raising awareness of these group-level processes among corporate stakeholders could substantially change prevailing perceptions about the adequacy of corporate control mechanisms, and increase pressures for new governance reforms.

9

The Social Psychological Dynamics of Symbolic Management

In previous chapters we examined dyad-level and group-level behavioral processes that support symbolic management in firm governance. In this chapter we examine processes of symbolic management at a more micro-level of analysis. Although our theory has considered psychological mechanisms that influence the behavior of managers, directors, and constituents, we have focused primarily on social beliefs (e.g., beliefs about colleagues and shared beliefs about strategy), and given less attention to individual-level cognitions (e.g., beliefs about the self). Moreover, our research has tended to examine change in social beliefs and behavior over relatively long and arbitrarily defined periods of time (e.g., change in ingratiation, advice seeking, or beliefs about strategy over the course of a year following the disclosure of poor firm performance). Our studies, like the larger literature on firm leadership, governance, and strategy, have devoted very little theoretical or empirical attention to the intertemporal dynamics of leader psychology or behavior. We know little about how the psychological states and behaviors of leaders may change over relatively short periods of time. In this chapter we begin to address these gaps in the literature by examining changes in the individual-level cognitions of executives and directors that occur before and after social interaction, and then consider how these micro-level, intertemporal dynamics may moderate the behavioral processes of symbolic management.

Self-Regulated Cognition and Interpersonal Influence

We begin by describing patterns of cognition that occur among executives and directors in anticipation of social interaction, and then examine how such cognitions moderate interpersonal influence processes discussed in previous chapters. In Chapter 7 we described a fundamental paradox facing social actors in exercising interpersonal influence known as the "ingratiator's dilemma," wherein the most attractive influence targets (e.g., high-status actors) are the most difficult to influence successfully, because they tend to be especially vigilant for flattery or other attempts to curry favor (Jones and Pittman, 1982; Leary, 1995; Schlenker, 2003). People are generally capable of discerning insincere or exaggerated flattery when they are alert to inconsistencies between verbal and non-verbal behavior

Symbolic Management: Governance, Strategy, and Institutions. James Westphal and Sun Hyun Park,
Oxford University Press (2020). © James Westphal and Sun Hyun Park.
DOI: 10.1093/oso/9780198792055.001.0001

(Jones, 1990), and when people express liking or admiration that exaggerates their inner feelings, those true feelings tend to leak through non-verbally (Ekman, 2001; Jones, 1990). Many non-verbal behaviors associated with specific emotions are hard to perform agentically, such that the overall constellation of behavior may appear unnatural to the observer (DePaulo et al., 2003; Ekman, 1993). For example, smiles may appear feigned or forced due to micro-facial expressions, gestures, or other body language that appears discrepant with positive affect. Because high-status actors are frequent targets of ingratiation, they are likely to be especially vigilant for such discrepancies.

We suggested that one "solution" to the ingratiator's dilemma is to engage in relatively sophisticated social influence behavior. In particular, we explained how some managers and directors engage in subtle and sophisticated forms of flattery that are unlikely to be interpreted by the influence target as attempts to curry favor. Although our theory offered a social psychological explanation for effective social influence, the focus of our theory was the psychology of the influence target. In this chapter we reveal a second way in which social actors can circumvent the ingratiator's dilemma by focusing on the psychology of the influence *agent*. In particular, we explain how self-regulated cognition in anticipation of social inter-action with a high-status person ("alter") can reduce the likelihood that expres-sions of liking, admiration, and respect will be interpreted cynically as attempts to curry favor. Our theory suggests that when people anticipate social interaction with a relatively high-status alter, they are prone to reflecting on personal and social characteristics that they share in common with alter, while avoiding thoughts about characteristics that they do *not* share (Westphal and Shani, 2016). For example, when a director with a background in finance anticipates meeting with a high-status colleague who has a background in marketing, but who also has prior management experience in the same industry, the director will be especially likely to reflect on his or her management experience, and that of their colleague, and especially unlikely to reflect on their functional backgrounds.

This pattern of cognition activates the well-known similarity-attraction prin-ciple in the service of social influence. People feel positive affect toward those with whom they share salient personal attributes, social affiliations, or group identities (Hogg and Terry, 2000; Montoya and Horton, 2004). They also tend to express more admiration for those who are similar on salient characteristics, as perceived similarity tends to promote internal attributions for successes (e.g., attributing career success to talent and hard work), and reduces the likelihood of external attributions (e.g., attributing success to luck, help, or special advantages). By extension, the salience or cognitive accessibility of shared personal and social attributes strongly moderates the effects of demographic similarity on positive affect and admiration (Pulakos and Wexley, 1983; Hogg and Terry, 2000). Among the strongest and most reliable findings in the social psychological literature is that when people are primed to consider personal or social attributes they hold in common with another person, they are more likely to report feelings of positive affect toward that person (Montoya and Horton, 2004). Thus, by reflecting on personal and social characteristics shared with a colleague, one increases the salience or cognitive accessibility of those attributes, which should amplify feelings of positive affect and respect or admiration toward the colleague in subsequent interaction. Psychological research on self-regulation suggests that people tend to regulate their cognitions prior to important tasks in a way that prepares them psychologically and emotionally for an effective performance. For example, on the day of an important exam, one might frame the exam as similar to tests that one has taken successfully before, to diminish anxiety and boost confidence (Fitzsimmons and Bargh, 2004). Such anticipatory cognitive reappraisal of the situation may be more effective in regulating emotion and increasing per-formance than suppressing emotions during the task itself (Sheppes et al., 2011). Anticipatory self-regulation involves storing useful information in one's working memory, where it becomes cognitively accessible during task performance (Baddeley, 1986; Fitzsimmons and Bargh, 2004).

Thus, when an individual reflects on characteristics shared with a colleague, and avoids thoughts about characteristics not shared, the shared attributes and the identities attached to them are stored in working memory and become more cognitively accessible during subsequent social interaction. As a result, the indi-vidual is primed to feel more positive affect and respect toward his or her colleague, which should be manifested in more sincere verbal and non-verbal expressions of liking and admiration during interaction. These relatively genuine communications should be more likely to elicit reciprocal attraction and a sense of psychological indebtedness, especially among high-status actors who tend to be vigilant for signs of ingratiation. In fact, our empirical research has provided systematic evidence that many corporate directors are prone to engaging in such self-regulated cognitions prior to meetings with high-status colleagues. Using longitudinal survey data in which 434 directors responded to surveys at regular intervals before and after meetings, we found (1) a positive interaction between anticipation of social interaction with another director (alter) and alter's relative status in the corporate elite on the extent to which the focal director reflects on personal and social characteristics held in common with alter, and (2) a negative interaction between anticipation of social interaction with alter and alter's relative status on the extent to which the director reflects on characteristics not shared. Relevant characteristics included aspects of the director's personal background, experience, group memberships and affiliations, and personality attributes, as well as professional characteristics such as functional background. Examples include perceived class background (e.g., perceiving that a colleague shares the focal manager's middle-class or working-class background), religious affiliation (e.g., perceiving that a colleague shares the focal manager's devotion to a particular faith), political party (perceiving the colleague as a fellow democrat or republican), perceived introversion versus extroversion, or sports fandom.

Further analysis indicated that directors were especially likely to engage in this pattern of reflection when they anticipated interaction with high-status colleagues who were relatively dissimilar from them across multiple demographic attributes. Our theory suggests that engaging in anticipatory, self-regulated cognition is especially important prior to interacting with dissimilar others, because otherwise demographic differences would impede genuine expressions of positive affect and respect.

Our analyses confirmed that reflecting on characteristics held in common with a fellow director, and avoiding thoughts about characteristics not shared, increases self-reported liking and admiration for the director. As shown in Figure 9.1, moreover, on average positive affect toward another director (alter) increases as social interaction with alter approaches, and then drops after interaction. The pattern is very similar for change in admiration over time. In addition, the pattern is particularly pronounced when alter is relatively high in status and demographically dissimilar from the focal director. Positive affect toward high-status colleagues who are demographically dissimilar tends to be lower than positive affect toward other colleagues when interaction is not anticipated, but just before interaction, positive affect toward high-status, dissimilar colleagues tends to be

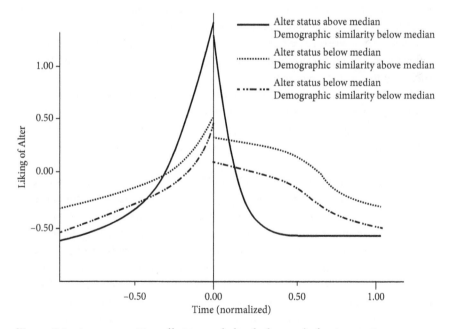

Figure 9.1. Average positive affect toward alter before and after interaction

higher than positive affect toward others. Thus, most of the time demographic dissimilarity is negatively associated with liking and admiration, consistent with standard theories of similarity attraction and intergroup bias. However, just prior to meetings with high-status persons, the effects are reversed: Dissimilarity is positively associated with liking and admiration, and our analyses suggest that the reversal is attributable to self-regulated cognition in anticipation of social interaction.

Our findings further showed that anticipatory self-regulated cognition is generally effective in inducing more genuine expressions of affect and respect for colleagues during interaction, which in turn increases interpersonal influence with high-status colleagues. Expressions of liking and admiration by a focal director (A) about another director (B) have a more positive effect on the likelihood that B would recommend A for a board appointment, to the extent that A reflects on attributes shared with B and does not reflect on attributes not shared, just prior to meeting with B. Moreover, the interactions between director cognition and flattery on board recommendations were significantly mediated by survey measures of perceived liking and admiration; that is, alter (B) was more likely to perceive that the focal director (A) likes and admires them to the extent that A engaged in self-regulated cognition prior to expressing liking and admiration for B. Again, these mediating effects were especially strong for relatively high-status, dissimilar alters.

The capacity for self-regulated cognition is likely acquired through a reinforcement learning process. Engaging in such cognition prior to social interaction results not only in more successful social influence behavior, but also in more enjoyable social interaction. There are both hedonic and instrumental rewards attached to anticipatory self-regulation, such that managers who have regular opportunities to interact with dissimilar, high-status persons should tend to learn such cognitive behavior over time.

The self-regulated cognition that we describe is related to Hochschild's (1983) notion of "deep acting," which entails indirect management of one's behavior by altering one's inner feelings or attitudes prior to a performance (also Grandey, 2003; Grandey et al., 2005). This research has examined how service workers such as flight attendants "psych themselves up" to feel socially approved emotions in the presence of customers (Hochschild, 1983: 33). Although these studies reveal a kind of anticipatory self-regulation, they have not addressed the fundamental cognitive processes that underlie deep acting. At the same time, while psychologists have identified cognitive reappraisal as a mechanism of self-regulation, they have not examined cognitive processes that prepare actors to engage in social interaction. Thus, research has not examined important forms of self-regulated *social* cognition, or cognitions about another individual that regulate one's feelings or attitudes about him or her. Our survey data from a large, representative sample of top managers and directors suggest that self-regulated social cognition is common among corporate leaders. The prevalence of such adaptive, cognitive tendencies among other populations is a promising topic for future research.

As shown in Figure 9.1, positive affect and admiration tend to return to their baseline levels fairly quickly after social interaction, especially for high-status alters. Further analysis of the survey data suggested that directors often engaged in self-regulated cognition shortly *after* meetings with high-status alters that involved reflecting on shared *and unshared* characteristics, and that such reflections partially mediated the decreases in liking and admiration that frequently occurred after social interaction. For dissimilar alters, such reflections were weighted toward unshared characteristics, resulting in larger drops in liking and admiration. In effect, while pre-meeting reflections were distorted toward shared characteristics, post-meeting reflections tended to represent the actual level of (dis)similarity between the focal director and alter. Although further research is needed on these psychological dynamics, the tendency to engage in cognitive reflections that more accurately represent the social attributes of high-status alters shortly after social interaction may function as a kind of "social reality check" that keeps directors from placing too much trust in their high-status colleagues. For example, if directors engaged in self-regulated cognition that resulted in more positive affect and admiration toward high-status colleagues on an ongoing basis, they might solicit more task-related help or career advice from those colleagues, or otherwise rely more on those colleagues than is warranted by their capabilities and expertise. They might also make less accurate predictions or assumptions about their colleagues' behavior; for example, they might underestimate their colleagues' potential to engage in political or unethical behavior. Moreover, in the absence of a "social reality check," managers may be prone to issuing overly positive or optimistic recommendations or referrals for positions at other firms or leadership roles within the firm, resulting in ill-advised appointments, and damaging the focal manager's reputation and social capital.

A realistic perspective on colleagues also motivates managers to actively maintain their interpersonal influence. Rather than counting on the ongoing support of dissimilar colleagues based on a single meeting, managers who remain cognizant of their differences from high-status colleagues are more likely to recognize the need for regular meetings with these colleagues in order to maintain their interpersonal influence over time. Our survey data indicate that a manager's propensity to engage in self-regulated social cognition not only amplifies the effect of flattery toward the interlocutor on positive affect toward the manager after a meeting, but also predicts the number of meetings scheduled by the manager with high-status, demographically dissimilar colleagues over extended periods of time. Thus, managers who engage in high levels of self-regulated cognition are not only more effective ingratiators, but they tend to arrange more opportunities to ingratiate their most important colleagues. Accordingly, the accumulated effects of self-regulated cognition on interpersonal influence are very strong.

We discussed these results in subsequent interviews with twenty-six managers and directors who participated in the original study, and most agreed with our interpretation. As one manager put it, "It makes sense that successful managers do this. It's a kind of people skill, and that's critical to advancing in corporate leadership, if not to surviving. You look on the bright side of your [colleagues] when you need to, and you look at them objectively the rest of the time."

None of these managers were conscious about their self-regulated cognition, and only four had noticed their tendency to engage in anticipatory self-regulation. Moreover, only one manager had noticed his tendency to engage in self-regulated cognition shortly after social interaction. These managers were also not conscious or aware of their tendency to engage in this pattern of cognition before or after interaction with demographically dissimilar colleagues. Interestingly, nearly all of these managers felt that they were likely above average in their tendency to engage in self-regulated cognition, and yet they were nearly uniform in expressing some level of cognitive dissonance about such behavior. All of the managers agreed that self-regulated cognition is adaptive in the workplace, or at least in corporate leadership, but they also generally viewed such behavior as unsavory and/or unsettling. When asked to what extent such behavior is "consistent with your self-concept," twenty-two of the twenty-six managers and directors replied that it was "somewhat" or "very inconsistent." The inconsistent self-perceptions that result from self-regulated cognition appear to conflict with managers' desire for authenticity in their social selves. Thus, the firm leaders whom we interviewed were fundamentally conflicted about self-regulated social cognition. We discuss the behavioral implications of such cognitive dissonance further below.

Our survey data also provided evidence that CEOs and other corporate officers engaged in self-regulated social cognition prior to anticipated interactions with outside directors. They were especially likely to reflect on characteristics held in common with an outside director prior to anticipated interaction, and less likely to reflect on characteristics not shared with the director, to the extent that the director had relatively high social status in the corporate elite and was dissimilar from the officer on multiple demographic dimensions. To the extent that self-regulated cognition resolves the ingratiator's dilemma and enhances interpersonal influence, it helps to explain the success of top executives at many companies in exerting social influence over outside directors, which in turn has contributed to the symbolic decoupling of executive incentive plans, structural board independence, and other corporate governance reforms described in Chapter 2.

Self-Regulated Cognition and Social Influence with External Stakeholders

In addition, our survey data included questions on self-regulated cognition before and after meetings with security analysts and representatives of institutional investors for a smaller sample of eighty-nine corporate officers. This sample was representative of all officers in the larger dataset, with respect to demographic characteristics (e.g., age, tenure in the organization, the level of prior management experience, and functional background) and employer characteristics (e.g., size and profitability of the focal firm). There was a general tendency for officers to engage in self-regulated cognition before and after meetings with security analysts who had been selected as members of the "All-America Research Team" by *Institutional Investor* magazine, considered to be an important source of status in the financial community (Hayward and Boeker, 1998; Hong et al., 2000), or who work at the largest, most prestigious brokerage firms (Clement and Tse, 2003). There was no evidence of self-regulated cognition before or after meetings with analysts from smaller firms who did not have All-America status. Demographic dissimilarity between officers and analysts was also associated with higher levels of self-regulated cognition. For example, prior to meetings, male officers engaged in more cognitive reflection about personal and social characteristics held in common with female versus male analysts.

We included our measures of self-regulated cognition prior to meetings in models of earnings forecasts and stock recommendations that also included measures of favor rendering, IM, and the full set of control variables from our previous analyses of leader–analyst relations, discussed in Chapters 2 and 7 (Westphal and Clement, 2008; Westphal and Graebner, 2010). We estimated these models for the subsample of firm-analyst dyads that included analysts who had All-America status and/or who work at the largest, most prestigious brokerage firms. Results indicated that self-regulated cognition interacted with measures of ingratiation (favor rendering, formal board independence, and verbal IM about board control remained strongly significant in these models) to predict more positive earnings forecasts and stock recommendations.

There was a similarly pronounced tendency for CEOs and chief financial officers to engage in self-regulated cognition prior to meetings with representatives of relatively powerful institutional investors. The level of ownership by institutional investors was a strong predictor of self-regulated cognition in models that included the full set of controls from Westphal and Bednar's (2008) study. Although it was not possible to examine the effects of self-regulated cognition on the particular strategic changes and corporate governance reforms examined by Westphal and Bednar, we did examine whether self-regulated cognition predicted the responses of institutional investors to survey questions that directly measured their level of satisfaction with firm leadership (e.g., "How satisfied are you with [the focal CEO's] strategic decision making?" (five-point scale: not at all... somewhat... very much so); "To what extent are you comfortable with the leadership of [the focal firm]?"). In models that included the full set of independent and control variables from Westphal and Bednar's analyses of corporate governance reforms, our measures of self-regulated cognition prior to meetings with representatives of institutional investors interacted with measures of ingratiatory behavior by CEOs and chief financial officers to increase the investors' reported level of satisfaction with firm leadership.

Who Engages in Self-Regulated Social Cognition?

Although our survey data revealed a general tendency toward self-regulated social cognition among the top managers and directors in our representative sample, there was variation among directors in their propensity to self-regulate. Our research indicates that the vocational and socio-economic backgrounds of firm leaders explains much of the variance in self-regulated cognition around social interaction. Most of the characteristics that predict the use of sophisticated ingratiation tactics described in Chapter 7 also predict self-regulated cognitions in anticipation of social interaction. In particular, top managers and directors with backgrounds in sales, marketing, or politics were more likely than managers and directors with backgrounds in finance, accounting, or engineering to engage in the pattern of cognitions described above when they anticipated social interaction with a high-status colleague (a legal background predicted the use of sophisticated forms of ingratiation, but was not associated with self-regulated cognition). Socio-economic background was also a significant predictor of self-regulated cognition. A traditional measure of upper-class background—whether the individual is listed in the Social Register or attended an exclusive preparatory ("prep") school—positively interacted with the anticipation of social interaction with alter to predict the degree to which an individual reflected on characteristics held in common with alter. This measure also *negatively* interacted with anticipation of social interaction to predict reflection on characteristics *not* shared with alter. A survey measure of class background yielded similar results: Managers and directors who perceived themselves to have a middle-class or working-class background were less likely to engage in this pattern of reflections prior to social interactions with colleagues. Moreover, further analysis of our survey data indicated that managers whose prior positions involved frequent interactions with demographically different and/or high-status colleagues were especially prone to engaging in self-regulated cognition, consistent with our suggestion that managers acquire this cognitive tendency through a reinforcement learning process.

In general, these background characteristics had an especially strong effect on the tendency to engage in self-regulated cognition shortly after interaction (i.e., the "social reality check" described above). As a result, managers and directors with an upper-class background, or a background in sales, marketing, or politics, exhibited a much steeper drop in positive affect and admiration following interaction with high-status, dissimilar alters. Managers and directors with a middle- or working-class background, or a background in finance, accounting, or engineering, were more likely to exhibit a persistent increase in positive affect and admiration for dissimilar alters following social interaction.

Moreover, further analysis of the survey data indicated that managers who had prior experience in sales positions that did not involve ongoing interactions with the same customers or the same individuals (e.g., "rainmaker" positions), were prone to engaging in self-regulated cognition prior to social interaction, but were significantly less likely to engage in self-regulation after interaction. This again supports the reinforcement learning explanation for self-regulated social cognition, in that managers whose prior positions did not place a premium on maintaining realistic perceptions of social influence targets appear less likely to learn to engage in such behavior after social interaction.

Further analyses also indicated that individuals with a background in sales, marketing, or politics exhibited a steeper increase in positive affect and admiration prior to interaction with high-status, dissimilar alters. Individuals with these backgrounds anticipate social interaction for a shorter period of time before meetings on average, and yet their self-regulated cognitions generate somewhat higher average levels of positive affect and admiration toward these alters. The affect and admiration curves for these individuals are more peaked around social interaction (i.e., compared to the solid line curve in Figure 9.1). These results appear to suggest that managers and directors with these backgrounds are both relatively efficient and effective at self-regulated social cognition. They require less time to prepare psychologically for social interaction, and yet their cognitive reflections have particularly strong, positive effects on their feelings toward alters. Accordingly, these individuals are especially "productive" self-regulators.

Given that self-regulated cognition augments the effect of interpersonal influence behavior on recommendations for prestigious appointments, we should expect that individuals who occupy high-status positions in corporate leadership tend to be relatively proficient self-regulators. In fact, corporate officers who hold positions at relatively large firms and who serve on multiple boards engage in higher levels of self-regulated social cognition prior to anticipated interaction with high-status, demographically dissimilar outside directors. Moreover, the affect and admiration curves for high-status officers tend to be more peaked around social interaction, suggesting that they are relatively efficient and effective at self-regulated social cognition. Just as our earlier research showed that ingratiation toward CEOs and other high-status leaders is among the strongest behavioral predictors of advancement in the corporate elite, this research indicates that proficiency at self-regulated cognition is a particularly strong psychological predictor of advancement to the most prominent positions in corporate leadership. In our models estimating recommendations for board appointments and other prestigious positions in corporate leadership, we have controlled for a variety of established survey measures that could plausibly influence advancement in corporate leadership, including self-monitoring, internal locus of control, tolerance for ambiguity, and cognitive complexity. Of these measures, only tolerance for ambiguity has consistently predicted measures of advancement, and its effects are much weaker in magnitude than the effects of self-regulated cognition (Westphal and Shani, 2016). Thus, while psychological characteristics such as cognitive complexity and tolerance for ambiguity may be important to the quality of strategic decision making by corporate leaders, the evidence thus far suggests that managers are selected for high-status leadership positions more on the basis of their psychological aptitude for engaging in effective interpersonal influence behavior. Such skill in self-regulated cognition not only results in more successful interpersonal influence behavior, but it also mitigates the side effects of self-regulation discussed further below.

The Side Effects and Benefits of Self-Regulated Cognition

Self-regulated cognition by firm leaders has a variety of side effects for the leaders themselves and their firms, some negative and some positive, that go well beyond the moderating effects on ingratiation. One side effect relates to strategic decision making. The literature on "ego depletion" has provided some evidence that the capacity for self-regulation is a limited resource, and that cognitive effort devoted to self-regulation can impair performance on other cognitive tasks (Baumeister et al., 1996). Although some have questioned the reliability and strength of empirical evidence for ego depletion (Carter and McCullough, 2014), there is at least sufficient evidence to suggest that self-regulated cognition can impair per-formance on cognitively demanding tasks that require focused attention and effort. Our surveys about self-regulated cognition also included a series of ques-tions about the extent to which managers and directors had recently reflected on strategic issues facing the firm (e.g., "Have you reflected on strategic challenges, vulnerabilities, and opportunities facing your firm (i) over the prior day; (ii) since [the prior survey]; (iii) since [meeting with a colleague]," "To what extent have you reflected on strategic challenges, vulnerabilities, and opportunities facing your firm (i) over the prior day; (ii) since [the prior survey]; (iii) since [meeting with a colleague]" (five-point scales: not at all ... to some extent ... a great deal)). Antici-pation of social interaction with a relatively high-status, demographically dissimi-lar colleague was negatively related to self-reported reflection on strategic challenges, vulnerabilities, or opportunities from the day before a scheduled meeting with the colleague to the time of the meeting. The results suggest that managers and directors tend to shift their focus of attention away from strategic issues and toward social relations prior to interacting with important colleagues.

On one level, this tradeoff between strategic reflection and self-regulated social cognition can be viewed as a hidden side effect of diversity. Interaction among colleagues who are dissimilar in social status and on salient demographic characteristics is cognitively taxing, and leaves less attention and information-processing capacity for other important tasks, including reflection on strategic issues. At the same time, self-regulated cognition is preferable to the absence of psychological preparation for social interaction in diverse groups, for a number of reasons. First, such cognition should tend to mitigate the side effects of social influence discussed in Chapter 7. We explained how ingratiation toward higher-status colleagues can trigger resentment, which increases the likelihood of social undermining behavior in communications with important third parties (e.g., journalists who cover the firm). Moreover, these side effects were especially pronounced for ingratiation toward dissimilar alters (e.g., flattery by white males toward female and racial minority CEOs). Self-regulated cognition prior to social interaction should tend to mitigate these effects of ingratiation. We argued that ingratiation triggers resentment in part because it threatens positive self-regard by violating one's preferred self-image as authentic and genuine in communicating with others. In effect, our research identified another dimension to the ingratiator's dilemma: Managers feel a need to ingratiate in order to realize their aspirations, but they compromise their desired self-identity in the process. Self-regulated social cognition partially resolves this dilemma by enabling one to express more genuine liking and admiration for high-status, dissimilar alters in the moment of communication. The focal actor is able to ingratiate more successfully without compromising his or her desired self-identity as an authentic communicator.

Self-Regulated Cognition and Burnout

Moreover, self-regulated cognition may also mitigate the broader side effects of interaction with high-status, demographically dissimilar colleagues, while enabling managers to capture the potential benefits of such interaction. Managers and directors who participated in the self-regulation study also responded to multi-item survey scales that measure feelings of burnout. Items in the scales were adapted from items in the Maslach Burnout Inventory (Maslach, 1982; Jackson et al., 1986; Schaufeli et al., 2002; Bria et al., 2014) and Farber's Burnout Scale (Farber, 1984).[1] Consistent with prior research, the survey items loaded onto two different factors, interpreted as energy depletion and cynicism, which are considered to be core components of burnout (Schaufeli et al., 2002; Bria et al., 2014).

---

[1] For example, survey items included the following five-point Likert-type scales: "I feel emotionally drained from my work"; "I have become less enthusiastic about my work"; "I have had time and energy for friends and family"; "I feel energized by my work"; "I accomplish many worthwhile things through my work."

We also conducted a second-order factor analysis, which indicated that the factor scores loaded onto a single, second-order factor.

We expected that the frequency of interaction with relatively high-status, demographically dissimilar colleagues would tend to promote feelings of burnout, which in turn would be negatively associated with discretionary behaviors that are known to enhance leader effectiveness. In particular, we hypothesized that feeling of burnout would reduce a top manager's propensity to (1) mentor lower-level managers, (2) provide encouragement to lower-level managers, (3) seek input from lower-level managers in making strategic decisions, and (4) seek information from lower-level managers about their progress on implementing corporate strategies (see McDonald and Westphal, 2011 for a discussion of how these behaviors contribute to leader effectiveness). Intergroup relations theory suggests that demographic differences on salient dimensions such as functional background, gender, and race provide a basis for in-group/out-group categorization, which reduces interpersonal liking, admiration, and trust (Tsui and O'Reilly, 1989; Kramer, 2001; Hewstone et al., 2002). Thus, regular interaction with higher-status colleagues who are demographically dissimilar has the potential to be energy depleting for many corporate managers. They feel impelled to convey liking and respect to ensure the support of powerful colleagues, which creates some level of dissonance with their actual sentiments. Moreover, reduced trust in dissimilar colleagues amplifies the perceived need to convey liking and respect, and creates some level of anxiety about the success of their interactions in ensuring their colleagues' support. Such cognitions and emotions are not only energy depleting, but may also trigger cynicism about collegial interaction.

Our analyses supported these conjectures. The results indicated that, controlling for the focal manager's status and demographic profile, the frequency of interaction with higher-status colleagues who are demographically dissimilar with respect to functional background, age, gender, and race is positively and significantly associated with reported feelings of burnout, including both energy depletion and cynicism. The effects were particularly strong for functional background, gender, and race, and they held for different demographic combinations (e.g., marketing managers interacting with higher-status finance managers and vice versa; men interacting with higher-status women and vice versa). Moreover, the frequency of flattery toward higher-status, dissimilar colleagues was strongly related to feelings of burnout, and this relationship was significantly mediated by a survey measure of felt authenticity.[2] That is, managers who engaged in flattery toward higher-status, dissimilar colleagues on a frequent basis reported

---

[2] The survey scale included several Likert-type items ("I feel like a real person at work"; "I feel in touch with myself at work"; "I can be myself at work" (five-point scale: strongly disagree...neither agree nor disagree...strongly agree)). Factor analysis indicated that these items loaded on the same construct with acceptable inter-item reliability.

feeling less authentic at work, which in turn was significantly associated with feelings of burnout (both energy depletion and cynicism).

At the same time, further analyses indicated that these effects were significantly moderated by self-regulated cognition. Although self-regulation is not a panacea (the effects of interaction with dissimilar colleagues on burnout were significant at average levels of self-regulated cognition), it nonetheless substantially dampened these important side effects. For example, an increase in self-regulated cognition of one standard deviation reduced the effect of interaction with higher-status, demographically dissimilar colleagues on symptoms of burnout by an average of 86 per cent. The moderating effects of self-regulated cognition on burnout were especially strong for individuals with a background in sales, marketing, or politics, consistent with the evidence cited above that managers and directors with these backgrounds are relatively efficient and effective self-regulators.

Self-regulated cognition also moderated the mediated relationship between flattery, reduced feelings of authenticity, and burnout. For the subset of managers who engaged in relatively high levels of self-regulated cognition (e.g., above the median level for the sample), the frequency of flattery toward higher-status, dissimilar colleagues was not significantly related to reduced feelings of authenticity. Interestingly, managers in relatively diverse top management teams who engage in high levels of self-regulated cognition reported lower levels of felt authenticity than managers in relatively homogenous teams who reported low levels of such cognition. As discussed above, the inconsistent self-perceptions that result from self-regulated cognition appear to reduce feelings of authenticity. When managers engage in self-regulated cognition on a regular basis in diverse groups, there will tend to be greater variance in salient dimensions of their self-identity, resulting in a somewhat less coherent sense of self. Yet, these negative direct effects appear to be more than offset by the moderating effects on flattery. In effect, managers are willing to trade some degree of consistency in their sense of self in order to remain true to *a* salient dimension of the self during social interactions. Thus, managers who engage in high levels of self-regulated cognition in diverse groups experience more satisfying and successful interactions with their colleagues, and this more than compensates for the psychological side effects that we have described.

Moreover, feelings of burnout were a strongly negative determinant of three discretionary leader behaviors that are associated with leader effectiveness: mentoring of lower-level managers, the provision of encouragement to lower-level managers, and seeking input from lower-level managers in making strategic decisions. Feelings of burnout were a weaker, though still statistically significant determinant of seeking information from lower-level managers about their progress on implementing corporate strategies. These models included the full set of independent variables from McDonald and Westphal's (2011) study of corporate leader effectiveness. In addition, feelings of burnout were a very strong predictor of subsequent turnover in models that controlled for a variety of factors that have been shown to predict voluntary or involuntary departure of top managers and directors, including multiple measures of firm performance, measures of manager/director power (Finkelstein, 1992), and interactions between performance and power. Moreover, the average level of self-regulated cognition was negatively associated with the rate of turnover, and this relationship was significantly mediated by feelings of burnout. The mediated relationship between self-regulated cognition, burnout, and turnover is especially strong for cases of turnover in which the manager or director disappears from the population of corporate leaders at large and mid-sized companies for at least three years after departing the firm.

Thus, self-regulated cognition not only enhances the effectiveness of social influence toward colleagues and important external stakeholders, but it increases the longevity of effective symbolic managers in their positions. Accordingly, the total, accumulated value of self-regulated cognition to the social influence of firm leaders is very substantial. Moreover, each of the discretionary leader behaviors described above is important to developing the leadership capabilities of top management teams. By exerting strong, indirect effects on several of these behaviors, while also increasing the duration of these effects (i.e., by reducing the rate of turnover), self-regulated cognition has important, secondary effects on firm leadership capabilities.

In addition, our survey data indicate that top executives who engage in relatively high levels of self-regulated cognition are especially likely to mentor subordinates and other top managers about communication with external stakeholders. Such communications are a critical function of top management (Mintzberg, 1983), and yet many managers have little if any direct experience with this role when first appointed to the top management team. Managers tend to learn about the norms of communication with external stakeholders, including IM, from their senior colleagues, and self-regulating executives devote disproportionate time to mentoring other managers about these external communications. Thus, self-regulated social cognition is critical to the success of symbolic management in corporate leadership. It is not only a critical enabler of successful social influence in dyadic communications with important external stakeholders, but it also promotes leader behaviors that help develop the communication capabilities of the larger top management team.

Self-Regulated Cognition and Conflict

Self-regulated cognition is likely to have a variety of other positive externalities for top management teams that should be examined further in future studies. One potentially important set of consequences relates to intragroup conflict. The upper echelon and organizational demography literatures have long suggested that the potential benefits of demographic diversity in top management teams, boards, and other work groups are often significantly constrained by interpersonal frictions or "relationship conflict" among group members (Jehn, 1995: 258; Hambrick et al., 1996; Pelled et al., 1999). Self-regulated social cognition may be a critical means of reducing such conflict. Our survey data indicate that executives who engage in relatively high levels of self-regulated cognition perceive less interpersonal conflict in their relationships with other top managers, and conversely that top managers perceive less conflict in their relationships with other managers who engage in relatively high levels of self-regulated cognition.

Moreover, there is suggestive evidence that the presence of top executives who engage in high levels of self-regulated cognition can reduce interpersonal conflict at the *group* level. Although we cannot yet develop precise measures of average self-regulated cognition for a large sample of top management teams, we have examined the relationship between self-regulated cognition by individual top managers and the perception of other responding executives at the same firm that their team has relatively high or low levels of relationship conflict and task conflict, using an adapted version of Jehn's (1995) intragroup conflict scale.[3] The small groups literature generally suggests that relationship conflict is negatively related to group effectiveness, and that task-based conflict is positively related to effectiveness, especially in groups that are engaged in relatively subjective and complex decision-making tasks (such as top management teams engaged in strategic decision making) (Hambrick et al., 1996; Pelled et al., 1999; Simons and Peterson, 2000). Moreover, the potential benefits of task conflict appear to be contingent on interpersonal trust among team members (Simons and Peterson, 2000; Dirks and Ferrin, 2001; De Dreu and Weingart, 2003). Our results indicate that the presence of at least one top management team member who engages in relatively high levels of self-regulated cognition (at least one standard deviation above the mean) significantly and negatively moderates the effects of demographic diversity on the level of relationship conflict in the team, as reported by other top managers (controlling for the self-regulated cognition of the responding manager). More specifically, while top management team diversity is positively related

---

[3] We adapted each of the survey items from Jehn's (1995) measure of intragroup conflict for top management teams. The adapted items for relationship conflict include the following: "How much friction is there among members in your top management team?"; "How much are personality conflicts evident in your top management team?"; "How much tension is there among members in your top management team?"; "How much emotional conflict is there among members in your top management team?" The adapted items for task conflict include: "How often do individuals in your top management team disagree about issues under discussion?"; "How frequently are there conflicts about ideas in your top management team?"; "How much conflict about strategic issues is there in your top management team?"; "To what extent are there differences of opinion in your top management team?" Factor analysis indicated that these items loaded onto two different factors as expected, with acceptable inter-item reliability (one of the task conflict items had a factor loading below 0.5; the results described here were robust to including or excluding this item).

to relationship conflict across multiple demographic characteristics, including functional background, gender, race, and age, these effects are significantly weaker if at least one top management team member engages in relatively high levels of self-regulated cognition.[4]

Our results also indicated that the presence of at least one top management team member who engages in relatively high levels of self-regulated cognition positively moderates the effects of demographic diversity on the level of task conflict in the team. The relationship between self-regulated cognition and task conflict appears to result from an increased frequency and duration of meetings among top management team members. Teams that include at least one manager who engages in self-regulated cognition tend to meet more frequently and for longer periods of time, which provides more opportunity for debate on strategic issues. Although our data do not yet allow a definitive assessment of the perform- ance consequences of task conflict among top managers, the presence of at least one top manager who engages in self-regulated cognition is positively related to survey measures of interpersonal trust among top managers, which is believed to positively moderate the effects of task conflict on group effectiveness (Simons and Peterson, 2000; Dirks and Ferrin, 2001). Moreover, in the following section we explain how self-regulated cognition can enhance the effectiveness of top man- agement teams in their IM activities. As discussed below, IM about strategy is increasingly conducted by groups of top executives and directors, and groups that include self-regulating leaders are more likely to work together effectively and capture the benefits of diversity in preparing for IM episodes.

Average levels of demographic diversity on top management teams and boards have gradually increased over the past two decades, and are expected to increase further over time. As diversity increases, the propensity for executives and direct- ors to engage in self-regulated cognition is also likely to increase. Accordingly, the side effects and benefits of self-regulated cognition are likely to become more pronounced over time.

Self-Regulation and Symbolic Management about Strategy, Leadership, and Governance

While self-regulated cognition can resolve the ingratiator's dilemma that the most important targets of ingratiation are also the most vigilant for insincere flattery, we further suggest how self-regulation can help resolve the broader dilemma that

---

[4] Our survey data from top management teams with multiple respondents indicate that if one team member engages in high levels of self-regulated cognition, other responding team members are more likely to engage in such cognition (and vice versa; if one team member does not engage in self-regulated cognition, others are less likely to engage in such cognition). Thus, it is likely that the moderating effect of self-regulated cognition reflects the influence of multiple team members.

attractive targets of social influence tend to be especially vigilant for exaggerated claims of any kind (Jones and Pittman, 1982), including exaggerated claims about the quality of strategy, leadership, and governance. In discussing the apparent limitations of symbolic management, Suchman (1995: 577) noted, "I adopt a somewhat skeptical attitude toward the autonomy, objectivity, and potency of managers. Managers do enunciate supportive myths and prescribe culturally congruent rituals; however, managers rarely convince others to believe much that the managers do not believe themselves."

The self-regulation that we have described thus far involves the regulation of social cognitions: reflections about the personal and social characteristics of oneself and others that increase the salience of similarities and reduce the salience of differences. In recent work we extend the construct of self-regulated social cognition to self-regulation of cognitions about organizational characteristics, including firm strategy and governance, and explain how such self-regulation can help resolve the dilemma of how to manage impressions of relatively power-ful, and thus skeptical stakeholders.

Recent research suggests that, in the post-Regulation Fair Disclosure environ-ment, security analysts are increasingly concerned with diagnosing the sincerity of top management's claims about their firm's conditions and prospects, and that they interpret verbal and non-verbal cues in making this diagnosis (Mayew and Venkatachalam, 2012; Brown et al., 2015). In revealing how important such cues have become to analysts, Brown et al. (2015; see also Mayew and Venkatachalam, 2012) quoted an analyst as stating that:

> We had an FBI profiler come in, and all the analysts and portfolio managers spent four hours with this profiler trying to understand how to read management teams, to tell when they're lying, to tell when they were uncomfortable with a question. That's how serious this whole issue has become.

It is especially important for top management to convey sincerity and conviction in managing the impressions of relatively powerful stakeholders, such as high-status security analysts and large institutional owners. These constituents are more likely to ask critical questions in conference calls and other communications with management, and as frequent targets of social influence attempts, they are also especially vigilant for IM, and prone to scrutinizing managers' verbal com-munications for indications of sincerity and conviction in their descriptions of the firm's strategy and performance prospects (Reingold, 2007; Mayew and Venkatachalam, 2012). As one analyst whom we interviewed put it,

> Of course when I'm speaking with [an executive] I'm interested in the reasoning, the logic [for the strategy]...what they say is important, but really more than that I'm interested in how they say it. Is there a genuine confidence there?

Do they mean what they say?...They know my opinion carries weight so they're going to give me a positive story, so I have to look them in the eye to figure out if it's the real story.

Our interviews suggested that representatives of powerful institutional investors have similar objectives in their meetings with top executives and directors. Thus, just as the most attractive targets of ingratiation are the most difficult to influence successfully, because they tend to be especially vigilant for attempts to curry favor, so the most attractive targets of IM are especially difficult to persuade. In the same way that people can discern insincere flattery when they are looking for inconsistencies between verbal and non-verbal behavior (Jones, 1990), so they can discern IM when looking for non-verbal cues of insincerity or exaggerated claims. When people convey confidence verbally in ways that exaggerate their true beliefs, their inner sentiments tend to leak through non-verbally (Ekman, 2001; Jones and Pittman, 1982). Non-verbal and paraverbal behaviors associated with confidence and optimism are difficult for most people to perform strategically, such that feigned expressions of confidence appear dissonant with micro-facial expressions, gestures, or other body language that subtly betray doubts (DePaulo et al., 2003; Ekman, 1993). Because they are frequent targets of IM, high-status actors are especially vigilant for such non-verbal cues. Moreover, this dilemma is exacerbated following the disclosure of low firm performance (e.g., unexpectedly low corporate earnings), which can trigger doubt and concern about the current strategy among firm leaders and stakeholders, while also increasing the need for IM. Under such conditions, external stakeholders will be especially vigilant for IM from firm leaders, and leaders may have greater difficulty conveying genuine confidence and optimism about the firm's performance prospects.

We suggest how firm leaders can circumvent this dilemma by engaging in self-regulated cognition prior to IM episodes. Our interviews and surveys indicate that prior to opportunities for IM with important firm stakeholders, including high-status security analysts and representatives of powerful institutional investors, top executives and directors often engage in a sequential process of reflection that prepares them to express genuine confidence in the firm's strategy, governance, and leadership. In particular, they initiate a reflective process that involves first considering possible weaknesses and vulnerabilities of the current strategy and governance, then reflecting on advantages and strengths, and finally affirming to themselves and each other that the strengths outweigh the weaknesses. Our surveys indicate that top managers and directors increasingly engage in this reflective process as a group or subgroup, prior to the IM episodes. As a result of this process, the top managers and directors are not only better prepared to answer critical questions about the firm's strategy, leadership, and governance, but they are also prepared to express genuine confidence in the firm's strategy, governance, and performance prospects. One top executive whom we interviewed described this process as an "analytical cheerleading" session:

> If the recent news [regarding firm performance] has been weak, and we're meeting with [analysts], we need to be prepared. We review possible criticisms [of our strategy], and then we review the rationale for our strategy in specific terms. We prepare for questions, but we're also getting behind the strategy … as a team, and as individuals. Everyone hears everyone else voicing confidence in the strategy, and so as a member of the team, you feel confident going into the meeting. When the meeting starts … everyone is feeling positive and believing strongly in the strategy.

Top managers also sometimes reflect on the strengths of their firm's corporate governance. For example, they may affirm the formal independence of outside directors and the role of the board in objectively monitoring and evaluating corporate strategy. This not only prepares executives to defend the quality of their firm's corporate governance in communicating with analysts and investors, but also bolsters their confidence in the firm's strategic decision making.

Our interviews and survey data also indicate that some teams engage in a further process of reflection soon after meeting with important stakeholders. One objective of this process is to ensure that managers and directors have a realistic and balanced perspective on the firm's strategy going forward. A number of managers described this process as a "reality check." As one top executive put it:

> We need to be confident with analysts, but then we need to be realistic about [the strategy] going forward, so we can recognize improvements and implement them. We need a reset. [When asked if analysts would want to be informed of executives' concerns:] Analysts want to see confidence, and then they want to see better performance. The reality check is very important to improving performance, and to continuous improvement overall.

Thus, especially in the context of disappointing firm performance, executives and directors often engage in self-regulated cognition about strategy and governance shortly before and after meetings with powerful stakeholders that directly parallels the self-regulated *social* cognition described above. At the same time, approximately half the top management teams in our sample that engaged in self-regulation prior to meetings with powerful stakeholders did not engage in compensatory self-regulation after meetings. This raises the possibility that self-regulated cognition about strategy and governance may sometimes contribute to executive overconfidence about strategy during periods of poor firm performance.

Our surveys indicate that processes of self-regulated cognition about strategy and governance have evolved and become more prevalent over time. In 2007 less than half of the corporate officers in our sample (37 per cent) engaged in self-regulation of this kind before meetings with security analysts or institutional investors, and only about 16 per cent of respondents engaged in self-regulated cognition shortly after these meetings. By 2015, a majority of responding officers in our sample (58 per cent) engaged in self-regulated cognition about strategy before meetings with these important stakeholders, and nearly half (46 per cent) engaged in self-regulation after meetings.

Moreover, self-regulated cognition evolved to become a more group-oriented activity over time. In 2007 about half of corporate officers who engaged in self-regulated cognition about strategy did so individually, while in 2015 nearly all the officers in our study engaged in self-regulated cognition as a subgroup or team (e.g., they engaged in a group discussion process that involved considering possible weaknesses and vulnerabilities of the current strategy and governance, reflecting on advantages and strengths, and then affirming to themselves and each other that the strengths outweigh the weaknesses). Corporate officers who engaged in self-regulated cognition about strategy and governance as a team reported significantly higher levels of confidence in the firm's strategy going into meetings with security analysts than officers who engaged in such cognition individually, especially during periods of low firm performance.

At the same time, the frequency of verbal communication by officers with security analysts, representatives of institutional investors, and other external stakeholders increased dramatically over this time period. While there was con-siderable variance among respondents in the frequency of such communications, the average frequency of verbal communication with security analysts and repre-sentatives of institutional investors increased by approximately 240 per cent and 185 per cent respectively over this time period. Moreover, 89 per cent of respond-ing officers communicated with analysts and institutional investors more fre-quently in 2015 than in 2007. When these trends are considered together, they suggest that the frequency of self-regulated cognition about strategy and govern-ance by corporate officers before and after meetings with external stakeholders has increased exponentially over the past decade. These trends have also contributed to a substantial increase in the intertemporal variance of officers' confidence in their firms' strategy and governance. That is, due to the combination of (1) more frequent verbal communication with external stakeholders, (2) more frequent "analytical cheerleading" about strategy and governance before these communi-cations, and (3) more frequent "reality checks" after these communications, in recent years corporate officers' reported level of confidence in their firms' strategy and governance has tended to fluctuate more dramatically over relatively short periods of time.

Although our research on self-regulation is ongoing, initial analyses suggest that at least some of the determinants and consequences of self-regulated cogni-tion about strategy parallel the determinants and consequences of self-regulated social cognition discussed above. Top management teams in which multiple executives have a background in sales, marketing, or politics are more likely than teams composed of executives with other backgrounds (e.g., finance, accounting, or engineering) to engage in self-regulation prior to meetings with powerful stakeholders. These backgrounds were also statistically significant, though weaker determinants of self-regulation after meetings.

There is a clear need for further research on the consequences of self-regulatory processes by firm leaders around IM episodes. Self-regulated cognition about strategy enables executives to compartmentalize the internal and external components of their jobs. Self-regulation prior to meetings with important stakeholders puts executives in the proper frame of mind for successful external communications, and self-regulation shortly after these communications puts them in the right mindset for internal, strategic decision-making processes. Future research could examine the consequences of self-regulation after IM episodes. Firm leaders who engage in a cognitive "reality check" after IM may be more likely to notice strategic opportunities and to initiate significant and/or timely changes in strategic direction. Given the potential importance of this form of self-regulation, we need research that explains variance in the propensity for leaders to correct for their biases after IM. More generally, we need a better understanding of why and how some leaders learn to adjust for individual and group-level biases in strategic decision making.

Self-regulation may interact with the diversity of top management teams to predict the success of IM with analysts, institutional investors, and other stakeholders. Diverse teams may especially benefit from the reflective process described above, in which executives first consider possible weaknesses and vulnerabilities of the current strategy and governance, then reflect on advantages and strengths, and then affirm to each other that the strengths outweigh the weaknesses. Team diversity on characteristics such as functional background may promote a deeper analysis of potential weaknesses in the strategy, while the social process of mutually affirming or "getting behind" the strategy prior to IM may be especially important in diverse teams. Research should examine whether diversity interacts with self-regulation to predict the valence of security analysts' recommendations and the positivity of their forecasts and reports.

Self-regulated cognition about strategy and governance may also have side benefits that parallel the effects of self-regulated social cognition. For example, self-regulation surrounding IM may reduce executive burnout and dampen conflict in diverse teams. Our analyses indicate that the frequency of IM with analysts, institutional investors, and other external stakeholders is a significant predictor of CEO responses to multi-item survey scales that measure feelings of burnout (the survey scales are described above). After controlling for a variety of firm-level and executive-level characteristics, including firm performance, executive experience, and the demographic characteristics described above, an increase in the frequency with which the CEO communicates with security analysts and institutional investors about firm strategy and governance of one standard deviation increases reported feelings of burnout by 96 per cent, including symptoms of energy depletion and cynicism. However, CEOs who engage in self-regulated cognition about strategy and governance with members of their management team prior to communications with analysts and institutional investors are substantially less likely to report feelings of burnout.

Our interviews with CEOs have also validated the strong main effects of IM demands on burnout, as well as the value of self-regulation in mitigating these effects. As one CEO told us:

> Communicating with [analysts] is an important part of my job, but it's draining. You're going from strategist to salesman. You're presenting the plan with complete confidence, but the reality strategically is complex. You're smart and you have the inside information. The complexities are in the back of your mind, but they're not in your speech. The speech has to be positive and it has to be simple. That conflict between what you know and what you have to communicate...it wears you down.

This CEO did not engage in the self-regulated cognition about strategy and governance described above. When people convey confidence verbally in ways that exaggerate their true beliefs, they tend to feel cognitive and emotive dissonance, which contributes to stress and emotional exhaustion (Hochschild, 1983; Grandey, 2003; Grandey et al., 2005). In the absence of self-regulation, this CEO felt cognitive and emotive dissonance from exaggerating their confidence in the firm's strategy. Another CEO who did engage in such self-regulation described the impression demands of the job differently:

> There's definitely a cheerleading side to these communications. [When asked if he finds it tiring]: not particularly...in some respects I draw energy from those [communications]. When I go in there I believe 100 percent in the strategy. I might have doubts the day before, and I might have doubts the day after. In the [meeting] I have no doubts. That makes analysts feel good about the strategy, and it makes me feel good. What's not to like?

Self-regulated cognition temporarily reduces decoupling between IM and executives' beliefs about strategy, and this ameliorates the psychological side effects of IM on the executives, while also increasing the influence of IM on stakeholders. As discussed above, our analyses indicated that symptoms of burnout predict discretionary leader behaviors such as mentoring and seeking input from lower-level managers, as well as the rate of turnover. Thus, in the absence of self-regulated cognition, the psychological side effects of IM can bleed over to reduce executives' effectiveness in their internal leadership roles. This is another way in which self-regulated cognition about strategy helps executives to compartmentalize the internal and external dimensions of their jobs. To the extent that self-regulated cognition reduces voluntary turnover by ameliorating symptoms of burnout, it not only increases the day-to-day effectiveness of top executives as leaders, but it also increases the duration of their contributions to IM and strategic decision making.

The effects of IM demands on executive burnout and turnover are an under-appreciated cost of external monitoring of firm leadership and strategy (e.g., in the form of assessments by security analysts and control by powerful institutional investors). The governance and strategy literatures tend to examine leader effect-iveness over relatively short and discrete time windows, and they likewise examine the behavioral effects of internal and external control mechanisms over relatively short periods of time. Our research suggests the importance of examining the cumulative contributions of top executives and directors to firm leadership and strategy, and the long-term effects of internal and external controls on executive leadership. By extension, there is a need for research on psychological and behavioral mechanisms such as self-regulated cognition that enhance the cumu-lative contributions of top executives, and that positively moderate the long-term effects of internal and external controls on firm leadership and strategy.

Self-regulated cognition prior to meetings with stakeholders may also reduce the likelihood of interpersonal conflict on diverse top management teams. The process of "getting behind the strategy . . . as a team" should tend to promote social cohesion and group identification, which should blur the faultlines that can otherwise form in diverse teams. Theory and research in the upper echelon and small group literatures suggest that diverse teams with weak faultlines experience less interpersonal conflict and better group outcomes, including a greater capacity for learning, a sense of psychological safety, and higher levels of group satisfaction (Smith et al., 1994; Lau and Murnighan, 1998, 2005; Jehn and Bezrukova, 2010).

Conclusion

In this chapter we have examined how different forms of self-regulated cognition by top managers and directors enhance the efficacy of social influence processes in symbolic management. We described a kind of self-regulated social cognition in which top managers and directors reflect on personal and social characteristics held in common with a colleague, and avoid thoughts about attributes not shared, prior to interacting with the colleague. We explained how self-regulated cognition of this kind increases the efficacy of ingratiation toward higher-status, demo-graphically dissimilar colleagues, and how such cognitions may increase the efficacy of ingratiation by firm leaders toward influential security analysts and representatives of relatively powerful institutional investors. We also revealed important side benefits of self-regulated cognition, including reduced symptoms of burnout in top executives and reduced interpersonal conflict in diverse top management teams. While self-regulated social cognition involves the regulation of thoughts and feelings about colleagues, a second form involves the regulation of cognitions about organizational characteristics, including firm strategy and governance, prior to opportunities for IM. We explained how self-regulated cognition prior to meetings with security analysts and institutional investors can enhance the efficacy of IM by preparing top executives to express genuine confidence in the firm's strategy, governance, and performance prospects. We further proposed that this form of self-regulation has side benefits for executives and top management teams that parallel the benefits of self-regulated social cognition, including a reduction in symptoms of burnout and dampened interpersonal conflict on diverse top management teams.

Thus, self-regulated cognition increases the efficacy of both ingratiation and persuasion attempts with powerful colleagues and stakeholders, the two most important forms of interpersonal influence in symbolic management. By reducing the effects of social influence behavior on symptoms of burnout, such as energy depletion and cynicism, self-regulated cognition increases the persistence of firm leaders in their symbolic management activities, as well as their day-to-day effectiveness as symbolic managers. It also helps top executives compartmentalize symbolic management from their internal leadership roles, dampening the tendency for symbolic management to bias strategic decision making and reduce executive engagement in discretionary leader behaviors such as mentoring and input seeking. By reducing the effect of demographic differences on interpersonal conflict, self-regulated cognition also has the side benefit of improving the quality of strategic decision making on diverse top management teams.

Social influence scholars have devoted little research attention to understanding how individuals prepare for IM. Goffman (1959: 112) distinguished between the "backstage" or "back regions" in which individuals prepare for social performances, and the front region in which IM takes place, but he stopped short of describing the social or psychological preparation that occurs in the back regions. Moreover, Goffman described the back region as a place where the performer "can relax ... drop his front ... and step out of character." The social and psychological preparation that we describe blurs the distinction between front and back, reduces the stress of performance, and averts the need to step into (or out of) character.

Self-regulated cognition not only enhances the effectiveness of social influence processes in symbolic management, but it also creates intertemporal variance in the social and strategic perceptions of firm leaders. In a sense, self-regulated cognition creates a subtle kind of decoupling between leaders' perceptions about their colleagues at the time of social interaction, or their perceptions about firm strategy and governance at the time of IM, and their perceptions at other points in time. We suggested that as demographic diversity on top management teams and boards increases over time, and the frequency of verbal IM toward external stakeholders continues to increase, the frequency of self-regulated cognition is likely to increase dramatically. As a result, the intertemporal variance in executives' social and strategic perceptions can be expected to increase as well. Executives' perceptions of their colleagues, and their level of confidence in firm strategy and governance, will increasingly oscillate over a relatively short period of time. The implications of such variance for firm leadership, governance, and strategic decision making are almost entirely unexplored, and represent an important topic for future research.

10

Conclusions, Future Research Directions, and Policy Implications

Symbolic management is the lynchpin of corporate governance. It is an agentic, political process that is informed by institutional logics in the broader culture, which exerts substantial influence on the perceptions of firm stakeholders. Thus, symbolic management effectively integrates political, socio-cognitive, and sociological perspectives on firm leadership, governance, and strategy. It is also a multi-level perspective that explains social and economic behavior at each level of the governance system. Our theory and research have suggested how symbolic decoupling operates at different levels of analysis, from dyadic relations between leaders within organizations, to relations between firm leaders and external stakeholders, to relations between groups of leaders and groups of stakeholders. There is decoupling at the most micro level, in the changing perceptions of individual leaders about high-status colleagues and firm characteristics before and after episodes of social influence, and at the most macro level there is decoupling between appearances and reality in the overall system of governance.

Just as decoupling spans levels of analysis, the mechanisms and consequences of symbolic management also operate at multiple levels. Our theory has described mechanisms that range from individual cognitive biases (e.g., attribution errors and egocentric biases), to group-level biases and influence processes (e.g., pluralistic ignorance and social distancing), to the social structure of firm leadership and institutionalization. The consequences of symbolic management range from individual-level outcomes such as leader reputation, to group-level behavior such as board monitoring and conflict, to change in the prevailing institutional logics of governance. Thus, our theory broadens the scope of sociological perspectives on governance, which have focused on the symbolic management of firm-level policies and structures, consistent with traditional, neo-institutional perspectives on management and organization.

Symbolic management not only provides a broader, more integrative alternative to extant behavioral theories of governance, but it incorporates and subsumes economic perspectives on governance such as agency theory. In the symbolic management perspective, agency theory is defined as a historically dependent, institutional logic. It is an endogenous manifestation of social values, assumptions, and prescriptions that became taken for granted for an extended period of time among segments of the professional community. Due in part to the symbolic

Symbolic Management: Governance, Strategy, and Institutions. James Westphal and Sun Hyun Park,
Oxford University Press (2020). © James Westphal and Sun Hyun Park.
DOI: 10.1093/oso/9780198792055.001.0001

management activities of firm leaders, the agency logic of governance has yielded over time to an alternative, neo-corporate logic that reinterprets agency prescriptions in ways that support management autonomy and control.

While our focus is on symbolic management as an integrative, behavioral theory of governance, our multi-level perspective ultimately suggests a powerful approach to the study of organizational behavior more generally. Symbolic decoupling is not limited to firm governance and strategy, but is pervasive at every level of the organization, and in virtually all forms of organization-environment relations. Wherever culture exerts an influence, and wherever politics can occur, symbolic management and decoupling are likely to play an important role in explaining organizational behavior and outcomes.

Future Research on the Symbolic Management Perspective

Our theoretical framework suggests a variety of promising directions for future research on firm leadership, governance and strategy, as well as research in organization studies more broadly. The extant literature has focused largely on firm-level IM and the symbolic decoupling of formal policies and structures. There is a need for further research on the symbolic management of organizational processes, as well as various forms of symbolic management that cross organizational boundaries. While our theory and research has begun to address the symbolic management of strategic decision-making processes, there is much work to be done on the variety of potential audiences for such symbolic management. For example, there is surprisingly little systematic research on how top executives manage the impressions of lower-level managers and staff about strategic decision making. Moreover, while our work examines symbolic management about input seeking and participation in decision making, research is also needed on how managers describe other phases of the decision-making process, including information processing and the incorporation of performance feedback. Our focus on the initial, input-seeking phase of decision making is shared by the larger literature on organizational decision-making processes, which has devoted disproportionate theoretical and empirical attention to organizational search, at the expense of other important phases of strategic decision making. In fact, the behavioral strategy literature sometimes appears to equate information search with decision making.

Top executives engage in symbolic management about a wide variety of other organizational processes beyond strategic decision making, including performance evaluation, management succession and promotion processes (Cannella and Shen, 2001), and cooperation across divisions or other formal groups in the organization. As with symbolic management about PSDM programs, communication about these processes may be framed as increasing "transparency," and yet may often be decoupled from the actual day-to-day processes in organizations. There is also symbolic management about broader characteristics of organizations such as an organizational culture. There would be value in future research that categorizes (1) the different types of organizational processes and characteristics that are potential subjects of symbolic management, (2) the relevant institutional logics that may enhance or limit the effectiveness of each form of symbolic management in conferring legitimacy, and (3) the relevant audiences for each form of symbolic management.

There is also a need for further theory and research on cooperation and competition in symbolic management. Although IM support and other cooperative forms of symbolic management appear to be the norm, negative IM about the leadership and strategy of competitors does sometimes occur. There is a clear need for research on when and why competitive symbolic management occurs, and its impact on leader and firm reputation.

Further research is also needed on how advice networks influence symbolic management. For example, outside directors who are experienced in communicating with particular stakeholder groups sometimes mentor or advise top executives on the content of verbal IM about firm strategy, governance, and performance. While a growing body of research has examined how and when firm leaders provide each other with advice about the content of firm policy and strategy, very little research has examined the provision of advice and mentoring about stakeholder relations. Our interviews suggest that firm leaders may seek advice and counsel from outside directors about stakeholder relations more often than they seek advice about strategy. Moreover, there is anecdotal evidence for a kind of generalized reciprocity in mentoring about stakeholder relations, including routine processes of IM with information intermediaries such as journalists and analysts, in which leaders who received mentoring about such communications earlier in their careers are motivated to reciprocate by providing similar mentoring to their junior colleagues. This generalized exchange network not only channels best practice information about effective processes of communication with different stakeholder groups, but it also diffuses assumptions and advice about appropriate topics of communication. It may help explain the surprising consistency across firm leaders in the content of symbolic management about governance and strategy. Accordingly, there would be considerable value in systematic research on the structure of this advice network, as well as its influence on the level, form, and effectiveness of symbolic management activity by firm leaders.

There would also be value in further research on the role of consultants and other third-party service providers in symbolic management. Our research has revealed how consultants facilitate symbolic decoupling in strategic decision making and director selection, while advising top managers on how to communicate with firm stakeholders in ways that should enhance the reputation of firm leadership and strategy. However, while our research has implicated consultants in some forms of symbolic decoupling, it has not yet provided direct, systematic evidence that consultants amplify the organizational benefits of symbolic action.

Moreover, while our theoretical framework encompasses a variety of specific forms of symbolic management at different levels of analysis, it does not fully address how these various activities may cohere into firm-level, symbolic management strategies. For example, scholars could examine whether firms tend to engage in patterns of symbolic management activity that resemble the "generic" strategies identified in classic strategic management research (Miles and Snow, 1978; Miller et al., 1984; Zajac and Shortell, 1989). Evidence that firms which engage in symbolic decoupling in one domain are more likely to engage in decoupling subsequently in other domains begins to address this issue (Westphal and Zajac, 2001), but little theory or research has sought to identify variation in patterns of symbolic management activity across firms. Some firms may tend to be early movers in developing new and innovative forms of symbolic management, while other firms tend to be fast followers that imitate and improve upon promising approaches, and still others are more reactive or less strategic in their symbolic management activity. Such a typology of symbolic management strategies could make multiple theoretical contributions above and beyond extant sociological perspectives, which tend to focus on specific practices and decisions rather than larger strategies, and which often make oversimplified distinctions between early and late adopters of particular practices.

Strategy scholars could also examine the potential for firms to realize competitive advantages from symbolic management strategies. While a considerable body of research has examined the impact of symbolic management on firm reputation and legitimacy, surprisingly little work has investigated the effects of symbolic management on firm performance, and even less has examined the potential consequences for competitive advantage. Scholars have tended to focus on forms of symbolic management that are widely diffused and/or easily imitated, and which therefore offered limited potential for sustainable differentiation from competitors. In fact, the limited prior research on performance consequences of symbolic management has examined institutionalized practices that enhance firm legitimacy at the *expense* of profitability (Westphal et al., 1997). Our recent research on symbolic PSDM programs is an exception, as this form of symbolic management is relatively subtle and complex, and thus not easily imitated without exclusive access to private information from fellow leaders and assistance from specialized consultants (Westphal and Zhu, 2019a). Our theory and findings suggest that the relational and structural embeddedness of firm leadership is one important determinant of competitive advantage from symbolic management.

There is also a need for further research on the side effects of symbolic management activity. Some forms of symbolic management may have negative consequences for lower-level managers and other staff in organizations. For example symbolic PSDM programs give the appearance of including lower-level managers and staff in strategic decision making, while actually solidifying the control of top executives. It would be interesting to examine whether symbolic PSDM programs are associated with strategic decisions that ultimately have negative consequences for lower-level employees, or whether the supposed intangible benefits of participation in decision making are provided to employees in lieu of more tangible benefits such as pay increases and generous benefits.

At the same time, symbolic management may also have adverse side effects on firm leaders. Our research suggests that symbolic management about governance and strategy often involves a combination of verbal IM and decoupling, which implies that firm leaders who engage in symbolic management are frequently in the position of exaggerating, distorting, or otherwise misleading firm constituents about strategic practices. Over time such communications could take a psychological and emotional toll on firm leaders. Our preliminary research suggests that symbolic decoupling is associated not only with more positive appraisals of firm leadership and strategy by information intermediaries, but also with higher rates of executive turnover. Studies could examine whether this surprising effect of decoupling on turnover is mediated by symptoms of executive burnout, including energy depletion and cynicism (Schaufeli et al., 2002; Bria et al., 2014). Symbolic management activity could also have side effects on firm leaders that parallel the side effects of ingratiation, including feelings of resentment toward the organization. In addition, it would be interesting to examine whether the different forms of self-regulated cognition that we have described, including self-regulated cognition about firm strategy, governance, and performance prospects prior to IM episodes, negatively moderate the side effects of symbolic management on firm leaders.

While scholars have sometimes characterized symbolic management as a kind of agency problem, wherein top executives benefit themselves at the expense of shareholders and other stakeholders, this is likely a gross oversimplification. Research has shown that symbolic management can enhance shareholder returns (Westphal and Zajac, 1998), and we expect that future research will demonstrate that symbolic management activity has complex consequences for firms, leaders, lower-level employees, and other stakeholders. Symbolic management is likely to have both benefits and costs, or at least unanticipated side effects, for every stakeholder group. An important objective for academic research is to develop a more detailed and nuanced understanding of these benefits and costs, and the conditions under which the benefits are more or less likely to outweigh the costs for each stakeholder group.

A longstanding gap in the behavioral literature on corporate governance, as well as the overlapping literature on symbolic management, is the shortage of systematic empirical research conducted in non-Western cultures. However, this gap has been narrowed significantly in recent years by comparative corporate governance scholars (e.g., Aguilera et al., 2018). There have now been quite a few studies on symbolic management in developing countries, especially in China (e.g., Soundarajan et al., 2018; Wang et al., 2018; Guo et al., 2017a) and how companies in emerging countries engage in systematic symbolic management activities when they cross cultural boundaries, for instance, getting listed on foreign stock exchanges (Park and Zhang, 2019. Although it is perhaps too early to conduct a systematic review of this burgeoning literature, there appears to be growing evidence for various forms of symbolic decoupling that parallel the decoupling of firm-level policies and structures demonstrated in the U.S. and other Anglo-Saxon countries, for instance, in corporate social responsibility reporting (Marquis and Qian, 2013; Zhang et al., 2019), corporate diversification (Wang and Luo, 2018), and inter-organizational network building (Guo et al., 2017b; Haveman et al., 2017). While symbolic management and decoupling will naturally be instantiated differently in developing countries and non-Western cultures, we anticipate that fundamental principles of our symbolic management framework are likely to generalize across cultures, in part because culture is integral to the framework itself. In particular, a fundamental proposition of our theory is that the form and consequences of symbolic action are conditioned by institutional logics at the societal level.

We have suggested that symbolic management theory provides a powerful approach to the study of organizational behavior more generally, beyond research on governance and strategy. Future research could examine symbolic decoupling at lower levels of organizations, and in other forms of organization–environment relations. For example, the symbolic management of participation in strategic decision making that we described is likely to be replicated in various forms at lower levels of organizations. Committees and task forces often employ devices such as online surveys of employees or other stakeholders to give the appearance of an inclusive and/or scientific approach to problem solving. Such processes may serve to rationalize the solution favored by a manager who formed the committee, while also enhancing the manager's reputation as an effective leader. There is also an element of symbolic decoupling in superior-subordinate relationships that parallels the decoupling in CEO–board relationships and other stakeholder relationships that we described. Much as the board's apparent independence from management is often not reflected in actual CEO–board relationships, formal procedures for mentoring, performance appraisals, and supervision are often not reflected in actual superior–subordinate relationships. Moreover, many of the social and psychological processes that support decoupling at the dyadic and group levels can occur in superior–subordinate relations at lower levels of the organization, including ingratiation, self-regulation, social distancing, and pluralistic ignorance. There are significant opportunities for scholars to explore the various manifestations of symbolic management in organizations, as well as important contingency factors and any boundary conditions on the occurrence and effectiveness of symbolic management.

Managerial and Public Policy Implications
of the Symbolic Management Perspective

Although further research is needed on the consequences of symbolic management for different stakeholder groups, our theory and research clearly suggest that firm leaders engage in a variety of different forms of symbolic action that benefit themselves and certain powerful stakeholders (e.g., large shareholders) at the expense of at least some, less powerful stakeholders (e.g., customers). There is now compelling evidence that symbolic decoupling often compromises the productive efficiency of organizations and the allocative efficiency of capital markets. Our research has identified multiple forms of symbolic management wherein top executives attract financial capital to their firms by adopting policies, programs, and structures that promise improvements in governance, strategy, and performance, but neglect to implement the initiatives, such that the improvements never materialize. In effect, symbolic management often misdirects economic resources to less productive uses. While some investors share the market returns from symbolic management, the vast majority of employees, customers, potential entrepreneurs, and other business owners are adversely affected by symbolic decoupling. Thus, symbolic management not only compromises allocative efficiency and productivity, but it also plays a part in increasing social inequality.

Accordingly, our research calls for action by regulators and other public policy makers to limit or discourage the various forms of symbolic decoupling described in this book. For example, firms that adopt PSDM programs might be required to document how strategic input from lower-level managers and staff is used in strategic decision making. Members of board-nominating committees might be required to certify that nominees for board seats do not have a personal *or* professional connection to top executives of competitor firms. Admittedly such measures will never be foolproof in preventing symbolic decoupling. If top executives are sufficiently motivated, they can find new ways to decouple a policy, or they can devise new policies and programs that are amenable to decoupling, staying one step ahead of regulators. However, requiring firm leaders to certify or demonstrate faithful implementation of policies and programs can at least raise the costs of decoupling, and provide a means of educating stakeholders about the potential for decoupling. Requiring firms to provide specific information about policy implementation would not only signal the importance of decoupling to journalists, other information intermediaries, and consumer advocates, but also cue them about specific questions to ask, which might also discourage or mitigate some forms of decoupling by firm leaders.

Educators and administrators at colleges and universities also have an important role to play in reducing negative forms of symbolic management. Students in a variety of fields ranging from business, law, public policy, journalism, communication, sociology, and economics should be exposed to theory and research on the forms and processes of symbolic management and the economic and social costs of symbolic decoupling. Such widespread education about symbolic management should increase monitoring of decoupling by journalists and their audiences, regulators, and consumer groups. And, educating current and future managers and financial market actors about the costs of symbolic management may deter firm leaders from engaging in decoupling, and deter analysts and lenders from endorsing or subsidizing decoupling.

Another approach to reducing symbolic decoupling is to disrupt or correct the social and psychological processes that help perpetuate decoupling. We have described social influence processes and social psychological biases at multiple levels of analysis that compromise the independence or vigilance of actors who are in a position to monitor or control symbolic decoupling. Relevant social influence processes include sophisticated forms of ingratiatory behavior and reciprocity by firm leaders toward corporate directors, information intermediaries and institutional investors, and social distancing of directors or information intermediaries who challenge or fail to endorse symbolic action. Social psychological biases include pluralistic ignorance among peripheral members of top management, outside directors, and information intermediaries, as well as groupthink among corporate officers. As discussed in previous sections, some of these processes are relatively straightforward to change, while others will be more challenging to address. Since pluralistic ignorance is rooted in a shared misunderstanding (i.e., a collective failure to recognize shared concerns about governance or strategy), it can be substantially reduced by simply increasing awareness of the bias among corporate directors and information intermediaries. Ingratiation is a powerful and insidious form of social influence, but its effectiveness can at least be reduced by educating directors, information intermediaries, and other relevant stakeholders about the sophisticated forms of flattery and opinion conformity identified in our research. Although groupthink is notoriously difficult to correct or avoid, structured processes such as forming a devil's advocate subcommittee of outside directors to challenge management's strategic assumptions may be effective in some cases (Eisenhardt and Zbaracki, 1992; Lorsch, 1993).

At the same time, our symbolic management framework also includes micro-level processes that have important side benefits for firms and their stakeholders. We described the psychological and social benefits of self-regulated cognition in which top managers and directors reflect on personal and social characteristics held in common with a colleague, and avoid thoughts about attributes not shared, prior to interacting with the colleague. We explained how self-regulated cognition of this kind can reduce symptoms of burnout in top executives and dampen interpersonal conflict in diverse top management teams.

More generally, many of the psychological and social processes that we have described could in principle be leveraged for the benefit of firm stakeholders. For example, participation process mentoring of first-time directors could be used to inculcate normative expectations that outside directors challenge the strategic assumptions of firm leaders, rather than warning directors to check with top managers before raising concerns in board meetings. Generalized exchange networks could be used to diffuse strategic wisdom rather than decoupling and IM support. Recommendations and referrals could be used to reward directors who provide valuable strategic information and advice rather than directors who ingratiate the CEO. Social distancing could be used to control self-interested, political behavior, rather than penalizing directors who challenge high-status leaders. These and other micro-processes that we have described are very powerful tools that can be deployed for good or ill, depending on the intentions of firm leaders and information intermediaries.

References

AESC (2011) "The association of executive search and leadership consultants outlook report." https://www.aesc.org/insights/thought-leadership/aesc-insights/2011-aesc-out look-report.

Afuah, Allan, and Christopher L. Tucci (2012) "Crowdsourcing as a solution to distant search." *Academy of Management Review* 37, no. 3: 355–75.

Aguilera, Ruth V., Kurt Descender, Michael K. Bednar, and Jun Ho Lee (2015) "Connecting the dots: Bringing external corporate governance in the corporate governance puzzle." *Academy of Management Annals* 9: 483–573.

Aguilera, Ruth V., William Q. Judge, and Siri A. Terjesen (2018) "Corporate governance deviance." *Academy of Management Review* 43, no. 1: 87–109.

Aguinis, Herman, Luis R. Gomez-Mejia, Geoffrey P. Martin, and Harry Joo (2018) "CEO pay is indeed decoupled from CEO performance: Charting a path for the future." *Management Research: Journal of the Iberoamerican Academy of Management* 16, no. 1: 117–36.

Alchian, Armen A., and Harold Demsetz (1972) "Production, information costs, and economic organization." *American Economic Review* 62, no. 5: 777–95.

Alinsky, Saul (1971) *Rules For Radicals: A Practical Primer for Realistic Radicals*. New York: Random House.

Allen, Michael Patrick (1974) "The structure of interorganizational elite cooptation: Inter-locking corporate directorates." *American Sociological Review*: 393–406.

Allport, Floyd Henry (1924) *Social Psychology*. Boston, MA: Houghton Mifflin.

Anderson, Ronald C., and David M. Reeb (2004) "Board composition: Balancing family influence in SandP 500 firms." *Administrative Science Quarterly* 49, no. 2: 209–37.

Anderson, Ronald C., Sattar A. Mansi, and David M. Reeb (2004) "Board characteristics, accounting report integrity, and the cost of debt." *Journal of Accounting and Economics* 37, no. 3: 315–42.

Andrews, Kenneth T., and Michael Biggs (2006) "The dynamics of protest diffusion: Movement organizations, social networks, and news media in the 1960 sit-ins." *American Sociological Review* 71, no. 5: 752–77.

Angst, Corey M., Emily S. Block, John D'arcy, and Ken Kelley (2017) "When do IT security investments matter? Accounting for the influence of institutional factors in the context of healthcare data breaches." *Mis Quarterly* 41, no. 3.

Arrfelt, Mathias, Robert M. Wiseman, and G. Tomas M. Hult (2013) "Looking backward instead of forward: Aspiration-driven influences on the efficiency of the capital allocation process." *Academy of Management Journal* 56, no. 4: 1081–103.

Ashforth, Blake E., and Ronald H. Humphrey (1997) "The ubiquity and potency of labeling in organizations." *Organization Science* 8, no. 1: 43–58.

Axelrod, Robert M. (1984) *The Evolution of Cooperation*. New York: Basic Books.

Baddeley, Alan D. (1986) *Working Memory*. Oxford: Clarendon Press.

Baker, Wayne E., and Sheen S. Levine (2013) "Mechanisms of generalized exchange: Towards an integrated model." Working paper, University of Michigan.

Baltzell, E. Digby (1958) *Philadelphia Gentlemen: The Making of a National Upper Class.* New York: Free Press.

Bansal, Pratima, and Geoffrey Kistruck (2006) "Seeing is (not) believing: Managing the impressions of the firm's commitment to the natural environment." *Journal of Business Ethics* 67, no. 2: 165–80.

Barkow, Jerome H. (1974) "Evaluation of character and social control among the Hausa." *Ethos* 2, no. 1: 1–14.

Barley, Stephen R., and Gideon Kunda (1992) "Design and devotion: Surges of rational and normative ideologies of control in managerial discourse." *Administrative Science Quarterly*: 363–99.

Barroso-Castro, Carmen, Mª Mar Villegas-Periñan, and Marta Dominguez (2017) "Board members' contribution to strategy: The mediating role of board internal processes." *European Research on Management and Business Economics* 23, no. 2: 82–9.

Bartlett, Christopher A., and Sumantra Ghoshal (1994) "Changing the role of top management: Beyond strategy to purpose." *Harvard Business Review* 72, no. 6: 79–88.

Bassili, John N. (2003) "The minority slowness effect: Subtle inhibitions in the expression of views not shared by others." *Journal of Personality and Social Psychology* 84, no. 2: 261.

Baumeister, Roy F. (1998) "The self." In S.T. Gilbert, S.T. Fiske, and G. Lindzey (eds), *Handbook of Social Psychology*, 4th edn: 680–740. New York: McGraw-Hill.

Baumeister, Roy F., and M.R. Leary (1995) "The need to belong: Desire for interpersonal attachments as a fundamental human motivation." *Psychological Bulletin* 117: 497–529.

Baumeister, Roy F., Laura Smart, and Joseph M. Boden (1996) "Relation of threatened egotism to violence and aggression: The dark side of high self-esteem." *Psychological Review* 103, no. 1: 5.

Bazerman, Max H., and Don A. Moore (2013) *Judgment in Managerial Decision Making*, 8th edn. New York: Wiley.

Beatty, Randolph P., and Edward J. Zajac (1994) "Top management incentives, monitoring, and risk sharing: A study of executive compensation, ownership and board structure in initial public offerings." *Administrative Science Quarterly* 39: 313–36.

Bednar, Michael K. (2012) "Watchdog or lapdog? A behavioral view of the media as a corporate governance mechanism." *Academy of Management Journal* 55, no. 1: 131–50.

Belliveau, Maura A., Charles A. O'Reilly III, and James B. Wade (1996) "Social capital at the top: Effects of social similarity and status on CEO compensation." *Academy of Management Journal* 39, no. 6: 1568–93.

Benner, Mary J., and Ram Ranganathan (2012) "Offsetting illegitimacy? How pressures from securities analysts influence incumbents in the face of new technologies." *Academy of Management Journal* 55, no. 1: 213–33.

Benton, Richard A. (2016) "Corporate governance and nested authority: Cohesive network structure, actor-driven mechanisms, and the balance of power in American corporations." *American Journal of Sociology* 122, no. 3: 661–713.

Bhagat, Sanjai, and Bernard Black (2001) "The non-correlation between board independence and long-term firm performance." Journal of Corporation Law l, no. 27: 231.

Bhojraj, Sanjeev, and Partha Sengupta (2003) "Effect of corporate governance on bond ratings and yields: The role of institutional investors and outside directors." *Journal of Business* 76, no. 3: 455–75.

Bidwell, Matthew (2011) "Paying more to get less: The effects of external hiring versus internal mobility." *Administrative Science Quarterly* 56, no. 3: 369–407.

Birmingham, S. (1987) *America's Secret Aristocracy.* New York: Little, Brown.

Bizjak, John, Michael Lemmon, and Ryan Whitby (2009) "Option backdating and board interlocks." *Review of Financial Studies* 22, no. 11: 4821–47.

Blasi, Gary, and John T. Jost (2012) *System Justification Theory and Research*. New York: Oxford University Press.

Blau, P.M. (1964) *Exchange and Power in Social Life*. New York: Wiley.

Bogardus, Emory S. (1959) *Social Distance*. Columbia, SC: University of South Carolina Press.

Boltanski, Luc, and Laurent Thévenot (2006) *On Justification: Economies of Worth*. Princeton, NJ: Princeton University Press.

Bonabeau, Eric (2009) "Decisions 2.0: The power of collective intelligence." *MIT Sloan Management Review* 50, no. 2: 45.

Boon, Susan D., and John G. Holmes (1991) "The dynamics of interpersonal trust: Resolving uncertainty in the face of risk." In Robert A. Hinde and Joe Groebel (eds), *Cooperation and Prosocial Behavior*: 190–211. New York: Cambridge University Press.

Boudana, Sandrine (2011) "A definition of journalistic objectivity as a performance." *Media, Culture and Society* 33, no. 3: 385–98.

Bouwman, Christa H.S. (2011) "Corporate governance propagation through overlapping directors." *Review of Financial Studies* 24, no. 7: 2358–94.

Brabham, Daren C. (2012) "The myth of amateur crowds: A critical discourse analysis of crowdsourcing coverage." *Information, Communication and Society* 15, no. 3: 394–410.

Brass, Daniel J., Joseph Galaskiewicz, Henrich R. Greve, and Wenpin Tsai (2004) "Taking stock of networks and organizations: A multilevel perspective." *Academy of Management Journal* 47, no. 6: 795–817.

Brealy, Richard A., and Stewart C. Myers (1991) *Principles of Corporate Finance*, 4th edn. New York: McGraw-Hill.

Brewer, Marilynn B. (1979) "In-group bias in the minimal intergroup situation: a cognitive-motivational analysis." *Psychological Bulletin* 86, no. 2: 307–24.

Brewer, Marilynn B., and Michael D. Silver (2000) "Group distinctiveness, social identification, and collective mobilization." In S. Stryker, T.J. Owens, and R.W. White (eds), *Self, Identity, and Social Movements*, Vol. 13: 153–71. Minneapolis, MN: University of Minnesota Press.

Bria, Mara, Florina Spânu, Adriana Băban, Dan L. Dumitrașcu (2014) "Maslach burnout inventory—general survey: Factorial validity and invariance among Romanian healthcare professionals." *Burnout Research* 1: 103–11.

Bromley, Patricia, and Walter W. Powell (2012) "From smoke and mirrors to walking the talk: Decoupling in the contemporary world." *Academy of Management Annals* 6, no. 1: 483–530.

Brown, Lawrence D., Andrew C. Call, Michael B. Clement, and Nathan Y. Sharp (2015) "Inside the 'black box' of sell-side financial analysts." *Journal of Accounting Research* 53, no. 1: 1–47.

Brown, Lawrence D., Andrew C. Call, Michael B. Clement, and Nathan Y. Sharp (2016) "The activities of buy-side analysts and the determinants of their stock recommendations." *Journal of Accounting and Economics* 18: 139–56.

Brown, Shona L., and Kathleen M. Eisenhardt (1997) "The art of continuous change: Linking complexity theory and time-paced evolution in relentlessly shifting organizations." *Administrative Science Quarterly*: 1–34.

Brozovsky, John A., and Parvez R. Sopariwala (1995) "The determinants of performance plan adoption." *Journal of Accounting, Auditing and Finance* 10, no. 3: 655–76.

Buch-Hansen, Hubert (2014) "Interlocking directorates and collusion: An empirical analysis." *International Sociology* 29, no. 3: 249–67.

Buchan, Nancy R., Rachel T.A. Croson, and Robyn M. Dawes (2002) "Swift neighbors and persistent strangers: A cross-cultural investigation of trust and reciprocity in social exchange." *American Journal of Sociology* 108, no. 1: 168–206.

Burt, Nathaniel (1963) *The Perennial Philadelphians: The Anatomy of an American Upper Class*. Philadelphia, PA: University of Pennsylvania Press.

Burt, R.S. (1983) *Corporate Profits and Cooptation: Networks of Market Constraints and Directorate Ties in the American Economy*. New York: Academic Press.

Burt, R.S. (1987) "Social contagion and innovation: Cohesion versus structural equivalence." *American Journal of Sociology* 92: 1287–335.

Burt, R.S. (2005) *Brokerage and Closure: An Introduction to Social Capital*. Oxford: Oxford University Press.

Byrne, D. (1971) *The Attraction Paradigm*. New York: Academic.

Camerer, Colin F., and Ernst Fehr (2004) "Measuring social norms and preferences using experimental games: A guide for social scientists." In J.P. Henrich, R. Boyd, S. Bowles, C. Camerer, E. Fehr, and H. Gintis (eds), *Foundations of Human Sociality: Economic Experiments and Ethnographic Evidence from Fifteen Small-Scale Societies*: 55–95. Oxford: Oxford University Press.

Camillus, John C. (2008) "Strategy as a wicked problem." *Harvard Business Review* 86, no. 5: 98.

Cannella, Jr., Albert A., and Wei Shen (2001) "So close yet so far: Promotion versus exit for CEOs heirs apparent." *Academy of Management Journal*, 44: 252–70.

Carlos, W. Chad, and Ben W. Lewis (2017) "Strategic silence: Withholding certification status as a hypocrisy avoidance tactic." *Administrative Science Quarterly*, 63: 130–69.

Carpenter, Jeffrey P., and Peter Hans Matthews (2004) "Why punish? Social reciprocity and the enforcement of prosocial norms." *Journal of Evolutionary Economics* 14, no. 4: 407–29.

Carpenter, Mason A., and James D. Westphal (2001) "The strategic context of external network ties: Examining the impact of director appointments on board involvement in strategic decision making." *Academy of Management Journal* 44, no. 4: 639–60.

Carter, Evan C., and Michael E. McCullough (2014) "Publication bias and the limited strength model of self-control: Has the evidence for ego depletion been overestimated?" *Frontiers in Psychology* 5: 823.

Chabot, Sean (2010) "Dialogue matters: Beyond the transmission model of transnational diffusion between social movements." In Rebecca Kolins Givan, Kenneth M. Roberts, and Sarah A. Soule (eds), *The Diffusion of Social Movements: Actors, Mechanisms, and Political Effects*. Cambridge: Cambridge University Press.

Chaiken, Shelly, and Charles Stangor (1987) "Attitudes and attitude change." *Annual Review of Psychology* 38, no. 1: 575–630.

Chandler, Alfred Dupont (1962) *Strategy and Structure: Chapters in the History of the American Industrial Enterprise*. Cambridge, MA: MIT Press.

Chen, Chao C., and James R. Meindl (1991) "The construction of leadership images in the popular press: The case of Donald Burr and People Express." *Administrative Science Quarterly*: 521–51.

Chen, Shuping, and Dawn A. Matsumoto (2006) "Favorable versus unfavorable recommendations: The impact on analyst access to management-provided information." *Journal of Accounting Research* 44, no. 4: 657–89.

Chesbrough, Henry W., and Melissa M. Appleyard (2007) "Open innovation and strategy." *California Management Review* 50, no. 1: 57–76.

Chu, Johan S.G., and Gerald F. Davis (2016) "Who killed the inner circle? The decline of the American corporate interlock network." *American Journal of Sociology* 122, no. 3: 714–54.

Chua, Roy Y.J., Michael W. Morris, and Paul Ingram (2009) "Guanxi vs networking: Distinctive configurations of affect-and cognition-based trust in the networks of Chinese vs American managers." *Journal of International Business Studies* 40, no. 3: 490–508.

Cialdini, Robert B. (2008) *Influence: Science and Practice*. New York: Pearson.

Cialdini, Robert B., and Noah J. Goldstein (2004) "Social influence: Compliance and conformity." *Annual Review of Psychology* 55: 591–621.

Cikara, M., M.M. Botvinick, and S.T. Fiske (2011) "Us versus them: Social identity shapes neural responses to intergroup competition and harm." *Psychological Science* 22: 306–13.

Clement, Michael B., and Senyo Y. Tse (2003) "Do investors respond to analysts' forecast revisions as if forecast accuracy is all that matters?" *Accounting Review* 78, no. 1: 227–49.

Cole, G. (1979) "Classifying research units by patterns of performance and influence: A typology of the Round 1 data." In Frank M. Andrews and George Aichholzer (eds), *Scientific Productivity: The Effectiveness of Research Groups in Six Countries*: 353–404. Cambridge: Cambridge University Press.

Cole, Jonathan, and Steve Cole (1973) *Social Stratification in Science*. Chicago, IL: Chicago University Press.

Coleman, J.S. (1990) *Foundations of Social Theory*. Cambridge, MA: Belknap Press.

Coleman, J.S. (1994) *Foundations of Social Theory*, 2nd edn. Cambridge, MA: Harvard University Press.

Coombes, Paul, and Mark Watson (2000) "Three surveys on corporate governance." *McKinsey Quarterly* 4: 74–74.

Corporate Board (2006) Survey finds corporate governance practices are improving. 27 (May–June): 25–7.

Cosmides, Leda, and John Tooby (1992) "Cognitive adaptations for social exchange." In Jerome H. Barkow, Leda Cosmides, and John Tooby (eds), *The Adapted Mind: Evolutionary Psychology and the Generation of Culture*. Oxford: Oxford University Press.

Crandall, Christian S., Paul J. Silvia, Ahogni Nicolas N'gbala, Jo-Ann Tsang, and Karen Dawson (2007) "Balance theory, unit relations, and attribution: The underlying integrity of Heiderian theory." *Review of General Psychology* 11, no. 1: 12.

Cross, Susan E., Jonathan S. Gore, and Michael L. Morris (2003) "The relational-interdependent self-construal, self-concept consistency, and well-being." *Journal of Personality and Social Psychology* 85, no. 5: 933.

Crystal, Graef S. (1991) *In Search of Excess: The Overcompensation of American Executives*. New York: Norton.

Cuddy, Amy J.C., Susan T. Fiske, and Peter Glick (2007) "The BIAS map: Behaviors from intergroup affect and stereotypes." *Journal of Personality and Social Psychology* 92, no. 4: 631.

Dalton, Dan R., Catherine M. Daily, Alan E. Ellstrand, and Jonathan L. Johnson (1998) "Meta-analytic reviews of board composition, leadership structure, and financial performance." *Strategic Management Journal* 19, no. 3: 269–90.

Daniel, Kent, David Hirshleifer, and Avanidhar Subrahmanyam (1998) "Investor psychology and security market under-and overreactions." *Journal of Finance* 53, no. 6: 1839–85.

D'Aveni, Richard A. (1990) "Top managerial prestige and organizational bankruptcy." *Organization Science* 1, no. 2: 121–42.

David, Parthiban D., Matthew Bloom, and Amy J. Hillman (2007) "Investor activism, managerial responsiveness, and corporate social performance." *Strategic Management Journal* 28: 91–100.

Davis, Allison, Burleigh Bradford Gardner, and Mary R. Gardner (1941) *Deep South: A Social Anthropological Study of Caste and Class.* Columbia, SC: University of South Carolina Press.

Davis, Gerald F. (2005) "New directions in corporate governance." *Annual Review of Sociology* 31: 143–62.

Davis, Gerald F., and Henrich R. Greve (1997) "Corporate elite networks and governance changes in the 1980s." *American Journal of Sociology* 103, no. 1: 1–37.

Davis, Gerald F., and Tracy A. Thompson (1994) "A social movement perspective on corporate control." *Administrative Science Quarterly*: 141–73.

Davis, Gerald F., Mina Yoo, and Wayne E. Baker (2003) "The small world of the American corporate elite, 1982–2001." *Strategic Organization* 1, no. 3: 301–26.

Davis, James H., F. David Schoorman, and Lex Donaldson (1997) "Toward a stewardship theory of management." *Academy of Management Review* 22, no. 1: 20–47.

De Dreu, Carsten K.W., and Laurie R. Weingart (2003) "Task versus relationship conflict, team performance, and team member satisfaction: A meta-analysis." *Journal of Applied Psychology* 8, no. 4: 741.

De Tocqueville, Alexis (2003) *Democracy in America,* trans. Gerald E. Bevan. New York: Penguin.

Dearborn, D.C., and Simon, H. (1958) "Selective perceptions: A note on the departmental identification of executives." *Sociometry* 21: 140–4.

Deephouse, David L. (1999) "To be different, or to be the same? It's a question (and theory) of strategic balance." *Strategic Management Journal* 20, no. 2: 147–66.

Deephouse, David L. (2000) "Media reputation as a strategic resource: An integration of mass communication and resource-based theories." *Journal of Management* 26, no. 6: 1091–112.

DePaulo, Bella M., James J. Lindsay, Brian E. Malone, Laura Muhlenbruck, Kelly Charlton, and Harris Cooper (2003) "Cues to deception." *Psychological Bulletin* 129, no. 1: 74.

Desai, Vinit M. (2011) "Mass media and massive failures: Determining organizational efforts to defend field legitimacy following crises." *Academy of Management Journal,* 54: 263–78.

DeWall, N.C., and Richman, S.B. (2011) "Social exclusion and the desire to reconnect." *Social and Personality Psychology Compass* 5: 919–32.

Diekmann, Andreas (2004) "The power of reciprocity: Fairness, reciprocity, and stakes in variants of the dictator game." *Journal of Conflict Resolution* 48, no. 4: 487–505.

DiMaggio, Paul (1997) "Culture and cognition." *Annual Review of Sociology* 23, no. 1: 263–87.

DiMaggio, Paul J., and Walter W. Powell (1983) "The iron cage revisited: Institutional isomorphism and collective rationality in organizational fields." *American Sociological Review* 48, no. 5: 147–60.

Dirks, Kurt T., and Donald L. Ferrin (2001) "The role of trust in organizational settings." *Organization Science* 12, no. 4: 450–67.

Domhoff, G.W. (2002) *Who Rules America? Power and Politics,* 4th edn. New York: McGraw Hill.

Dorfman, Peter W., Paul J. Hanges, and Felix C. Brodbeck (2004) "Leadership and cultural variation: The identification of culturally endorsed leadership profiles." *Culture, Leadership, and Organizations: The GLOBE Study of 62 Societies*: 669–719.

Douglas, M. (1990) Foreword: No free gifts. In M. Mauss and W.D. Halls (eds), *The Gift: The Form and Reason for Exchange in Archaic Societies*: 7–18. New York: W.W. Norton.

Dovidio, J.F., and Gaertner, S.L. (2010) "Intergroup bias." In S.T. Fiske, D.T. Gilbert, and G. Lindzey (eds), *Handbook of Social Psychology*, Vol. 2. Chichester: John Wiley and Sons.

Du Bois, Cora (1955) "The dominant value profile of American culture." *American Anthropologist* 57, no. 6: 1232–9.

Duffy, Michelle K., Kristin L. Scott, Jason D. Shaw, Bennett J. Tepper, and Karl Aquino (2012) "A social context model of envy and social undermining." *Academy of Management Journal* 55, no. 3: 643–66.

Dunbar, R. (1998) *Grooming, Gossip, and the Evolution of Language*. Cambridge, MA: Harvard University Press.

Dunn, Barnaby D., Davy Evans, Dasha Makarova, Josh White, and Luke Clark (2012) "Gut feelings and the reaction to perceived inequity: The interplay between bodily responses, regulation, and perception shapes the rejection of unfair offers on the ultimatum game." *Cognitive, Affective, and Behavioral Neuroscience* 12, no. 3: 419–29.

Eisenhardt, Kathleen M. (1989) "Agency theory: An assessment and review." *Academy of Management Review* 14, no. 1: 57–74.

Eisenhardt, Kathleen M., and Mark J. Zbaracki (1992) "Strategic decision making." *Strategic Management Journal* 13, no. S2: 17–37.

Ekeh, P.P. (1974) *Social Exchange Theory: The Two Traditions*. Cambridge, MA: Harvard University Press.

Ekman, Paul (1993) "Facial expression and emotion." *American Psychologist* 48, no. 4: 384.

Ekman, Paul (2001) *Telling Lies: Clues to Deceit in the Marketplace, Politics, and Marriage*. New York: W.W. Norton and Company.

Elsbach, Kimberly D. (1994) "Managing organizational legitimacy in the California cattle industry: The construction and effectiveness of verbal accounts." *Administrative Science Quarterly* 39: 57–88.

Elsbach, Kimberly D., and Greg Elofson (2000) "How the packaging of decision explanations affects perceptions of trustworthiness." *Academy of Management Journal* 43, no. 1: 80–9.

Eminet, Aurélien, and Zied Guedri (2010) "The role of nominating committees and director reputation in shaping the labor market for directors: An empirical assessment." *Corporate Governance: An International Review* 18, no. 6: 557–74.

Erikson, E.H. (1994) *Identity and the Life Cycle*. New York: W.W. Norton and Company.

Esser, James K. (1998) "Alive and well after 25 years: A review of groupthink research." *Organizational Behavior and Human Decision Processes* 73, no. 2–3: 116–41.

Fama, Eugene F. (1970) "Efficient capital markets: A review of theory and empirical work." *Journal of Finance* 25: 383–417.

Fama, Eugene F. (1980) "Agency problems and the theory of the firm." *Journal of Political Economy* 88, no. 2: 288–307.

Fama, Eugene F., and Michael C. Jensen (1983) "Separation of ownership and control." *Journal of Law and Economics* 26, no. 2 (1983): 301–25.

Farber, Barry A. (1984) "Farber burnout scale." *Journal of Educational Research* 77: 325–31.

Fehr, Beverley (2004) "Intimacy expectations in same-sex friendships: A prototype interaction-pattern model." *Journal of Personality and Social Psychology* 86, no. 2: 265.

Fehr, Ernst, and Klaus M. Schmidt (2006) "The economics of fairness, reciprocity and altruism: Experimental evidence and new theories." In Serge-Christophe Kolm and Jean Mercier Ythier (eds), *Handbook of the Economics of Giving, Altruism and Reciprocity: Foundations*, Vol. 1. North Holland: Elsevier.

Fehr, Ernst, Urs Fischbacher, and Simon Gächter (2002) "Strong reciprocity, human cooperation, and the enforcement of social norms." *Human Nature* 13, no. 1: 1–25.

Feldman, Martha S., and James G. March (1981) "Information in organizations as signal and symbol." *Administrative Science Quarterly*: 171–86.

Ferro, M. (2010) *Resentment in History*. Cambridge: Polity.

Finkelstein, Sydney (1992) "Power in top management teams: Dimensions, measurement, and validation." *Academy of Management Journal* 35: 505–38.

Finkelstein, Sydney, Donald C. Hambrick, and Albert A. Cannella (2009) *Strategic Leadership: Theory and Research on Executives, Top Management Teams, and Boards*. Oxford: Oxford University Press.

Fiske, Susan T. (2010) "Envy up, scorn down: How comparison divides us." *American Psychologist* 65, no. 8: 698.

Fiss, Peer C. (2006) "Social influence effects and managerial compensation evidence from Germany." *Strategic Management Journal* 27, no. 11: 1013–31.

Fiss, Peer C., and Paul M. Hirsch (2005) "The discourse of globalization: Framing and sensemaking of an emerging concept." *American Sociological Review* 70, no. 1: 29–52.

Fiss, Peer C., and E.J. Zajac (2004) "The diffusion of ideas over contested terrain: The (non) adoption of a shareholder value orientation among German firms." *Administrative Science Quarterly* 49, no. 4: 501–34.

Fitzsimons, Gráinne M., and John A. Bargh (2004) "Automatic self-regulation." In Kathleen D. Vohs and Roy F. Baumeister (eds), *Handbook of Self-Regulation: Research, Theory, and Applications*, 2nd edn: 151–70. New York: Guilford Press.

Fligstein, Neil (1990) *The Transformation of Corporate Control*. Cambridge, MA: Harvard University Press.

Fligstein, Neil, and Taekjin Shin (2007) "Shareholder value and the transformation of the US economy, 1984–2000." *Sociological Forum* 22, no. 4: 399–424.

Friedland, Roger, and Robert R. Alford (1991) "Bringing society back in: Symbols, practices and institutional contradictions." In Walter W. Powell and Paul J. DiMaggio (eds), *The New Institutionalism in Organizational Analysis*: 232–63. Chicago, IL: University of Chicago Press.

Friedman, Daniel, and Nirvikar Singh (2004) "Negative reciprocity: The coevolution of memes and genes." *Evolution and Human Behavior* 25, no. 3: 155–73.

Frijda, Nico H. (1986) *The Emotion*. Cambridge: Cambridge University Press.

Garfinkel, Harold (1967) *Studies in Ethnomethodology*. Englewood Cliffs, NY: Prentice Hall.

Gast, Arne, and Michele Zanini (2012) "The social side of strategy." *McKinsey Quarterly* 2, no. 1: 82–93.

Gersh, David (1987) "The corporate elite and the introduction of IQ testing in American public schools." In M. Schwartz (ed.), *The Structure of Power in America*: 163–94. New York: Holmes and Meier.

Gintis, Herbert (2000) *Strong Reciprocity and Human Sociality*. Working Paper No. 2000–02, University of Massachusetts, Department of Economics.

Gintis, Herbert, Samuel Bowles, Robert Boyd, and Ernst Fehr (2003) "Explaining altruistic behavior in humans." *Evolution and Human Behavior* 24, no. 3: 153–72.

Gintis, Herbert, Joseph Henrich, Samuel Bowles, Robert Boyd, and Ernst Fehr (2008) "Strong reciprocity and the roots of human morality." *Social Justice Research* 21, no. 2: 241–53.

Gluckman, Max (1963) "Papers in honor of Melville J. Herskovits: Gossip and scandal." *Current Anthropology* 4, no. 3: 307–16.

Goffman, E. (1959) *The Presentation of Self in Everyday Life.* New York: Anchor Books.

Goffman, E. (1963) *Stigma: Notes on the Management of Spoiled Identity.* Englewood Cliffs, NJ: Prentice-Hall.

Gordon, R.A. (1996) "Impact of ingratiation on judgments and evaluations: A meta-analytic investigation." *Journal of Personality and Social Psychology* 71, no. 1: 54–70.

Gouldner, A.W. (1960) "The norm of reciprocity: A preliminary statement." *Sociological Review* 25: 161–78.

Graffin, S.D., J.B. Wade, J.F. Porac, and R.C. McNamee (2008) "The impact of CEO status diffusion on the economic outcomes of other senior managers." *Organization Science* 19: 457–74.

Grandey, Alicia A. (2003) "When 'the show must go on': Surface acting and deep acting as determinants of emotional exhaustion and peer-rated service delivery." *Academy of Management Journal* 46, no. 1: 86–96.

Grandey, Alicia A., Glenda M. Fisk, and Dirk D. Steiner (2005) "Must 'service with a smile' be stressful? The moderating role of personal control for American and French employees." *Journal of Applied Psychology* 90, no. 5: 893.

Granovetter, M. (1973) "The strength of weak ties." *American Journal of Sociology* 78: 1360–80.

Granovetter, M. (1985) "Economic action and social structure: The problem of embeddedness." *American Journal of Sociology* 91, no. 3: 481–510.

Granovetter, M. (2017) *Society and Economy: Framework and Principles.* Cambridge, MA: Harvard University Press.

Greenwood, Royston, and Roy Suddaby (2006) "Institutional entrepreneurship in mature fields: The big five accounting firms." *Academy of Management Journal* 49, no. 1: 27–48.

Greiner, Ben, and M. Vittoria Levati (2005) "Indirect reciprocity in cyclical networks: An experimental study." *Journal of Economic Psychology* 26, no. 5: 711–31.

Greve, Henrich R. (1998) "Performance, aspirations and risky organizational change." *Administrative Science Quarterly* 43: 58–86.

Greve, Henrich R., Donald Palmer, and Jo-Ellen Pozner (2010) "Organizations gone wild: The causes, processes, and consequences of organizational misconduct." *Academy of Management Annals* 4, no. 1: 53–107.

Grosser, Travis J., Virginie Lopez-Kidwell, and Giuseppe Labianca (2010) "A social network analysis of positive and negative gossip in organizational life." *Group and Organization Management* 35, no. 2: 177–212.

Guo, Rui, Lan Tao, Caroline Bingxin Li, and Tao Wang (2017) "A path analysis of greenwashing in a trust crisis among Chinese energy companies: The role of brand legitimacy and brand loyalty." *Journal of Business Ethics* 140, no. 3: 523–36.

Guo, Yidi, Quy Nguyen Huy, and Zhixing Xiao (2017) "How middle managers manage the political environment to achieve market goals: Insights from China's state-owned enterprises." *Strategic Management Journal* 38, no. 3: 676–96.

Gurven, Michael (2004) "To give and to give not: The behavioral ecology of human food transfers." *Behavioral and Brain Sciences* 27, no. 4: 543–59.

Hall, D.T. (2002) *Careers in and out of Organizations.* Thousand Oaks, CA: Sage.

Hallett, Tim (2010) "The myth incarnate: Recoupling processes, turmoil, and inhabited institutions in an urban elementary school." *American Sociological Review* 75, no. 1: 52–74.

Hambrick, Donald C., Theresa Seung Cho, and Ming-Jer Chen (1996) "The influence of top management team heterogeneity on firms' competitive moves." *Administrative Science Quarterly*: 659–84.

Hamel, Gary (2007) *The Future of Management*. Boston, MA: Harvard Business School Press.

Harkins, Stephen G., and Richard E. Petty (1981) "The multiple source effect in persuasion: The effects of distraction." *Personality and Social Psychology* Bulletin 7, no. 4: 627–35.

Hautz, Julia, David Seidl, and Richard Whittington (2017) "Open strategy: Dimensions, dilemmas, dynamics." *Long Range Planning* 50, no. 3: 298–309.

Hayes, A.F. (2013) *Introduction to Mediation, Moderation and Conditional Process Analysis: A Regression-Based Approach*. New York: Guilford Press.

Hayward, Mathew L.A., and Warren Boeker (1998) "Power and conflicts of interest in professional firms: Evidence from investment banking." *Administrative Science Quarterly*: 1–22.

Haveman, Heather A., Nan Jia, Jing Shi, and Yongxiang Wang (2017) "The dynamics of political embeddedness in China." *Administrative Science Quarterly* 62, no. 1: 67–104.

Heath, Chip, and Rich Gonzalez (1995) "Interaction with others increases decision confidence but not decision quality: Evidence against information collection views of interactive decision making." *Organizational Behavior and Human Decision Processes* 61, no. 3: 305–26.

Heider, Fritz (1958) *The Psychology of Interpersonal Relations*. Hillsdale, NJ: Lawrence Erlbaum.

Heppner, Whitney L., Michael H. Kernis, John B. Nezlek, Joshua Foster, Chad E. Lakey, and Brian M. Goldman (2008) "Within-person relationships among daily self-esteem, need satisfaction, and authenticity." *Psychological Science* 19, no. 11: 1140–5.

Heron, Randall A., and Erik Lie (2009) "What fraction of stock option grants to top executives have been backdated or manipulated?" *Management Science* 55, no. 4: 513–25.

Hewstone, Miles (1990) "The 'ultimate attribution error'? A review of the literature on intergroup causal attribution." *European Journal of Social Psychology* 20: 311–35.

Hewstone, Miles, Mark Rubin, and Hazel Willis (2002) "Intergroup bias." *Annual Review of Psychology* 53, no. 1: 575–604.

Hill, Kim (2002) "Cooperative food acquisition by Ache foragers." *Human Nature* 13: 105–28.

Hillman, Amy J., and Thomas Dalziel (2003) "Boards of directors and firm performance: Integrating agency and resource dependence perspectives." *Academy of Management Review* 28, no. 3: 383–96.

Hochschild, A.R. (1983) "The managed heart: Commercialization of human feeling." Berkeley, CA: University Press.

Hogg, Michael A., and Deborah I. Terry (2000) "Social identity and self-categorization processes in organizational contexts." *Academy of Management Review* 25, no. 1: 121–40.

Hollinger, Richard C., and John P. Clark (1982) "Formal and informal social controls of employee deviance." *Sociological Quarterly* 23, no. 3: 333–43.

Hollyer, James R., B. Peter Rosendorff, and James Raymond Vreeland (2011) "Democracy and transparency." *Journal of Politics* 73, no. 4: 1191–205.

Hong, Harrison, Jeffrey D. Kubik, and Amit Solomon (2000) "Security analysts' career concerns and herding of earnings forecasts." *Rand Journal of Economics*: 121–44.

Hornborg, Alf (2014) "Technology as fetish: Marx, Latour, and the cultural foundations of capitalism." *Theory, Culture and Society* 31, no. 4: 119–40.

Horne, C., Dodoo, F.N.-A., and Dodoo, N.D. (2013) "The shadow of indebtedness: Bridewealth and norms constraining female reproductive autonomy." *American Sociological Review* 78, no. 3: 503–20.

House, Robert J., Paul J. Hanges, Mansour Javidan, Peter W. Dorfman, and Vipin Gupta (eds) (2004) *Culture, Leadership, and Organizations: The GLOBE Study of 62 Societies.* Thousand Oaks, CA: Sage.

House, Robert J., Peter W. Dorfman, Mansour Javidan, Paul J. Hanges, and Mary F. Sully de Luque (2013) *Strategic Leadership across Cultures: GLOBE Study of CEO Leadership Behavior and Effectiveness in 24 Countries.* London: Sage.

Hula, Kevin W. (1999) *Lobbying Together: Interest Group Coalitions in Legislative Politics.* Washington, DC: Georgetown University Press.

Ingram, Paul, and Arik Lifschitz (2006) "Kinship in the shadow of the corporation: The interbuilder network in Clyde River shipbuilding, 1711–1990." *American Sociological Review* 71, no. 2: 334–52.

Investor Relations Business (2000) "Good governance pays off." 5: 1–4.

Islam, M.R., and M. Hewstone (1993) "Intergroup attributions and affective consequences in majority and minority groups." *Journal of Personality and Social Psychology* 64: 936–50.

Jackson, Susan E., Richard L. Schwab, and Randall S. Schuler (1986) "Toward an understanding of the burnout phenomenon." *Journal of Applied Psychology* 71, no. 4: 630.

Jaher, Frederic Cople (1982) *The Urban Establishment: Upper Strata in Boston, New York, Charleston, Chicago, and Los Angeles.* Chicago, IL: University of Illinois Press.

James, W. (1890) *Principles of Psychology.* New York: Dover.

Jehn, Karen A. (1995) "A multimethod examination of the benefits and detriments of intragroup conflict." *Administrative Science Quarterly*: 256–82.

Jehn, Karen A., and Katerina Bezrukova (2010) "The faultline activation process and the effects of activated faultlines on coalition formation, conflict, and group outcomes." *Organizational Behavior and Human Decision Processes* 112, no. 1: 24–42.

Jensen, M.C. (1989) "The eclipse of the public corporation." *Harvard Business* 67, no. 5: 61–74.

Jensen, M.C., and William H. Meckling (1976) "Theory of the firm: Managerial behavior, agency costs and ownership structure." *Journal of Financial Economics* 3, no. 4: 305–60.

Jeong, Young-Chul, and Tai-Young Kim (2018) "Between legitimacy and efficiency: An institutional theory of corporate giving." *Academy of Management Journal.*

Jiraporn, Pornsit, Wallace N. Davidson III, Peter DaDalt, and Yixi Ning (2009) "Too busy to show up? An analysis of directors' absences." *Quarterly Review of Economics and Finance* 49, no. 3: 1159–71.

Johansson, Lars-Olof, and Henrik Svedsäter (2009) "Piece of cake? Allocating rewards to third parties when fairness is costly." *Organizational Behavior and Human Decision Processes* 109, no. 2: 107–19.

Johnson, Jonathan L., Alan E. Ellstrand, Dan R. Dalton, and Catherine M. Dalton (2005) "The influence of the financial press on stockholder wealth: The case of corporate governance." *Strategic Management Journal* 26, no. 5: 461–71.

Johnson, Scott G., Karen Schnatterly, and Aaron D. Hill (2013) "Board composition beyond independence: Social capital, human capital, and demographics." *Journal of Management* 39, no. 1: 232–62.

Jones, E.E. (1964) *Ingratiation.* New York: Appleton-Century-Crofts.

Jones, E.E. (1990) *Interpersonal Perceptions.* New York: Freeman.

Jones, E.E., and Thane S. Pittman (1982) "Toward a general theory of strategic self-presentation." *Psychological Perspectives on the Self* 1, no. 1: 231–62.

Joseph, John, William Ocasio, and Mary H. McDonnell (2014) "The structural elaboration of board independence: Executive power, institutional logics, and the adoption of

CEO-only board structures in U.S. corporate governance." *Academy of Management Journal* 57: 1834–58.

Jost, John T., Aaron C. Kay, and Hulda Thorisdottir (2009) *Social and Psychological Bases of Ideology and System Justification*. Oxford: Oxford University Press.

Jung, J., and Shin, T. (2018) "Learning not to diversify: The transformation of graduate business education and the decline of diversifying acquisitions." *Administrative Science Quarterly*, 0001839218768520.

Kane, Emily W., and Kimberly J. Whipkey (2009) "Predictors of public support for gender-related affirmative action: Interests, gender attitudes, and stratification beliefs." *Public Opinion Quarterly* 73, no. 2: 233–54.

Keeves, Gareth D., James D. Westphal, and Michael L. McDonald (2017) "Those closest wield the sharpest knife: How ingratiation leads to resentment and social undermining of the CEO." *Administrative Science Quarterly* 62, no. 3: 484–523.

Kelly, Caroline (1993) "Group identification, intergroup perceptions and collective action." *European Review of Social Psychology* 4, no. 1: 59–83.

Keynes, John M. (1936) *The General Theory of Employment, Interest, and Money*. New York: Harcourt, Brace and Co.

Khurana R. (2002) *Searching for a Corporate Savior: The Irrational Quest for Charismatic CEOs*. Princeton, NJ: Princeton University Press.

Kilduff, Martin, and W. Tsai (2003) *Social Networks and Organizations*. London: Sage.

Kinzler, Katherine D., Kristin Shutts, and Joshua Correll (2010) "Priorities in social categories." *European Journal of Social Psychology* 40, no. 4: 581–92.

Kisfalvi, Veronika, and Steve Maguire (2011) On the nature of institutional entrepreneurs: Insights from the life of Rachel Carson. *Journal of Management Inquiry* 20, no. 2: 152–77.

Klandermans, Bert (1984) "Mobilization and participation: Social-psychological expansions of resource mobilization theory." *American Sociological Review*: 583–600.

Klandermans, Bert (2002) "How group identification helps to overcome the dilemma of collective action." *American Behavioral Scientist* 45, no. 5: 887–900.

Kluegel, James R., and Eliot R. Smith (1986) *Beliefs about Inequality: Americans' Views of What Is and What Ought to Be*. New York: de Gruyter.

Kosloff, Spee, Jeff Greenberg, Toni Schmader, Mark Dechesne, and David Weise (2010) "Smearing the opposition: Implicit and explicit stigmatization of the 2008 US presidential candidates and the current US president." *Journal of Experimental Psychology* 139, no. 3: 383.

Krackhardt, David (1992) "The strength of strong ties: The importance of philos in organizations." In N. Nohria and R.G. Eccles (eds), *Networks and Organizations: Structure, Form, and Action*: 216–39. Boston, MA: Harvard Business School Press.

Krackhardt, David (1998) "Simmelian ties: Super strong and sticky." In Roderick Kramer and Margaret Neale (eds), *Power and Influence in Organizations*: 21–38. London: Sage.

Kramer, Roderick M. (2001) "Identity and trust in organizations: One anatomy of a productive but problematic relationship." In M.A. Hogg and D.J. Terry (eds), *Social Identity Processes in Organizational Contexts*: 167–80. Oxford: Blackwell.

Krause, Ryan (2017) "Being the CEO's boss: An examination of board chair orientations." *Strategic Management Journal* 38: 697–713.

Krause, Ryan, and Matthew Semadeni (2013) "Apprentice, departure, and demotion: An examination of the three types of CEO-board chair separation." *Academy of Management Journal* 56, 805–26.

Kroll, Mark, Bruce A. Walters, and Peter Wright (2008) "Board vigilance, director experience, and corporate outcomes." *Strategic Management Journal* 29, no. 4: 363–82.

Kumar, Kamalesh, and Michael Beyerlein (1991) "Construction and validation of an instrument for measuring ingratiatory behaviors in organizational settings." *Journal of Applied Psychology* 76, no. 5: 619.

Kumar, Raman, and Parvez R. Sopariwala (1992) "The effect of adoption of long-term performance plans on stock prices and accounting numbers." *Journal of Financial and Quantitative Analysis* 27, no. 4: 561–73.

Kuperman, Jerome C. (2003) "Using cognitive schema theory in the development of public relations strategy: Exploring the case of firms and financial analysts following acquisition announcements." *Journal of Public Relations Research* 15, no. 2: 117–50.

Kwan, Virginia S.Y., Oliver P. John, Richard W. Robins, and Lu Lu Kuang (2008) "Conceptualizing and assessing self-enhancement bias: A componential approach." *Journal of Personality and Social Psychology* 94, no. 6: 1062.

Labianca, Giuseppe, and Daniel J. Brass (2006) "Exploring the social ledger: Negative relationships and negative asymmetry in social networks in organizations." *Academy of Management Review* 31, no. 3: 596–614.

Lam, Wing, Xu Huang, and E.D. Snape (2007) "Feedback-seeking behavior and leader-member exchange: Do supervisor-attributed motives matter?" *Academy of Management Journal* 50, no. 2: 348–63.

Langevoort, Daniel C. (2006) "Beyond 'independent' directors: A functional approach to board independence." *Harvard Law Review* 119, no. 3: 1553–75.

Latour, Bruno (1993) *We Have Never Been Modern*. Cambridge, MA: Harvard University Press.

Lau, Dora C., and J. Keith Murnighan (1998) "Demographic diversity and faultlines: The compositional dynamics of organizational groups." *Academy of Management Review* 23, no. 2: 325–40.

Lau, Dora C., and J. Keith Murnighan (2005) "Interactions within groups and subgroups: The effects of demographic faultlines." *Academy of Management Journal* 48, no. 4: 645–59.

Lavie, Dovev, and Harbir Singh (2011) "The evolution of alliance portfolios: The case of Unisys." *Industrial and Corporate Change* 21, no. 3: 763–809.

Lawler, Edward J., Shane R. Thye, and Jeongkoo Yoon (2008) "Social exchange and micro social order." *American Sociological Review* 73, no. 4: 519–42.

Leach, Colin Wayne, Russell Spears, Nyla R. Branscombe, and Bertjan Doosje (2003) "Malicious pleasure: Schadenfreude at the suffering of another group." *Journal of Personality and Social Psychology* 84, no. 5: 932.

Leary, Mark R. (1995) *Self-presentation: Impression Management and Interpersonal Behavior*. Boulder, CO: Westview Press.

Leary, Mark R., E.S. Tambor, S.K. Terdal, and D.L. Downs (1995) "Self-esteem as an interpersonal monitor: The sociometer hypothesis." *Journal of Personality and Social Psychology* 68: 518–30.

Lee, Angela Y. (2001) "The mere exposure effect: An uncertainty reduction explanation revisited." *Personality and Social Psychology Bulletin* 27, no. 10 (2001): 1255–66.

Lee, James J., and Steven Pinker (2010) "Rationales for indirect speech: The theory of the strategic speaker." *Psychological Review* 117, no. 3: 785.

Leippe, Michael R., Andrew P. Manion, and Ann Romanczyk (1992) "Eyewitness persuasion: How and how well do fact finders judge the accuracy of adults' and children's memory reports?" *Journal of Personality and Social Psychology* 63, no. 2: 181.

Levine, Steven B. (1980) "The rise of American boarding schools and the development of a national upper class." *Social Problems* 28, no. 1: 63–94.

Levit, Doron, and Nadya Malenko (2016) "The labor market for directors and externalities in corporate governance." *Journal of Finance* 71, no. 2: 775–808.

Li, Weiwen, Ryan Krause, Xin Qin, Junsheng Zhang, Hang Zhu, Shanshan Lin, and Yuehua Xu (2018) "Under the microscope: A n experimental look at board transparency and director monitoring behavior." *Strategic Management Journal* 39, no. 4: 1216–36.

Liberman, Akiva, and Shelly Chaiken (2003) "Defensive processing of personally relevant health messages." In P. Salovey and A.J. Rothman (eds), *Social Psychology of Health*: 118–29. New York: Psychology Press.

Lord, Robert G., and Karen J. Maher (2002) *Leadership and Information Processing: Linking Perceptions and Performance.* New York: Routledge.

Lord, Robert G., Roseanne J. Foti, and James S. Phillips (1982) "A theory of leadership categorization." In James G. Hunt, Uma Sekaran, and Chester Schriesheim (eds), *Leadership: Beyond Establishment Views*: 121. Carbondale, IL: Southern Illinois University Press.

Lorsch, Jay W. (1993) "Lukens Inc.: The melters' committee (A)." *Harvard Business School* Case 493–070.

Lorsch, Jay W., and E. MacIver (1989) *Pawns or Potentates: The Reality of America's Corporate Hoards.* Boston, MA: Harvard Business School Press.

Lounsbury, Michael, and Mary Ann Glynn (2019) *Cultural Entrepreneurship: A New Agenda for the Study of Entrepreneurial Processes and Possibilities.* Cambridge: Cambridge University Press.

Love, E. Geoff, Lim, J., and Bednar, Michael K. (2017) The face of the firm: The influence of CEOs on corporate reputation. *Academy of Management Journal* 60, no. 4: 1462–81.

Lynall, Matthew D., Brian R. Golden, and Amy J. Hillman (2003) "Board composition from adolescence to maturity: A multitheoretic view." *Academy of Management Review* 28, no. 3: 416–31.

MacCannell, Dean (1973) "Staged authenticity: Arrangements of social space in tourist settings." *American Journal of Sociology* 79, no. 3: 589–603.

MacDonald, Geoff, and Mark R. Leary (2005) "Why does social exclusion hurt? The relationship between social and physical pain." *Psychological Bulletin* 131, no. 2: 202.

MacKinnon, David P., Chondra M. Lockwood, Jeanne M. Hoffman, Stephen G. West, and Virgil Sheets (2002) "A comparison of methods to test mediation and other intervening variable effects." *Psychological Methods* 7, no. 1: 83.

MacLean, Tammy L., and Michael Behnam (2010) "The dangers of decoupling: The relationship between compliance programs, legitimacy perceptions, and institutionalized misconduct." *Academy of Management Journal* 53, no. 6: 1499–520.

Mael, Fred, and Blake E. Ashforth (1992) "Alumni and their alma mater: A partial test of the reformulated model of organizational identification." *Journal of Organizational Behavior* 13, no. 2: 103–23.

Maner, Jon K., C. Nathan DeWall, Roy F. Baumeister, and Mark Schaller (2007) "Does social exclusion motivate interpersonal reconnection? Resolving the porcupine problem." *Journal of Personality and Social Psychology* 92, no. 1: 42.

March, James G., and Johan P. Olsen (1984) "The new institutionalism: Organizational factors in political life." *American Political Science Review* 78, no. 3: 734–49.

March, James G., Lee S. Sproull, and Michal Tamuz (1991) "Learning from samples of one or fewer." *Organization Science* 2, no. 1: 1–13.

Markóczy, Lívia, Sunny Li Sun, Mike W. Peng, Weilei Shi, and Bing Ren (2013) "Social network contingency, symbolic management, and boundary stretching." *Strategic Management Journal* 34, no. 11: 1367–87.

Marquis, Christopher, and Cuili Qian (2013) "Corporate social responsibility reporting in China: Symbol or substance?" *Organization Science* 25, no. 1: 127–48.

Maslach, Christina (1982) *Burnout: The Cost of Caring*. Englewood Cliffs, NJ: Prentice-Hall.

Mauss, Marcel (1990) *The Gift: The Form and Reason for Exchange in Archaic Societies*. New York: W.W. Norton.

Mayew, William J. (2008) "Evidence of management discrimination among analysts during earnings conference calls." *Journal of Accounting Research* 46, no. 3: 627–59.

Mayew, William J., and M. Venkatachalam (2012) "The power of voice: Managerial affective states and future firm performance." *Journal of Finance* 67: 1–43.

McAdam, Doug, S. Tarrow, and C. Tilly (2001) *Dynamics of Contention*. New York: Cambridge University Press.

McAllister, D.J. (1995) "Affect- and cognition-based trust as foundations for interpersonal cooperation in organizations." *Academy of Management Journal* 38: 24–59.

McDonald, Michael L., and James D. Westphal (2003) "Getting by with the advice of their friends: CEOs' advice networks and firms' strategic responses to poor performance." *Administrative Science Quarterly* 48, no. 1: 1–32.

McDonald, Michael L., and James D. Westphal (2010) "A little help here? The effects of independent board control on CEO helping networks: A social identification perspective." *Academy of Management Journal* 53: 343–70.

McDonald, Michael L., and James D. Westphal (2011) "My brother's keeper? CEO identification with the corporate elite, social support among CEOs, and leader effectiveness." *Academy of Management Journal* 54, no. 4: 661–93.

McDonald, Michael L., and James D. Westphal (2013) "Access denied: Low mentoring of women and minority first-time directors and its negative effects on appointments to additional boards." *Academy of Management Journal* 56, no. 4: 1169–98.

McDonald, Michael L., James D. Westphal, and Melissa E. Graebner (2008) "What do they know? The effects of outside director acquisition experience on firm acquisition performance." *Strategic Management Journal* 29, no. 11: 1155–77.

McDonald, Michael L., Gareth D. Keeves, and James D. Westphal (2018) "One step forward, one step back: White male top manager organizational identification and helping behavior toward other executives following the appointment of a female or racial minority CEO." *Academy of Management Journal* 61, no. 2: 405–39.

McDonnell, Mary H., and Brayden King (2013) "Keeping up appearances: Reputational threat and impression management after social movement boycotts." *Administrative Science Quarterly*, 58: 387–419.

McEvily, Bill, Vincenzo Perrone, and Akbar Zaheer (2003) "Trust as an organizing principle." *Organization Science* 14, no. 1: 91–103.

McKenna, Christopher D. (2006) *The World's Newest Profession: Management Consulting in the Twentieth Century*. Cambridge: Cambridge University Press.

Merton, Robert K. (1936) "The unanticipated consequences of purposive action." *American Sociological Review* 1: 894–904.

Merton, Robert K. (1957) *Social Theory and Social Structure*. New York: Free Press.

Merton, Robert K. (1968) "The Matthew effect in science: The reward and communication systems of science are considered." *Science* 159, no. 3810: 56–63.

Meyer, John W., and Brian Rowan (1977) "Institutionalized organizations: Formal structure as myth and ceremony." *American Journal of Sociology* 83, no. 2: 340–63.

Meyer, R.E., and M.A. Höllerer (2010) "Meaning structures in a contested issue field: A topographic map of shareholder value in Austria." *Academy of Management Journal* 53, no. 6: 1241–62.

Miles, R.E., and C.C. Snow (1978) *Organizational Strategy, Structure, and Process.* New York: McGraw-Hill.

Milkovich, George T., and Jerry M. Newman (1984) *Compensation.* Plano, TX: Business Publications.

Miller, Dale T., and Leif D. Nelson (2002) "Seeing approach motivation in the avoidance behavior of others: Implications for an understanding of pluralistic ignorance." *Journal of Personality and Social Psychology* 83, no. 5: 1066.

Miller, Dale T., Benoit Monin, and Deborah A. Prentice (2000) "Pluralistic ignorance and inconsistency between private attitudes and public behaviors." In Deborah J. Terry and Michael A. Hogg (eds), *Attitudes, Behavior, and Social Context: The Role of Norms and Group Membership.* London: Psychology Press.

Miller, Danny, Peter H. Friesen, and Henry Mintzberg (1984) *Organizations: A Quantum View.* Englewood Cliffs, NJ: Prentice Hall.

Mintzberg, Henry (1973) *The Nature of Managerial Work.* New York: Harper and Row.

Mintzberg, Henry (1983) *Power in and around Organizations.* Englewood Cliffs, NJ: Prentice-Hall.

Mizruchi, Mark S. (1996) "What do interlocks do? An analysis, critique, and assessment of research on interlocking directorates." *Annual Review of Sociology* 22, no. 1: 271–98.

Mizruchi, Mark S. (2013) *The Fracturing of the American Corporate Elite.* Cambridge, MA: Harvard University Press.

Molm, Linda D. (2003) "Theoretical comparisons of forms of exchange." *Sociological Theory* 21, no. 1: 1–17.

Molm, Linda D., Jessica L. Collett, and David R. Schaefer (2007) "Building solidarity through generalized exchange: A theory of reciprocity." *American Journal of Sociology* 113, no. 1: 205–42.

Montoya, R. Matthew, and Robert S. Horton (2004) "On the importance of cognitive evaluation as a determinant of interpersonal attraction." *Journal of Personality and Social Psychology* 86, no. 5: 696.

Moore, James H., and Matthew S. Kraatz (2011) "Governance form and organizational adaptation: Lessons from the savings and loan industry in the 1980s." *Organization Science* 22: 850–68.

Morozov, Evgeny (2012) *The Net Delusion: The Dark Side of Internet Freedom.* New York: Public Affairs.

Moscovici, Serge, and Willem Doise (1994) *Conflict and Consensus: A General Theory of Collective Decisions.* New York: Sage.

Noelle-Neumann, E. (1993) *The Spiral of Silence: Public Opinion—Our Social Skin.* Chicago, IL: University of Chicago Press.

Ocasio, W., and Joseph, J. (2005) "Cultural adaptation and institutional change: The evolution of vocabularies of corporate governance, 1972–2003." *Poetics* 33, no. 3–4: 163–78.

O'Gorman, Hubert J. (1975) "Pluralistic ignorance and white estimates of white support for racial segregation." *Public Opinion Quarterly* 39, no. 3: 313–30.

O'Gorman, Hubert J., and Stephen L. Garry (1976) "Pluralistic ignorance: A replication and extension." *Public Opinion Quarterly* 40, no. 4: 449–58.

O'Reilly III, Charles A., and Brian G.M. Main (2010) "Economic and psychological perspectives on CEO compensation: A review and synthesis." *Industrial and Corporate Change* 19, no. 3: 675–712.

O'Reilly III, Charles A., Brian G. Main, and Graef S. Crystal (1988) "CEO compensation as tournament and social comparison: A tale of two theories." *Administrative Science Quarterly*: 257–74.

O'Reilly III, Charles A., David F. Caldwell, and William P. Barnett (1989) "Work group demography, social integration, and turnover." *Administrative Science Quarterly*: 21–37.

O'Toole, J., and Bennis, W. (2009) "A culture of candor." *Harvard Business Review*, June: 1–7.

Pahl Ray E. (2000) *On Friendship*. Malden, MA: Polity Press.

Palmer, Donald, and Brad M. Barber (2001) "Challengers, elites, and owning families: A social class theory of corporate acquisitions in the 1960s." *Administrative Science Quarterly* 46, no. 1: 87–120.

Palmer, D., Friedland, R., and Singh, J.V. (1986) "The ties that bind: Organizational and class bases of stability in a corporate interlock network." *American Sociological Review* 51: 781–96.

Park, Sun Hyun, and James D. Westphal (2013) "Social discrimination in the corporate elite: How status affects the propensity for minority CEOs to receive blame for low firm performance." *Administrative Science Quarterly* 58, no. 4: 542–86.

Park, Sun Hyun, James D. Westphal, and Ithai Stern (2011) "Set up for a fall: The insidious effects of flattery and opinion conformity toward corporate leaders." *Administrative Science Quarterly* 56, no. 2: 257–302.

Park, Sun Hyun and Zhang Yanlong (2019) "Cultural Entrepreneurship in Corporate Governance Practice Diffusion: Framing of Independent Directors by U.S. Listed Chinese Companies", Working Paper, Seoul National University.

Patalano, Andrea L., and Zachary LeClair (2011) "The influence of group decision making on indecisiveness-related decisional confidence." *Judgment and Decision Making* 6: 163.

Pelled, Lisa Hope, Kathleen M. Eisenhardt, and Katherine R. Xin (1999) "Exploring the black box: An analysis of work group diversity, conflict, and performance." *Administrative Science Quarterly* 44, no. 1: 1–28.

Penner, Louis A., John F. Dovidio, Jane A. Piliavin, and David A. Schroeder (2005) "Prosocial behavior: Multilevel perspectives." *Annual Review of Psychology* 56: 365–92.

Pettigrew, T.F. (1979) "The ultimate attribution error: Extending Allport's cognitive analysis of prejudice." *Personality and Social Psychology Bulletin* 5: 461–76.

Petty, Richard E., and John T. Cacioppo (2012) *Communication and Persuasion: Central and Peripheral Routes to Attitude Change*. New York: Springer Science and Business Media.

Pfaffenberger, Bryan (1988) "Fetishised objects and humanised nature: Towards an anthropology of technology." *Man*: 236–52.

Pfaffenberger, Bryan (1992) "Social anthropology of technology." *Annual Review of Anthropology* 21, no. 1: 491–516.

Pfeffer, Jeffrey (1994) *Competitive Advantage through People*. Boston, MA: Harvard Business School Press.

Pinker, Steven, Martin A. Nowak, and James J. Lee (2008) "The logic of indirect speech." *Proceedings of the National Academy of Sciences* 105, no. 3: 833–8.

Podolny, Joel M. (1993) "A status-based model of market competition." *American Journal of Sociology* 98, no. 4: 829–72.

Podolny, Joel M. (2001) "Networks as the pipes and prisms of the market." *American Journal of Sociology* 107, no. 1: 33–60.

Pollock, Timothy G., and Violina P. Rindova (2003) "Media legitimation effects in the market for initial public offerings." *Academy of Management Journal* 46, no. 5: 631–42.

Pollock, Timothy G., Harald M. Fischer, and James B. Wade (2002) "The role of power and politics in the repricing of executive options." *Academy of Management Journal* 45, no. 6: 1172–82.

Pollock, Timothy G., Violina P. Rindova, and Patrick G. Maggitti (2008) "Market watch: Information and availability cascades among the media and investors in the US IPO market." *Academy of Management Journal* 51, no. 2: 335–58.

Portes, Alejandro (1998) "Social capital: Its origins and applications in modern sociology." *Annual Review of Sociology* 24, no. 1: 1–24.

Portes, Alejandro (2010) *Economic Sociology: A Systematic Inquiry*. Princeton, NJ: Princeton University Press.

Powell, Walter W., and Jeannette A. Colyvas (2008) "Microfoundations of institutional theory." In Royston Greenwood, Christine Oliver, Thomas B. Lawrence, and Renate E. Meyer (eds), *The Sage Handbook of Organizational Institutionalism*: 276–98. London: Sage.

Preacher, Kristopher J., and Andrew F. Hayes (2008) "Asymptotic and resampling strategies for assessing and comparing indirect effects in multiple mediator models." *Behavior Research Methods* 40, no. 3: 879–91.

Prentice, Deborah A., and Dale T. Miller (1996) "Pluralistic ignorance and the perpetuation of social norms by unwitting actors." In Mark P. Zanna (ed.), *Advances in Experimental Social Psychology*, Vol. 28: 161–209. San Diego, CA: Academic Press.

Pulakos, E.D., and K.N. Wexley (1983) "The relationship among perceptual similarity, sex and performance ratings in manager subordinate dyads." *Academy of Management Journal* 26: 129–39.

Quinn, C.G. (1996) "Introduction." In E. Wharton, *The Age of Innocence*. London: Penguin Books.

Rao, Hayagreeva (1994) "The social construction of reputation: Certification contests, legitimation, and the survival of organizations in the American automobile industry: 1895–1912." *Strategic Management Journal* 15, no. S1: 29–44.

Rao, Hayagreeva, Henrich R. Greve, and Gerald F. Davis (2001) "Fool's gold: Social proof in the initiation and abandonment of coverage by Wall Street analysts." *Administrative Science Quarterly* 46, no. 3: 502–26.

Rao, Hayagreeva, Philippe Monin, and Rodolphe Durand (2003) "Institutional change in Toque Ville: Nouvelle cuisine as an identity movement in French gastronomy." *American Journal of Sociology* 108, no. 4: 795–843.

Rao, Hayagreeva, Philippe Monin, and Rodolphe Durand (2005) "Border crossing: Bricolage and the erosion of categorical boundaries in French gastronomy." *American Sociological Review* 70, no. 6: 968–91.

Rediker, Kenneth J., and Anju Seth (1995) "Boards of directors and substitution effects of alternative governance mechanisms." *Strategic Management Journal* 16, no. 2: 85–99.

Reingold, Dan (2007) *Confessions of a Wall Street Analyst: A True Story of Inside Information and Corruption in the Stock Market*. New York: Harper Collins.

Reinhard J. (2002) "Persuasion in the legal setting." In James Price Dillard and Michael Pfau (eds), *The Persuasion Handbook: Developments in Theory and Practice*: 543–602. Thousand Oaks, CA: Sage.

Roseman, I.J., C. Wiest, and T.S. Swartz (1994) "Phenomenology, behaviors, and goals differentiate discrete emotions." *Journal of Personality and Social Psychology* 67: 206–21.

Rosen, Peter A. (2011) "Crowdsourcing lessons for organizations." *Journal of Decision Systems* 20, no. 3: 309–24.

Rosette, Ashleigh Shelby, Geoffrey J. Leonardelli, and Katherine W. Phillips (2008) "The White standard: Racial bias in leader categorization." *Journal of Applied Psychology* 93, no. 4: 758.

Ryan, Lori Verstegen, and Marguerite Schneider (2002) "The antecedents of institutional investor activism." *Academy of Management Review* 27, no. 4: 554–73.

Ryan, Michelle K., and S. Alexander Haslam (2007) "The glass cliff: Exploring the dynamics surrounding the appointment of women to precarious leadership positions." *Academy of Management Review* 32, no. 2: 549–72.

Sadler, Pamela, and Erik Woody (2003) "Is who you are who you're talking to? Interpersonal style and complementarily in mixed-sex interactions." *Journal of Personality and Social Psychology* 84, no. 1: 80.

Salancik, Gerald R., and James R. Meindl (1984) "Corporate attributions as strategic illusions of management control." *Administrative Science Quarterly*: 238–54.

Sanitioso, Rasyid, Ziva Kunda, and Geoffrey T. Fong (1990) "Motivated recruitment of autobiographical memories." *Journal of Personality and Social Psychology* 59, no. 2: 229–41.

Schank, Richard L. (1932) "A study of community and its group institutions conceived of as behavior of individuals." *Psychological Monographs* 43, no. 2: 1–133.

Schaufeli, Wilmar B., Marisa Salanova, Vicente González-Romá, and Arnold B. Bakker (2002) "The measurement of engagement and burnout: A two sample confirmatory factor analytic approach." *Journal of Happiness Studies* 3, no. 1: 71–92.

Schlenker, Barry R. (2003) "Self-presentation." In M.R. Leary and J.P. Tangney (eds), *Handbook of Self and Identity*: 429–518. New York: Guilford Press.

Schlenker, Barry R., and Michael F. Weigold (1992) "Interpersonal processes involving impression regulation and management." *Annual Review of Psychology* 43, no. 1: 133–68.

Schoeck, Helmut (1969) *Envy: A Theory of Social Behavior*. New York: Harcourt, Brace, and World.

Schudson, Michael (2003) *The Sociology of News*, 2nd edn. New York: W.W. Norton and Company.

Scott, M., and S.M. Lyman (1968) "Accounts." *American Sociological Review* 33: 46–62.

Scott, W. Richard (1987) "The adolescence of institutional theory." *Administrative Science Quarterly*: 493–511.

Scott, W. Richard (2001) *Institutions and Organizations*. 2nd edn. Thousand Oaks, CA: Sage.

Scott, W. Richard (2002) *Organizations: Rational, Natural, and Open Systems* 3rd edn. New York: Prentice-Hall.

Scott, W. Richard, and G.F. Davis (2007) *Organizations and Organizing: Rational, Natural and Open Systems*. New York: Routledge.

Sedikides, Constantine, and Aiden P. Gregg (2008) "Self-enhancement: Food for thought." *Perspectives on Psychological Science* 3, no. 2: 102–16.

Segal, M.W. (1979) "Varieties of interpersonal attraction and their interrelationships in natural groups." *Social Psychology Quarterly* 42: 253–61.

Segev, Eran, Joyce Chen, Brendan English, and Robert C. Johns (2014) "Impacts of participatory strategic planning on advancing innovation at the Volpe Center." *Transportation Research Record* 2420, no. 1: 45–54.

Seinen, Ingrid, and Arthur Schram (2006) "Social status and group norms: Indirect reciprocity in a repeated helping experiment." *European Economic Review* 50, no. 3: 581–602.

Shani, Guy, and James D. Westphal (2016) "Persona non grata? Determinants and consequences of social distancing from journalists who engage in negative coverage of firm leadership." *Academy of Management Journal* 59, no. 1: 302–29.

Sheldon, Kennon M., and Tim Kasser (2001) "Getting older, getting better? Personal strivings and psychological maturity across the life span." *Developmental Psychology* 37, no. 4: 491.

Sheldon, Kennon M., Richard M. Ryan, Laird J. Rawsthorne, and Barbara Ilardi (1997) "Trait self and true self: Cross-role variation in the Big-Five personality traits and its relations with psychological authenticity and subjective well-being." *Journal of Personality and Social Psychology* 73, no. 6: 1380.

Shelton, J.N., and J.A. Richeson (2005) "Intergroup contact and pluralistic ignorance." *Journal of Personality and Social Psychology* 88, no. 1: 91–107.

Sheppes, Gal, Susanne Scheibe, Gaurav Suri, and James J. Gross (2011) "Emotion-regulation choice." *Psychological Science* 22, no. 11: 1391–6.

Shi, Wei, Yan Zhang, and Robert E. Hoskisson (2019) "Examination of CEO-CFO social interaction through language style matching: Outcomes for the CFO and the organization." *Academy of Management Journal* 62: 383–414.

Shipilov, Andrew (2012) "Strategic multiplexity." *Strategic Organization* 10, no. 3: 215–22.

Siegel, Phyllis A., and Joel Brockner (2005) "Individual and organizational consequences of CEO claimed handicapping: What's good for the CEO may not be so good for the firm." *Organizational Behavior and Human Decision Processes* 96, no. 1: 1–22.

Silver, Allan (1990) "Friendship in commercial society: Eighteenth-century social theory and modern sociology." *American Journal of Sociology* 95, no. 6: 1474–504.

Simons, T.L., and R.S. Peterson (2000) "Task conflict and relationship conflict in top management teams: The pivotal role of intragroup trust." *Journal of Applied Psychology* 85: 102–11.

Sinclair, S., B.S. Lowery, C.D. Hardin, and A. Colangelo (2005) "Social tuning of automatic racial attitudes: The role of affiliative motivation." *Journal of Personality and Social Psychology* 89: 583–92.

Smith, Ken G., Ken A. Smith, Judy D. Olian, Henry P. Sims, Jr., Douglas P. O'Bannon, and Judith A. Scully (1994) "Top management team demography and process: The role of social integration and communication." *Administrative Science Quarterly*: 412–38.

Smith, Richard H. (2013) *The Joy of Pain: Schadenfreude and the Dark Side of Human Nature*. Oxford: Oxford University Press.

Smith, Richard H., and Sung Hee Kim (2007) "Comprehending envy." *Psychological Bulletin* 133, no. 1: 46.

Soltes, Eugene (2014) "Private interaction between firm management and sell-side analysts." *Journal of Accounting Research* 52, no. 1: 245–72.

Soundararajan, Vivek, Laura J. Spence, and Chris Rees (2018) "Small business and social irresponsibility in developing countries: Working conditions and 'evasion' institutional work." *Business and Society* 57, no. 7: 1301–36.

Stanca, Luca (2009) "Measuring indirect reciprocity: Whose back do we scratch?" *Journal of Economic Psychology* 30, no. 2: 190–202.

Staw, Barry M., Pamela I. McKechnie, and Sheila M. Puffer (1983) "The justification of organizational performance." *Administrative Science Quarterly*: 582–600.

Stephens, Clifford P., and Michael S. Weisbach (1998) "Actual share reacquisitions in open-market repurchase programs." *Journal of Finance* 53, no. 1: 313–33.

Stern, Ithai, and James D. Westphal (2010) "Stealthy footsteps to the boardroom: Executives' backgrounds, sophisticated interpersonal influence behavior, and board appointments." *Administrative Science Quarterly* 55, no. 2: 278–319.

Stevens, C.K., and A.L. Kristof (1995) "Making the right impression: A field study of applicant impression management during job interviews." *Journal of Applied Psychology* 80: 587–606.

Stickel, Scott E. (1995) "The anatomy of the performance of buy and sell recommendations." *Financial Analysts Journal*: 25–39.

Stieger, Daniel, Kurt Matzler, Sayan Chatterjee, and Florian Ladstaetter-Fussenegger (2012) "Democratizing strategy: How crowdsourcing can be used for strategy dialogues." *California Management Review* 54, no. 4: 44–68.

Stoker, Janka I., Mandy Van der Velde, and Joris Lammers (2012) "Factors relating to managerial stereotypes: The role of gender of the employee and the manager and management gender ratio." *Journal of Business and Psychology* 27, no. 1: 31–42.

Strang, David, and Wesley D. Sine (2002) "Interorganizational institutions." *Companion to Organizations*: 497–519.

Strang, David, and Sarah A. Soule (1998) "Diffusion in organizations and social movements: From hybrid corn to poison pills." *Annual Review of Sociology* 24, no. 1: 265–90.

Stuart, Toby E., Ha Hoang, and Ralph C. Hybels (1999) "Interorganizational endorsements and the performance of entrepreneurial ventures." *Administrative Science Quarterly* 44, no. 2: 315–49.

Stürmer, Stefan, Mark Snyder, and Allen M. Omoto (2005) "Prosocial emotions and helping: The moderating role of group membership." *Journal of Personality and Social Psychology* 88, no. 3: 532.

Suchman, Mark C. (1995) "Managing legitimacy: Strategic and institutional approaches." *Academy of Management Review* 20, no. 3: 571–610.

Suddaby, Roy, Alex Bitektine, and Patrick Haack (2017) "Legitimacy." *Academy of Management Annals* 11, no. 1: 451–78.

Suls, Jerry, and Peter Green (2003) "Pluralistic ignorance and college student perceptions of gender-specific alcohol norms." *Health Psychology* 22, no. 5: 479.

Swart, Hermann, Miles Hewstone, Oliver Christ, and Alberto Voci (2011) "Affective mediators of intergroup contact: A three-wave longitudinal study in South Africa." *Journal of Personality and Social Psychology* 101, no. 6: 1221.

Takahashi, N. (2000) "The emergence of generalized exchange." *American Journal of Sociology* 105: 1105–34.

Tarrow, Sidney (2010) "Dynamics of diffusion: Mechanisms, institutions, and scale shift." In Rebecca Kolins Givan, Kenneth M. Roberts, and Sarah A. Soule (eds), *The Diffusion of Social Movements: Actors, Mechanisms, and Political Effects*: 204–19. New York: Cambridge University Press.

Thornton, Patricia H. and William Ocasio (1999) "Institutional logics and the historical contingency of power in organizations: Executive succession in the higher education publishing industry, 1958–1990." *American Journal of Sociology* 105: 801–43.

Thornton, Patricia H., William Ocasio, and Michael Lounsbury (2012) *The Institutional Logics Perspective: A New Approach to Culture, Structure, and Process*. Oxford: Oxford University Press.

Tilcsik, András (2010) "From ritual to reality: Demography, ideology, and decoupling in a post-communist government agency." *Academy of Management Journal* 53, no. 6: 1474–98.

Tinsley, Catherine H., James B. Wade, Brian G.M. Main, and Charles A. O'Reilly (2017) "Gender diversity on US corporate boards: Are we running in place?" *ILR Review* 70, no. 1: 160–89.

Tittle, Charles R. (1980) *Sanctions and Social Deviance: The Question of Deterrence.* New York: Praeger.

Tittle, Charles R. (1995) *Control Balance: Toward a General Theory of Deviance (Crime and Society).* New York: Westview Press.

Tormala, Zakary L., Victoria L. DeSensi, Joshua J. Clarkson, and Derek D. Rucker (2009) "Beyond attitude consensus: The social context of persuasion and resistance." *Journal of Experimental Social Psychology* 45, no. 1: 149–54.

Tsui, Anne S., and Charles A. O'Reilly III (1989) "Beyond simple demographic effects: The importance of relational demography in superior-subordinate dyads." *Academy of Management Journal* 32, no. 2: 402–23.

Tsui, Anne S., Lyman W. Porter, and Terri D. Egan (2002) "When both similarities and dissimilarities matter: Extending the concept of relational demography." *Human Relations* 55, no. 8: 899–929.

Tuchman, Barbara G. (1978) *Making News: A Study in the Construction of Reality.* New York: Free Press.

Tuchman, G. (1972) "Objectivity as a strategic ritual: An examination of newsmen's notions of objectivity." *American Journal of Sociology* 77: 660–79.

Turban, D.B. and Jones, A.P. (1988) "Supervisor-subordinate similarity: types, effects, and mechanisms." *Journal of Applied Psychology* 73: 228–34.

Turner, John C., Michael A. Hogg, Penelope J. Oakes, Stephen D. Reicher, and Margaret S. Wetherell (1987) *Rediscovering the Social Group: A Self-Categorization Theory.* Oxford: Basil Blackwell.

Useem, Michael (1984) *The Inner Circle: Large Corporations and the Rise of Business Political Activity in the US and UK.* New York: Oxford University Press.

Useem, Michael (1993) *Executive Defense: Shareholder Power and Corporate Reorganization.* Cambridge, MA: Harvard University Press.

Useem, Michael (1996) *Investor Capitalism: How Money Managers Are Changing the Face of Corporate America.* New York: Basic Books.

Uzzi, Brian (1996) "The sources and consequences of embeddedness for the economic performance of organizations: The network effect." *American Sociological Review*: 674–98.

Vonk, Roos (1998) "The slime effect: Suspicion and dislike of likeable behavior toward superiors." *Journal of Personality and Social Psychology* 74, no. 4: 849.

Vonk, Roos (2002) "Self-serving interpretations of flattery: Why ingratiation works." *Journal of Personality and Social Psychology* 82: 515–26.

Wade, James B., Joseph F. Porac, and Timothy G. Pollock (1997) "Words, worth, and the justification of executive pay." *Journal of Organizational Behavior* 18: 641–64.

Walker, Edward T. (2014) *Grassroots for Hire: Public Affairs Consultants in American Democracy.* Cambridge, MA: Cambridge University Press.

Walster, Elaine, Ellen Berscheid, and G. William Walster (1973) "New directions in equity research." *Journal of Personality and Social Psychology* 25, no. 2: 151.

Wang, Danqing, and Xiaowei Rose Luo (2018) "Retire in peace: Officials' political incentives and corporate diversification in China." *Administrative Science Quarterly*: 0001839218786263.

Wang, Peng, Li-Fung Cho, and Ren Li (2018) "An institutional explanation of media corruption in China." *Journal of Contemporary China*: 1–15.

Wayne, Sandy J., and Robert C. Liden (1995) "Effects of impression management on performance ratings: A longitudinal study." *Academy of Management Journal* 38, no. 1: 232–60.

Weisbuch, Max, Diane M. Mackie, and Teresa Garcia-Marques (2003) "Prior source exposure and persuasion: Further evidence for misattributional processes." *Personality and Social Psychology Bulletin* 29, no. 6: 691–700.

Wesselmann, Eric D., Danielle Bagg, and Kipling D. Williams (2009) "'I feel your pain': The effects of observing ostracism on the ostracism detection system." *Journal of Experimental Social Psychology* 45, no. 6: 1308–11.

Westphal, James D. (1998) "Board games: How CEOs adapt to increases in structural board independence from management." *Administrative Science Quarterly*: 511–37.

Westphal, James D. (1999) "Collaboration in the boardroom: Behavioral and performance consequences of CEO-board social ties." *Academy of Management Journal* 42, no. 1: 7–24.

Westphal, James D. (2019) *Diversity without Inclusion in Corporate Leadership*. Ann Arbor, MI: University of Michigan Press.

Westphal, James D., and Michael K. Bednar (2005) "Pluralistic ignorance in corporate boards and firms' strategic persistence in response to low firm performance." *Administrative Science Quarterly* 50, no. 2: 262–98.

Westphal, James D., and Michael K. Bednar (2008) "The pacification of institutional investors." *Administrative Science Quarterly* 53, no. 1: 29–72.

Westphal, James D., and Michael B. Clement (2008) "Sociopolitical dynamics in relations between top managers and security analysts: Favor rendering, reciprocity, and analyst stock recommendations." *Academy of Management Journal* 51, no. 5: 873–97.

Westphal, James D., and David L. Deephouse (2011) "Avoiding bad press: Interpersonal influence in relations between CEOs and journalists and the consequences for press reporting about firms and their leadership." *Organization Science* 22, no. 4: 1061–86.

Westphal, James D., and Melissa E. Graebner (2010) "A matter of appearances: How corporate leaders manage the impressions of financial analysts about the conduct of their boards." *Academy of Management Journal* 53, no. 1: 15–44.

Westphal, James D., and Poonam Khanna (2003) "Keeping directors in line: Social distancing as a control mechanism in the corporate elite." *Administrative Science Quarterly* 48, no. 3: 361–98.

Westphal, James D., and Laurie P. Milton (2000) "How experience and network ties affect the influence of demographic minorities on corporate boards." *Administrative Science Quarterly* 45, no. 2: 366–98.

Westphal, James D., and Sun Hyun Park (2012) "Unintended agency: Impression management support as a trigger of institutional change in corporate governance." *Research in Organizational Behavior* 32: 23–46.

Westphal, James D., and Guy Shani (2016) "Psyched-up to suck-up: Self-regulated cognition, interpersonal influence, and recommendations for board appointments in the corporate elite." *Academy of Management Journal* 59, no. 2: 479–509.

Westphal, James D., and Ithai Stern (2006) "The other pathway to the boardroom: Interpersonal influence behavior as a substitute for elite credentials and majority status in obtaining board appointments." *Administrative Science Quarterly* 51, no. 2: 169–204.

Westphal, James D., and Ithai Stern (2007) "Flattery will get you everywhere (especially if you are a male Caucasian): How ingratiation, boardroom behavior, and demographic minority status affect additional board appointments at US companies." *Academy of Management Journal* 50, no. 2: 267–88.

Westphal, James D., and Edward J. Zajac (1994) "Substance and symbolism in CEOs' long-term incentive plans." *Administrative Science Quarterly* 39: 367–90.

Westphal, James D., and Edward J. Zajac (1995) "Who shall govern? CEO/board power, demographic similarity, and new director selection." *Administrative Science Quarterly*: 60–83.

Westphal, James D., and Edward J. Zajac (1998) "The symbolic management of stockholders: Corporate governance reforms and shareholder reactions." *Administrative Science Quarterly*: 127–53.

Westphal, James D., and Edward J. Zajac (2001) "Decoupling policy from practice: The case of stock repurchase programs." *Administrative Science Quarterly* 46, no. 2: 202–28.

Westphal, James D., and Edward J. Zajac (2013) "A behavioral theory of corporate governance: Explicating the mechanisms of socially situated and socially constituted agency." *Academy of Management Annals* 7, no. 1: 607–61.

Westphal, James D., and David H. Zhu (2019a) "Seeking input when the train has left the station: The symbolic decoupling of participative strategic decision making." Working paper, University of Michigan.

Westphal, James D., and David H. Zhu (2019b) "Under the radar: How firms manage competitive uncertainty by appointing friends of other CEOs to their boards." *Strategic Management Journal*.

Westphal, James D., Ranjay Gulati, and Stephen M. Shortell (1997) "Customization or conformity? An institutional and network perspective on the content and consequences of TQM adoption." *Administrative Science Quarterly*: 366–94.

Westphal, James D., Marc-David L. Seidel, and Katherine J. Stewart (2001) "Second-order imitation: Uncovering latent effects of board network ties." *Administrative Science Quarterly* 46, no. 4: 717–47.

Westphal, James D., Sun Hyun Park, Michael L. McDonald, and Mathew L.A. Hayward (2012) "Helping other CEOs avoid bad press: Social exchange and impression management support among CEOs in communications with journalists." *Administrative Science Quarterly* 57, no. 2: 217–68.

Westphal, James D., Rajyalakshmi Kunapuli, and Sun Hyun Park (2019) "Leveling the playing field: The diffusion of coordinated impression management support among minority leaders and the consequences for media coverage of firm leadership." Working paper, University of Michigan.

Wharton, E. (1996) *The Age of Innocence*. London: Penguin Books.

Whittington, Richard, Ludovic Cailluet, and Basak Yakis-Douglas (2011) "Opening strategy: Evolution of a precarious profession." *British Journal of Management* 22, no. 3: 531–44.

Wiersema, Margarethe, and Yan Zhang (2013) "Executive turnover in the stock option backdating wave: The impact of social context." *Strategic Management Journal* 34: 590–609.

Williams, Kipling D. (2007) "Ostracism." *Annual Review of Psychology* 58.

Williams, Kipling D. (2009) "Advances in experimental social psychology." In M.P. Zanna (ed.), *Ostracism: A Temporal Need—Threat model*: 275–314. New York: Academic Press.

Winner, Langdon (1977) *Autonomous Technology: Technics-out-of-Control as a Theme in Political Thought*. Cambridge, MA: MIT Press.

Winner, Langdon (1986) *Technology as forms of life. In The Whale and the Reactor: A Search for Limits in an Age of High Technology*. Chicago, IL: Chicago University Press.

Wood, Wendy (2000) "Attitude change: Persuasion and social influence." *Annual Review of Psychology* 51, no. 1: 539–70.

Yamagishi, Toshio, and Toko Kiyonari (2000) "The group as the container of generalized reciprocity." *Social Psychology Quarterly*: 116–32.

Yukl, G. (2006) *Leadership in Organizations*, 6th edn. Upper Saddle River, NJ: Pearson Prentice Hall.

Zajac, E.J., and Stephen M. Shortell (1989) "Changing generic strategies: Likelihood, direction, and performance implications." *Strategic Management Journal* 10, no. 5: 413–30.

Zajac, Edward J., and James D. Westphal (1994) "The costs and benefits of managerial incentives and monitoring in large US corporations: When is more not better?" *Strategic Management Journal* 15, no. S1: 121–42.

Zajac, Edward J., and James D. Westphal (1995) "Accounting for the explanations of CEO compensation: Substance and symbolism." *Administrative Science Quarterly*: 283–308.

Zajac, Edward J., and James D. Westphal (1996) "Director reputation, CEO-board power, and the dynamics of board interlocks." *Administrative Science Quarterly*, 41: 507–29.

Zajac, Edward J., and James D. Westphal (2004) "The social construction of market value: Institutionalization and learning perspectives on stock market reactions." *American Sociological Review* 69, no. 3: 433–57.

Zajonc, Robert B. (2001) "Mere exposure: A gateway to the subliminal." *Current Directions in Psychological Science* 10, no. 6: 224–8.

Zhang, Yanlong, Heli Wang, and Xiaoyu Zhou (2019) (In Press). "Dare to Be Different? Conformity vs. Differentiation in Corporate Social Activities of Chinese Firms and Market Responses." *Academy of Management Journal*. DOI: https://doi.org/10.5465/amj.2017.0412.

Zhu, David H., and James D. Westphal (2011) "Misperceiving the beliefs of others: How pluralistic ignorance contributes to the persistence of positive security analyst reactions to the adoption of stock repurchase plans." *Organization Science* 22, no. 4: 869–86.

Zhu, David H., and James D. Westphal (2014) "How directors' prior experience with other demographically similar CEOs affects their appointments onto corporate boards and the consequences for CEO compensation." *Academy of Management Journal* 57, no. 3: 791–813.

Zippelius, Reinhold (1986) "Exclusion and shunning as legal and social sanctions." *Ethology and Sociobiology* 7, no. 3–4: 159–66.

Zorn, Dirk M. (2004) "Here a chief, there a chief: The rise of the CFO in the American firm." *American Sociological Review* 69, no. 3: 345–64.

Zuckerman, Ezra W. (2000) "Focusing the corporate product: Securities analysts and de-diversification." *Administrative Science Quarterly* 45, no. 3: 591–619.

Zwiebel, Jeffrey (1995) "Corporate conservatism and relative compensation." *Journal of Political Economy* 103, no. 1: 1–25.

Index of Names

For the benefit of digital users, indexed terms that span two pages (e.g., 52–53) may, on occasion, appear on only one of those pages.

General Index

For the benefit of digital users, indexed terms that span two pages (e.g., 52–53) may, on occasion, appear on only one of those pages.